Born of a Woman

OTHER BOOKS BY JOHN SHELBY SPONG

Honest Prayer

This Hebrew Lord

Dialogue: In Search of Jewish-Christian Understanding
with Rabbi Jack Daniel Spiro

Christpower

Life Approaches Death: A Dialogue on Medical Ethics
with Dr. Daniel Gregory

The Living Commandments

The Easter Moment

Into the Whirlwind: The Future of the Church

Beyond Moralism
with the Venerable Denise G. Haines

*Consciousness and Survival—An Interdisciplinary
Inquiry into the Possibility of Life Beyond Biological
Death* (Editor and Contributor)

Living in Sin? A Bishop Rethinks Human Sexuality

*Rescuing the Bible from Fundamentalism:
A Bishop Rethinks the Meaning of Scripture*

Born of a Woman

A Bishop Rethinks the Birth of Jesus

John Shelby Spong

HarperSanFrancisco

A Division of HarperCollins*Publishers*

FIRST EDITION

Library of Congress Cataloging-in-Publication Data

Spong, John Shelby.
    Born of a woman : a bishop rethinks the birth of Jesus / John Shelby Spong. — 1st ed.
       p.   cm.
    Includes bibliographical references and index.
    ISBN 0–06–067513–6 (alk. paper)
    ISBN (INTL.) 0–06–067529–2
    1. Jesus Christ—Nativity. 2. Bible. N.T.—Criticism,
interpretation, etc. I. Title.
BT315.2.S66   1992
232.92′1—dc20   91–55087
                                                CIP

---

92 93 94 95 96 HAD 10 9 8 7 6 5 4 3 2 1

This edition is printed on acid-free, recycled paper that meets the American National Standards Institute Z39.48 Standard.

For
Katharine Shelby Catlett
and
John Baldwin Catlett III

*who have given to Chris and me
the joy of being grandparents*

Contents

Preface

As long ago as 1973, when I wrote *This Hebrew Lord*, I added a footnote to chapter 15 that said, "When this book was originally conceived I had planned to devote one unit to the interpretive envelope in which the Gospel story is wrapped: the birth narrative on one side and the resurrection on the other. But so massive was the material that I gathered that I decided to save it for a later publication." It amazes me even now that I laid out this future course for myself that long ago.

Seven years later I made good half of that commitment when, in 1980, *The Easter Moment* was published. This book was designed to explore that critical point in history at which the power of the gospel exploded onto the stage of the world. It focused on the nexus where faith and tradition intersect knowledge and secularity. My working title for that manuscript was "A Case for the Resurrection to the Modern Mind." I am particularly pleased that Harper & Row reissued it in a revised paperback edition in 1987, and that even now it is being completely rewritten for a new decade under the title *The Resurrection: Myth and Reality—A Bishop Rethinks the Meaning of Easter.*

Since *The Easter Moment* came out I have published five additional volumes. Never, however, did I lose the desire to look at the birth narratives of Jesus as intensely as I had examined the resurrection narratives, and to do it in a way that would be accessible to the average layperson.

Over the years since 1973, my theological and biblical conclusions have created wide debate, with responses ranging from hysterical anger to genuine appreciation. In those years I was significantly shaped by the feminist movement. It opened my eyes in new ways to see the oppression of women in both church and society, usually done in the name of God, the Bible, and sacred tradition. I was also drawn into an intense study of human sexuality and into the churchwide debate on changing patterns in sexual ethics. Particularly did my study lead me to a new understanding of the source and origin of homosexuality, which challenged all of my sexist and homophobic prejudices.

My conclusions in these areas, published under the title *Living in Sin? A Bishop Rethinks Human Sexuality*, had the effect of making me a symbol for moving beyond the conventional moral patterns and prevailing wisdom that mark the church's traditional understanding of both the role and place of women and the attitude toward our gay and lesbian brothers and sisters. Those who defined themselves as defenders of the faith of their fathers resisted my ideas with intensity and even with vicious personal attacks, but those who felt excluded from the traditions of the past saw in me a welcome sign of hope for a future inclusiveness in the body of Christ. Those whose ultimate loyalty is to an undisturbed ecclesiastical institution waffled as usual, in a vain search for some middle and safe ground. In a strange and fascinating way, the debate on human sexuality drove me back to the Bible. Those who supported the oppression and isolation of women in the church quoted the Bible to justify their continuing prejudice. Those who could not escape their deep, and in some cases unconscious, homophobia found in the literal texts of Scripture support for their condemnation of gay and lesbian people. So I wrote *Rescuing the Bible from Fundamentalism* to call the debate on Scripture to a new level of both scholarship and sanity. Once again the storms of controversy howled as would-be defenders of the Bible rose to attack my stance, usually without reading the book itself.

Finally, after those two best-selling volumes, I turned my attention once more to my long-yearned-for project of writing on the birth narratives of our Lord. I suppose I hoped that this endeavor would lower the decibels of the anger and enable me and others to engage the Bible on a level of significant scholarship. But, alas, there is no safe haven anywhere, and when consciousness is raised in one area, it is raised everywhere. In these familiar texts I now discovered definitions of women that were less than admirable. Even the poetry of the tales could not succeed in hiding that fact. The birth narratives also raised for me anew and in powerful ways the whole question of the authority and proper use of Holy Scripture in the life of the church. Even though I quite specifically addressed this theme in my last book, I could now take the tools developed in that volume and use them to bring the Christmas and Epiphany stories to a new level of intensity. When my diocese graciously created for me a sabbatical month each February, I took the opportunity to pursue this subject with total concentration at such wonderful places as Union Theological Seminary in New York City, Yale Divinity School in New Haven, Connecticut, Harvard Divinity School in Cambridge, Massachusetts, and Magdalen College at Oxford University.

In those great institutions I read the major contemporary voices in New Testament scholarship as they probed the truth of the birth narratives. The power of such male scholars as Raymond Brown, Edward Schillebeeckx, Joseph Fitzmyer, Michael Goulder, and Herman Hendrickx made significant contributions to my study; but so did the newly assertive feminine voices of Rosemary Radford Ruether, Anne Belford Ulanov, Elisabeth Schüssler Fiorenza, Jane Schaberg, Margaret Miles, and Phyllis Trible.

Beyond that, I explored various aspects of mother worship, ancient and modern. I came to know the likes of Isis, Cybele, Artemis and Diana, with whom I had almost no familiarity. I met the Black Madonna. I sought to separate the Mary of history from the virgin Mary of myth. I tried to place myself inside the mentality of the first generation of Christians in order to appreciate the way they used the Hebrew Scriptures. I read anew the early Fathers (there were no early Mothers who wrote) and listened for the meaning behind the words as the gradual divinization of Mary began to occur in Christian history. I focused on the impact of that movement on real women. Finally, I read deeply the writings of Carl G. Jung, and those who might be described as Jungians, looking especially for the way the concepts of male and female were related in the psychic history of humankind.

It is fair to say, however, that out of all this background study, two people have shaped my thought on this subject far beyond any others, and a sense of indebtedness and deep appreciation requires that they be treated in a class by themselves. So, out of my previous list, I lift them up for particular emphasis.

First and foremost is the Reverend Dr. Raymond E. Brown, professor of New Testament at Union Theological Seminary in New York City, and the person I regard as the ranking New Testament scholar in the world. Because Ray Brown is the godfather to the son of a priest formerly in my diocese, I utilized that relationship to secure him as a lecturer in the New Dimensions series in the Diocese of Newark in 1977, just before his book *The Birth of the Messiah* was published. Those lectures, which introduced me to the substance of that book, were so stimulating that I could not wait to add the book to my library.

My habit as a scholar is to take one major theological or biblical book and to live with it intensely as my teacher for a full year. In 1986 I installed Ray Brown's *Birth of the Messiah* into that powerful role. It became my primary study book. I read it over the course of a year in small portions, four or five pages a day, checking all of its references, taking copious notes, and interacting with it deeply. That book became part of me, and in many ways this volume leans heavily on Ray Brown's insights. I have sought to give him proper credit in the notes, but I cannot adequately describe in notes his research that suffuses this entire book. I simply acknowledge that the very thoughts I seek to popularize in this volume root more significantly in Raymond Brown than in anyone else. I do not altogether agree with Professor Brown, as the reader will discover. I value the challenge offered to his conclusions by Michael Goulder and others, but I have been exceedingly enriched by him and owe him much. Very few laypeople will, in my opinion, read Raymond Brown; if they do, his use of Hebrew and Greek and his system of abbreviations (JBAP for John the Baptist, for example) will put them off. But if my readers find their appetites whetted for the master, I am happy to direct them to Raymond Brown's book, which is, in my opinion, the classic, the masterpiece in the field.

The second person to whom I am deeply indebted is Jane Schaberg, professor of religion at the University of Detroit. I immediately ordered her book, *The Illegitimacy of Jesus,* when I saw it advertised in the *Christian Century.* It was also later commended to me by Phyllis Trible of the Union Seminary faculty in New York.

Jane Schaberg's book threw a brand-new light on the birth narratives for me. It illustrates the enrichment that is open to the church when a body of people, like women, once largely rejected and ignored by the church begins to be listened to with care.

How does a woman, a feminist biblical theologian, listen to the birth traditions as they are written, narrated, and interpreted historically only by men? How can we get behind the patriarchal prejudices and the male biases in order to hear, read, and interpret this story more objectively? Jane Schaberg's book was more exciting than any mystery I've ever encountered. She opened my eyes to clues in Holy Scripture that I had never seen.

Her book is brilliantly researched and extensively documented. She builds her case on material that is, quite frankly, very scanty, for prejudice and bias suppress so heavily. Yet her research and insights have made some parts of that story make sense to me where they never did before. The tension created in me by the dialogue between Raymond Brown and Jane Schaberg was vigorous, and that tension becomes my gift to my reading audience as it finds expression in this book. Schaberg is, for me, a wonderful challenge and corrective to Brown. She enjoys an independent freedom of inquiry where Raymond Brown is bound, I believe, more tightly than even he recognizes to the dogmatism of his Roman Catholic tradition. She offers a feminist perspective to that male construct of the virgin Mary that opens Mary to a real humanity. I have never met Jane Schaberg, but I look forward to the day when I will have that privilege. To his great credit, Raymond Brown, writing in *A Dictionary of Biblical Interpretation*, takes cognizance of the challenge to his point of view by feminist biblical scholars (p. 311). That is as far as one might logically expect him to go.

In all of this study I was seeking one thing only: a deeper knowledge of God as that knowledge is revealed in Jesus of Nazareth called Christ by those of us who acknowledge his

Lordship. I seek this revealing Christ in the pages of this volume through the legends of his birth, just as I had sought to find him in the Easter Moment through the narratives and legends about his resurrection. I have pursued boldly some startling possibilities. I have gone far beneath the level of biblical literalism that those familiar with my writings will recognize as a common theme. Some readers, not having the background to understand the Bible that they treasure, will be startled and perhaps even offended upon hearing my conclusions. It will be incomprehensible to them how one who calls himself a Christian and, even more, one who lives inside the structures of the church as an Anglican bishop, could entertain the possibilities this book suggests.

I grieve over the fact that I will cause some simple believers pain. I do not do so lightly. I cannot believe, however, that biblical ignorance will in the long run serve well the cause of Christ, and claims that the Bible constitutes the inerrant Word of God in literal detail can, in my mind, never be anything more than biblical ignorance.

Long ago I decided that I could no longer sacrifice scholarship and truth to protect the weak and religiously insecure. I see another audience that the church seems to ignore. That audience is made up of brilliantly educated men and women who find in the church a god too small to be the God of life for them, a knowledge too restricted to be compelling or a superstition too obvious to be entertained with seriousness. My now-grown daughters are part of that audience. I want them to find in the Christian church a gospel that takes seriously the world of their experience, that does not seek to bind their minds into premodern or ancient forms, that is not afraid to examine emerging truth from any source, whether from the world of science or the world of biblical scholarship. I want the church to proclaim a gospel that has contemporary power and to worship a God who does not need to be protected by hiding that God in some anti-intellectual pose, for fear that new truth will obliterate faith and devotion due such a God.

I hope this book will illumine the minds and hearts of those who still find the church to be their spiritual home. I know thousands who remain in the church out of habit or hope but at the price of turning off their minds. Beyond that audience, however, I hope this book will entice and invite those who are members of the church alumni association to take another look, to invest their lives anew in this institution. It does have within itself the capacity to challenge its own assumptions and stereotypes, to renew its own life, and to modify its theological understanding of both God and truth when new occasions teach new duties.

Finally, I hope this book will encourage Christians of all persuasions to take the Bible seriously, to study it deeply, to engage its truth significantly. For more than forty years I have spent some time each day in Bible study. That book never ceases to amaze me, for it constantly calls me to discover new and exciting treasures in passages that I must have read hundreds of times before and yet was not able to see. The one decision that has most dramatically affected my life as a priest and bishop has been my commitment to daily Bible study.

Fundamentalist Christians distort the Bible by taking it literally. Liberal Christians distort the Bible by not taking it seriously. If my years of ordination have had power and influence in the life of the church, the primary reason has been that as a liberal I have dedicated my intellectual energy to Bible study. I commend that practice to the new generation of clergy.

To many people I express my thanks for assistance in the preparation of this manuscript: first to my friends at Union

Theological Seminary in New York and most especially to academic dean and provost Milton McC. Gatch; head librarian Richard Spoor, and library research assistant Seth E. Kasten. The Burke Library at Union is a wonder and a gold mine, and Seth Kasten can find anything, no matter how obscure. Four faculty members at that institution—Tom Driver, Phyllis Trible, Christopher Morse, and Ann Belford Ulanov—were especially helpful in directing my reading; and Barry Ulanov, a professor at Barnard College who has the good fortune to be married to Ann, did his best to convince me that Augustine was not, in his heart of hearts, a flesh-denigrating Manichaean. He failed, but he was brilliant in the attempt.

Second, I acknowledge my debt to the people at Yale Divinity School, especially former deans Leander Keck and James Annand. The assistant dean at Berkeley (the Episcopal component at Yale) David Parachini, reference librarian John Bollier, circulation librarian Suzanne Estelle-Holmer, and library assistants Mark Jessiman, Mark Myers, Leslie Afford, and Dineen Dowling—all served my needs well.

Third, the Divinity School at Harvard and most especially the Divinity School library were for me another special resource. I express my appreciation to Dean Ronald Theiman, Chaplain Krister Stendahl, and Professor Gordon Kaufman, who were particularly helpful. Also, my thanks go to Dean Otis Charles and the students at Episcopal Divinity School, the Episcopal part of the Harvard consortium, who made me welcome.

My thanks go also to Dr. Jeffrey John, dean of the Chapel at Magdalen College, Oxford, the Reverend Peter Eaton, chaplain at Magdalen College, and the Reverend Dr. Stephen Tucker, dean of the Chapel at New College, Oxford, for their welcome and assistance during my stay at that great university as a visiting scholar and guest lecturer. I was especially grateful for their introduction to me of the work of Michael Goulder on Luke and for the sheer professionalism of the staff at the Bodleian Library at Oxford.

To the clergy and people of the Diocese of Newark I express an ever-deepening gratitude for their support as I have developed during my long years as their bishop an episcopal career based on serious scholarship. Major portions of this book became public first as lectures to the Diocese of Newark in our New Dimensions lecture series. Hosting those lectures were Christ Church in Short Hills, the Reverend David Ernest, rector, and the Reverend Philip Kasey and the Reverend Polly Kasey, assistants; the Church of the Epiphany, Orange, the Reverend Canon Gervais Clarke, rector; and St. Paul's Church, Chatham, the Reverend Dr. Franklin Vilas, rector.

The public nature of my life as the bishop of Newark has meant that my theological probings became newsworthy, even when I was speaking only to my official diocesan family. I have consciously and deliberately insisted on doing my theological and ethical thinking in public. It is the only way I know to break the Christian faith out of its confining religious ghetto. But to do so is a costly vocation for a bishop. It has made me a godsend to some and a source of anguish to others. It has also made me quite aware that this style of leadership demands of a diocese the expenditure of great amounts of energy. The clergy and laypeople of the Diocese of Newark have given me that gift as well as their love and encouragement in abundant measure. But of even greater value to me and to the diocese has been their gift of honest interaction. Theological agreement has never been a virtue that I have sought. Theological honesty, the contending of competing ideas, the willingness to seek truth in dialogue— these are virtues dear to me, and these virtues in great abundance mark the life of the Diocese of Newark. I am proud of that; indeed, I consider it my greatest episcopal contribution.

I also wish to thank the members of Trinity Presbyterian Church in Charlotte, North Carolina, and their pastor, Dr. Louis Patrick, among whom I tested this material on two occasions as the leader of their annual conference at the retreat center in Montreat, North Carolina. By their interaction many points in this volume were clarified. The opportunity to teach among Presbyterians is one way that I acknowledge my debt to my Presbyterian mother.

The community church at Point O'Woods, New York, and the clergy of the Diocese of El Camino Real in California also let me give this material trial runs. To John H. McCain at Point O'Woods and to the Right Reverend Richard L. Shimpfky, bishop of El Camino Real, go my gratitude for those opportunities.

My thanks go also to my staff, first to Wanda Hollenbeck, who runs the bishop's office and has facilitated in a mighty way my writing career for the past eight years. Wanda possesses sensitivity, competence, and integrity in such abundant measure that words cannot fully capture her importance to me. Suffice it to say that she fills that position with enormous talent and professional skill. This will be the fifth book that she has helped me produce. I would also like to thank her husband, Richard, for his infinitely wise career decision that caused him, along with his wife, to move to West Orange, New Jersey, and thus to become a significant part of my life.

The other members of my staff share with me fully in the responsibilities of the office of bishop. They are Suffragan Bishop Jack M. McKelvey, Assisting Bishop Walter C. Righter, and our three lay executives, John G. Zinn in finance, Michael P. Francaviglia in administration, and Karen K.

Lindley in communications and program. I like to demonstrate to the church at large that the bishop's office is a corporate, not a singular, office and that each of these people shares significantly in that corporateness. In liturgical events in the diocese I symbolize this by putting the members of my core staff behind the bishop's crozier in ecclesiastical processions where traditionally only the bishop walks. Most people think of that as an odd, perhaps incorrect, liturgical procedure. I think of it as a powerful symbol of the truth I seek to live out in my life as a bishop.

Others who work in Diocesan House and who grace our corporate life include Cecil Broner, Rupert Cole, Annemarie Cole, Gail Deckenbach, Yowanda Herring, Robert Lanterman, Karla Lerman, Barbara Lescota, Ginny Maiella, Pat McGuire, Brad Moor, William Quinlan, Joyce Riley, Lucy Sprague, Elizabeth Stone, Phillip Storm and Theresa Wilder. To all of them I express deep gratitude.

Finally, I salute my immediate family: my wonderful wife, Christine, who makes every day holy and happy; my Richmond, Virginia, daughters—Ellen and Katharine, with their respective husbands, Gus Epps and Jack Catlett; my California daughter, Jaquelin, and her husband, Todd Hylton; my two grandchildren, to whom by name this book is dedicated; Brian Barney, my stepson, who is a student at the University of Vermont; and Rachel Barney, my stepdaughter, who is a student in the engineering school at Columbia University in New York City. It is one of life's great privileges to enjoy the association and to love the members of one's primary and extended family. I live as such a privileged man.

John Shelby Spong
Newark, New Jersey
1992

Born of a Woman

1

Escaping Biblical Literalism

For most of the two thousand years of history since the birth of our Lord, the Christian church has participated in and supported the oppression of women. This oppression has been both overt and covert, conscious and unconscious. It has come primarily through the church's ability in the name of God to define a woman and to make that definition stick. It was grounded in a literalistic understanding of Holy Scripture thought of as the infallible word of God and produced in a patriarchal era.

Patriarchy and God have been so deeply and uncritically linked to gender by the all-male church hierarchy that men have little understood how this alliance has been used to the detriment of all women. In a unique and intriguing sense, the parts of the Bible that have contributed most to this negativity have been the birth narratives of Matthew and Luke. These stories, far more than is generally realized, assisted in the development of the ecclesiastical stereotype of the ideal woman against which all women came to be judged. The power of these birth narratives over women lies in their subtle illusions and romantic imagery. Those biblical passages

1

that contain obvious prejudice against women can be quickly confronted and easily laid aside. But subtle, unconscious definitions and traditional unchallenged patterns resist so simple an excising. So it is that through these passages of Holy Scripture the picture of a woman known as "the virgin" has found entry into the heart of the Christian story, and from that position she has exercised her considerable influence.

Each year at the Christmas season she is brought out of the church and placed in a position of public honor for about two weeks. She is dressed in pale blue, portrayed with demure, downcast eyes, and defined in terms of virgin purity. No female figure in Western history rivals her in setting standards. Since she is known as "the virgin," she has contributed to that peculiarly Christian pattern of viewing women primarily in terms of sexual function. Women may deny their sexuality by becoming virgin nuns, or women may indulge their sexuality by becoming prolific mothers. But in both cases, women are defined not first as persons and second as sexual beings but first and foremost as females whose sexuality determines their identity. This means, in my opinion, that the literalized Bible in general, and the birth narratives that turn on the person of the virgin in particular, are guilty of aiding and abetting the sexist prejudice that continues to live and to distort women even as late in history as these last years of the twentieth century.

I want to challenge publicly and vigorously this view of both the Bible and the virgin tradition and sexual images that gather around the stories of Jesus' birth. But I want to do this quite specifically as a Christian and as one who treasures the Scriptures. That task represents for me a willingness to walk the razor's edge of faith. I intend to claim the Bible as my ally in the struggle to end the oppression of women. I also intend to celebrate Christmas each year using the traditional readings and symbols of that season, but I will seek to

2

free that birth tradition from its destructive literalism. I do not believe that Mary was in any biological sense literally a virgin. I do not believe that someone known as a virgin mother can be presented with credibility to contemporary men or women as an ideal woman. I do not believe that the story of Mary's virginity enhanced the portrait of the mother of Jesus. To the contrary, I believe that story has detracted from Mary's humanity and has become a weapon in the hands of those whose patriarchal prejudices distort everyone's humanity in general but women's humanity in particular. But before examining the birth narratives specifically, it is necessary to look briefly at the Bible as a whole.

I am amazed that given the knowledge revolution of the last six hundred years anyone can still regard the Bible as the dictated words of God, inerrant and eternal. This claim, however, is still made with effective power and still finds a fertile field in the hearts of many who refer to themselves as simple believers. It is this audience to whom the television evangelists direct their appeal. These electronic "preachers of the Word" offer to their legions biblical security, certainty in faith, and even superiority in their sense of salvation. In return, their supporters provide the evangelists with a following that can be translated into political power and enormous financial resources. Neither the political power nor the financial resources are always used, history has revealed, in a responsible way.

In recent years I have been given the opportunity to engage two of America's better-known evangelists in televised debates about the Bible.[1] I am for them an interesting study, for I grew up as a biblical fundamentalist and had the content of the Bible made a part of my very being. I have read this wondrous book on a daily basis since I was twelve. The remarkable biographical detail of my spiritual journey is that when I ceased being a fundamentalist I did not cease to love the Bible. The Bible remains today the primary focus of my study. I am therefore a strange phenomenon, at least in Christian America. I am known as a theological liberal. Yet I dare to call myself a Bible-believing, Bible-based Christian. Such a combination is, for many, a contradiction in terms.

When I hear a public person suggest that the Bible means literally exactly what it says, I am so amazed that I have to remind myself that some seven decades have passed since the famous Scopes trial in Tennessee. That trial not only captured the nation's attention but it also actually found a young high school science teacher guilty of espousing evolution in his classroom in direct defiance of the truth of Holy Scripture. Such activity constituted a crime in Tennessee in the 1920s. In that trial Clarence Darrow was brilliant in his cross-examination of William Jennings Bryan, reducing his opponent to blathering ineptitude by asking such biblical questions as "Where did Cain get his wife?" and "Was it really possible for a human being named Jonah to live three days and three nights in the belly of a whale?" But the jury nonetheless voted to convict the high school teacher, for the commitment to biblical literalism was more deeply a part of the security system of the times than was the commitment to truth. So bizarre was their conclusion that it propelled Mr. Scopes, Mr. Darrow, and Mr. Bryan into the very folklore of America.

Yet, incredible though it is, the presentation of this kind of biblical literalism continues to live today, being regularly fed by the mass communication system called television. That electronic power assures that religious ignorance will continue to live for yet a while longer. Furthermore, it guarantees that this level of ignorance will continue to define many of the religious questions and the religious issues of our time, to the ultimate loss of credibility for all religious systems, I fear.

As a direct consequence of this activity, increasing numbers of the educated of our world will be convinced that organized religion is little more than a hysterical, superstitious system with no ability to compel either their response or allegiance. Those who seek to be citizens of this century as well as believing Christians will be a shriveling and sometimes almost invisible minority.

It is quite easy to dismiss biblical fundamentalism on intellectual grounds.[2] The Bible is full of contradictions. The same God who says in one place, "You shall not kill" (Exod. 20:13), in another place orders Israel to "slay the Amalekites, every man, woman and child" (1 Sam. 15:3ff). The God who seems to entertain a universal consciousness when heard to say, "My name shall be great among the gentiles" (Mal. 1:10) or "every valley shall be exalted" (Isa. 40:4), is also pictured as rejoicing over the drowning of the Egyptians in the Red Sea (Exodus 15) and allowing the heads of the Edomite children to be "dashed against the rocks" (Ps. 137:7–9). An entire manuscript filled with similar contradictions could be gathered quickly.

Beyond these anomalies, geological and astrophysical evidence has also challenged biblical "truth" successfully. That evidence reveals that this planet earth has been in existence for between four and five billion years and that human or near-human life itself is between five hundred thousand and two million years old. This documentable data should be able to take care of the literalization of the seven-day creation story and Irish Bishop James Ussher's biblical calculation that the earth was created in the year 4004 B.C.E. Since the sun does not revolve around the earth, as Joshua thought, it would be quite difficult to order it to stop in its journey across the sky. Yet Joshua did precisely that, according to the Bible, to enable Israel to win its battle before nightfall (Josh. 10:12–13).

5

We could also raise interesting questions as to what occurred in the digestive system of the great fish when Jonah entered that system whole and remained there for seventy-two hours (Jon. 1:17). At the very least, there would have been an acute fishy constipation. Did the graves really open at the time of the crucifixion and people long dead get up and walk into Jerusalem to be seen by many, as Matthew asserts (Matt. 27:51–53)? Did the waters of the Red Sea really part for Moses (Exod. 14:21ff)? Did manna really rain down from heaven only on six days so as not to violate the Sabbath by falling on the seventh day (Exod. 16:5)? Did Noah really gather all the animals of the world into that tiny boat, two by two (Gen. 7:6–10)? Did that include kangaroos, which no one knew existed until Australia was discovered centuries later? Did Jesus walk on the water (Mark 6:48, 49), still the storm (Mark 4:37–41), or feed the multitude with five loaves and two fish (John 6:1–14)? If grave clothes were left intact in Jesus' tomb when Jesus rose, as John asserts (John 20:7), are we to assume that his resurrected body was unclothed?

Belief in the historic accuracy of these texts no longer exists in academic circles, but it still enjoys a vigorous life in the pews of many of our churches. In a less blatant form this fundamentalistic attitude permeates not just the ranks of the unthinking masses but finds expression even in sophisticated, well-educated, high ecclesiastical circles.

No less a person than Pope John Paul II has supported a document and an attitude that proclaims, "Women will never be priests in the Roman Catholic Church because Jesus did not choose any women to be his disciples." I submit that this is a literal misuse of the Holy Scriptures. In the social order and mores of the first century, a woman as a member of a disciple band of an itinerant rabbi or teacher was inconceivable. The female role was too clearly circumscribed for that even to be imagined. Here, however, biblical literalism is ec-

6

lectic rather than thoroughgoing. Perhaps it has not yet occurred to the bishop of Rome that Jesus did not choose any Polish males to be disciples either, but this did not exclude from the priesthood the Polish boy Karol Jozef Wojtyla, who became John Paul II. Of course, this attitude toward women is changing everywhere, including all branches of the Christian church. Even those churches that still refuse to ordain women now allow them to serve the church as lay leaders and acolytes and on the governing boards. None of that was possible before World War II. All churches will surely have women pastors, priests, and bishops before long.

When I listen to Easter and Christmas sermons, I hear time after time a still-vibrant neoliteralism even in those mainline churches that would be embarrassed if someone suggested they were fundamentalistic. Likewise, the official documents, studies, and pastoral letters issued by ecclesiastical bodies or groups of bishops are often buttressed by straightforward appeals to the literalism of Scripture. One bishop was quoted in the press as asserting that in seven specific passages of the Bible homosexuality was condemned, as if that somehow guaranteed it to be so forever.[3] Every movement to end oppression in any form in Western history has had to overcome the authority of a literal Bible. Christianity, with its Scriptures intact, persecuted pagans and spawned a vicious anti-Semitism that fueled everything from the Crusades to the Holocaust to the defacement of synagogues. That demonic gift from biblical literalism plagues us even today. A literal Bible still sees the Jews as those evil people who killed Jesus. "His blood be on us and on our children" (Matt. 27:25) is a text frequently used to justify our prejudice. The Jews are called in the Bible "children of the devil" (John 8:44), and they are defined as possessing a God-given stupor: "eyes that cannot see and ears that cannot hear" (Rom. 11:8). There are times that I literally shudder

7

when I hear the Good Friday story read and realize once again that the biblical use of the words *the Jews* in that narrative will once more feed that dark stain on the historic soul of Christianity.

Other life-denying prejudices have been perpetuated throughout history as official "Christian" positions, buttressed by an appeal to the literal Bible. Included on that list would be the rejection of left-handed people as abnormal, the enslavement and segregation of non-white people as subhuman, the violation and murder of gay or lesbian people who are labelled sick or depraved, the repulsion from the sanctuaries of the church including the burial office of those who have committed suicide, and the rejection and excommunication through canon law of divorced persons regardless of the circumstances leading to the divorce. It always seemed strange to me that something called the Word of God became in fact again and again in the life of the church a weapon of oppression. But that is the judgment of history.

It is almost amusing to examine "biblical morality" as it is called by the literalists. They do not seem to understand how immoral, by our standards, many biblical attitudes are. For example, according to the older of the Hebrew creation myths, the woman was not created in the image of God but rather came into being as an afterthought to provide the male with a companion and a helpmate (Gen. 2:4–23). The woman was the property of the man. Lot, called righteous by the Bible, offered his virgin daughters to the angry mob in the city of Sodom (Gen. 19:8). Who will step forward to support that part of "biblical morality"? In the Ten Commandments, the quintessential part of the Jewish law still naively saluted as the essence of biblical morality, the wife was listed after a man's house and before a man's ox, as a possession not to be coveted by another man (Exod. 20:17). Moralists who quote the seventh commandment prohibiting adultery (Exod.

8

20:14) fail to realize that polygamy was the style of marriage abroad when that commandment was given. Indeed, three hundred years after the giving of the law at Mount Sinai, Solomon had seven hundred wives and three hundred concubines, says the Bible (1 Kings 11:3). What does adultery mean when one man possesses one thousand women? In its literal context the seventh commandment really enjoined one man from violating the woman who was the property of another man. A woman who was not so owned was, of course, fair game. That does not seem to be nearly so moral as the moralists would have us believe.

Beyond the naive literalism of the fundamentalists and the more subtle literalism of a broad segment of church leaders is still another level of biblical literalism. It is all but unchallenged even in religious and academic circles. This form of literalism is the assertion that the Bible's stories are absolutely unique, novel, and non-syncretistic, or the literalism that fails to see the universal aspects of all religious folklore. Joseph Campbell in his conversation with Bill Moyers, published under the title *The Power of Myth,* suggested that religious people should study the myths of religions other than their own because they tend to literalize the myths of their own religious systems.[4]

Many stories in the mythologies of the world, for example, parallel familiar parts of the Christian tradition. Divine figures are born of virgin mothers, mythic heroes die and are resurrected and return to heaven in cosmic ascensions. When we read of these traditions in the context of Egyptian sacred writings, it does not occur to us to literalize the stories of Osiris and Isis. We know we are dealing in that instance with ancient myths. However, we avoid making the same assumptions about our own faith story. In fact, among some Christians, anyone not affirming the total historicity of the Christian story is suspect and drummed out of the corps as

9

a nonbeliever or even a heretic. Most believing Christians have not yet come to recognize in their religious tradition the subjectivity of language, of history, of a particular value system, or of every specific mind-set.

Can the meaning of Jesus' ascension (Acts 1), which in its biblical context assumed a three-tiered universe—a flat earth and a literal heaven above the domed sky—be delivered from the words and thought forms of the era that first froze that experience into such stringent and dated concrete images? Can space-age people escape the conclusion that if Jesus literally rose from this earth, and even if he traveled at the speed of light (186,000 miles per second), he has still not escaped the boundaries of this single galaxy. Literalism leads to strange absurdities!

In the first century's view of genetics, the whole life of the infant was assumed to be genetically present in the sperm of the male, a concept referred to as a humuncleos.[5] The birth narratives written in that era, therefore, in order to assert Jesus' divine origin had only to displace the male, for the female was believed to offer nothing save the womb to serve as an incubator. That story, if literalized, can make no sense at all in a world that understands the genetic processes of both males and females quite differently. The framers of the birth narratives did not know about egg cells and the way zygotes are formed genetically. Literalize the birth legends of Matthew and Luke today and you will, according to such eminent theologians as Wolfhart Pannenberg and Emil Brunner, destroy the Christian concept of incarnation.[6] A Jesus who receives his human nature from Mary and his divine nature from the Holy Spirit cannot meet the test of being fully human and fully divine. He would, in fact, be neither fully human nor fully divine, both Pannenberg and Brunner have argued. If they are correct, then even Christianity itself cannot stand the continued literalization of the virgin birth tradition. Yet at lunch in the refectory of one of America's foremost divinity schools several years ago, the students with whom I talked were still treating the virgin story literally, and, perhaps more fearfully, they were quoting one of their professors to buttress their arguments.

When one Episcopal bishop told me that he accepted the virgin birth story literally because "if God wanted to be born of a virgin, he could have arranged that,"[7] or when another said, "If God created ex nihilo, the virgin birth would be a snap,"[8] I thought to myself, How will the church survive in this world with that lack of scholarship among its leaders? In those statements the bishops were asserting their belief in a God who was in fact a manipulative male person, who would set aside the processes of the world to produce a miracle in order to bring his (sic) divine presence into a human enterprise called life, from which this God was clearly separated. They also revealed no knowledge whatsoever of the biblical studies that have, for at least a century, thrown new light on the interpretation of these birth narratives.

Literalism masquerades under many forms—from the blatant to the subtle to the unconscious—but it is literalism nonetheless, and in every instance it is finally destructive to truth. Because the power of institutional Christianity has been assumed to rest upon the literal assertions of a fourth-century creed, it is easy to understand why biblical literalism continues to possess its tenacious hold upon ecclesiastical leadership, including those academicians who teach the clergy of the future in some of the seminaries of this land, particularly the denominationally based seminaries.

A literalized myth is a doomed myth. Its truth cannot be rescued. Literalism is not even a benign alternative for contemporary Christians. It is, in the modern world, nothing less than an enemy to faith in Jesus Christ. It is a belief system built on ignorance, which acts as if God, the infinite

11

mystery, can be defined in the words of any human being or in the thought forms of a particular era. Literalism is a claim that God's eternal truth has been, or can be, captured in the time-limited concepts of human history. It is to pretend that knowledge is finite and that knowledge does not therefore explode in infinite new directions daily. Biblical fundamentalism reduces the religious options for people to the shallow levels of propositional truth and then fills them with a religious certainty that can be maintained only by a defensive, aggressive hysteria. When that certainty explodes, fundamentalism leaves the would-be fundamentalist with no alternative save a Godless despair. The day has passed for me when, in the name of tolerance to the religious insecurities of others, I will allow my Christ to be defined inside a killing literalism.

So I turn to these questions: What does it take to understand those mythic dimensions that fill our religious story? Can the universal elements in the Christian myth be identified? Can they be lifted out of the tribal thinking of our limited minds until they touch the deep recesses of life, the depths of the human psyche, and even the mystical center of God? Can the religious traditions of Christianity be taken seriously but not literally? Can Christians be freed to explore the sacred writings of our faith story without being bound inside the prejudices, worldviews, and emotional pitfalls of another era? Can the Christian church at the dawn of the twenty-first century be called out of the literalism that if not escaped will finally be the cause of its death?

The time has come, I believe, for the church to launch into the deep, to give its people the courage to live with integrity and to search our sacred story with honesty for truth. The time has come for the church to recognize certainty as a vice and to dismiss it, and to embrace uncertainty as a virtue. The time has come for the church to surrender its neurotic pattern of trafficking in one feeble religious security system after another and to allow its people to feel the bracing wind of insecurity, so that Christians might understand what it means to walk by faith.

Can the church surrender its defining prejudices of a personalistic, masculine, and patriarchal worldview? Can we escape the stereotypes of the past that define gender, sexual orientation, and sexual morality in a way that has always violated women and now is seen increasingly to violate everyone? Can the church get out of the behavior-control business and into the business of calling people into being the holy and complete selves God has created them to be?

In this volume I have chosen to focus specifically on the role of church and Scripture in the oppression of women. In order to bring that focus into its clearest relief, I concentrate my study on the birth narratives that introduce the first and third Gospels in our standard biblical text.

At the beginning of this chapter, I stated my opinion that these narratives, more than any other parts of the Bible, have exercised a negative influence on women by providing a definition of ideal womanhood against which every woman must be compared. I therefore roam beneath the words of these familiar Christmas narratives. I examine this text by looking at similar stories in traditions quite different from my own. I face the implications of my claim that the story of the virgin birth is not literal, factual history. If there was no virgin birth, then either Joseph[9] or some other male was the earthly father of Jesus. If paternity belonged to one other than Joseph, then the question must be asked as to whether the liaison was accomplished with or without the consent of Jesus' mother. I examine the suggestion that Jesus might have been an "illegitimate" child, now being offered by feminist biblical scholars, and seek to understand the implications of that possibility for Christian theology. I ask why the

13

real woman who was at Jesus' side in life and death was replaced by an unreal sexless woman early in Christian history. Only in this manner, I am convinced, can we face, expose, and expunge the negativity toward women created by the literal Bible in general and the literalized birth narratives in particular. In the process, I hope to alert the church to the price it has had to pay for its embrace of fundamentalism.

As a new and promising doorway through which to walk into this task, I present first a method, a context, and a setting employed by the Bible's original authors that affect the Gospels in general and the birth stories specifically. By entering this doorway, I hope to provide a new option beyond the present sterile choices that so many feel the church today offers the world; namely, must I be premodern and prejudicial in order to be a Christian? or must I leave Christianity in order to escape my prejudices and take seriously my post-Christian world?

Perhaps I can open my readers' eyes to see that literalism in all its forms can die and yet God will continue to live. This journey will be, I believe, worth the reader's time and worth the believer's risk.

2

Approaching the Story Through Midrash

If the Bible is to be read today with intelligence, our knowledge of how it came to be written needs to be expanded. If I can offer that knowledge, then perhaps I can also offer enough security to enable the fundamentalists to listen and enough hope to enable those who have abandoned Christianity as premodern nonsense to look again. Perhaps both groups could then see that there is more to Christianity than that limiting literalism to which some cling and by which others are repelled.

Between the two sterile camps of believing literally or rejecting all, there is, in fact, a giant arena to explore. One cannot enter that arena, however, unless there is a doorway. One must also expect that beyond the doorway is a territory worth exploring, a territory that promises new meaning.

Some time ago while visiting a church in my diocese that was predominantly oriented toward literalistic Christianity, I tried at a luncheon meeting of the vestry in the rector's home to address these issues on a very elementary level. The result was revealing, to say the least. Luke's Gospel was the focus of my conversation. I talked about Luke's worldview, his audience, the issues alive in the church to which he wrote, and his way of addressing those issues.

I illustrated this by sketching briefly the impact of the figure Elijah on Luke's construction of Jesus' life story. I suggested that Luke, who is the only Gospel writer to give us a narrative of Jesus' ascension and a narrative of the Pentecost experience, developed both of these accounts by following the Elijah story line from 2 Kings. Elijah in the Hebrew Scriptures had bodily ascended into heaven via a fiery chariot drawn by fiery horses (2 Kings 2:11). He had also promised to bestow upon his single disciple, Elisha, a "double share" of his enormous but still-human spirit. The test for Elisha would be whether or not he saw his master Elijah's actual ascension. The narrative proclaimed that this "seeing" was accomplished, and Elisha walked away from that scene in the spirit and power of Elijah. Even the sons of the prophets affirmed this, for when Elisha returned to them they proclaimed, "The Spirit of Elijah rests upon Elisha" (2 Kings 2:15).

Elijah was known for his power to call down fire from heaven. He had done this in the contest with the prophets of Baal on Mount Carmel (1 Kings 18:20–39). He had also consumed with fire "a captain of fifty men with his fifty" and a second captain of fifty and his men sent to inquire about the status of the first group (2 Kings 1:9–12). In the folklore of Israel this fiery power belonged uniquely to Elijah.

Luke, aware of this Hebrew legend, had Jesus, in Elijah fashion, begin a journey with his disciples to his final destiny. As part of this final journey, Jesus sent his disciples ahead to prepare his way. When the Samaritan villages did not receive these disciples appropriately, they returned to

Jesus angry and requested that fire from heaven be called down to destroy these Samaritans (Luke 9:54). Jewish readers familiar with their traditions would recognize this as a request for the use of the Elijah power. Jesus, however, declined their request and even rebuked them (Luke 9:55).

In this narrative the figure of Elijah is clearly in the background. It should surprise no one therefore that Luke, seeking to present Jesus as the new and greater Elijah, suggested that since Elijah ascended into the sky as the climax of his life, Jesus did likewise (Acts 1:1–11). But note the contrast. Elijah needed a chariot. Jesus seemed to have ascended on his own power. Luke said that Jesus' disciples, like Elisha, witnessed the ascension so they were eligible to receive the Spirit of their master. Elijah bestowed a double portion of his enormous but still-human spirit on his single disciple, Elisha. Jesus, the new and greater Elijah, poured the infinite power of God's Holy Spirit upon the entire gathered Christian community (Acts 2:1ff). It came as a mighty rushing wind because the Hebrew word for spirit, *ruach*, is also the name for wind, which was thought to be nothing less than the breath of God. It also came as a tongue of fire, which lighted upon the disciples' heads but did not hurt or destroy them. It was the fire of Elijah lifted to a new dimension, not of destruction but of refining, by the new and greater Elijah.

As I sought to explain this biblical background, my friends around the room looked increasingly incredulous. "You mean," one of them said, "that maybe these things did not actually happen?"

"No," I suggested. "What we have in the Gospels is an interpretative narrative based on an earlier part of the tradition and designed to enable the reader to see the reality of God in Jesus and to be drawn to this reality in faith."

"This means," my questioner continued, "that you are saying that Luke was lying. He told these things as if they were true when he knew they were not!"

The luncheon would not be long enough to address these issues, I thought to myself in despair. This woman believed that the Gospels were something like a television documentary or a researched biography. She knew nothing about the style of writing that was in vogue in the Jewish world when the Gospels were written. She did not embrace the fact that when Jesus lived there was no electronic or print media.

It was inevitable that the first Christians, who were Jewish people, would interpret Jesus, organize their memory, and shape their religious life based on their Jewish religious heritage, which was the only tradition they knew. Luke in effect stated this in his resurrection narrative when he suggested that Jesus "opened the scriptures" to Cleopas and his partner in the Emmaus road story (Luke 24:27) and later when Luke has Jesus say, "These are the words that I spoke to you while I was yet with you, that all things must be fulfilled which were written in the law of Moses and in the prophets and in the psalms concerning me" (Luke 24:44).

The way the Jewish tradition viewed and treated Scripture was very clear. This method produced what was called midrash. Midrash represented efforts on the part of the rabbis to probe, tease, and dissect the sacred story looking for hidden meanings, filling in blanks, and seeking clues to yet-to-be-revealed truth. It was the assumption of the rabbis developing the midrash that the sacred text was timeless, that it was true in the past, true in the present, and true in the future.

Clues to understanding God's action today could be found in the ancient narratives. Christians were convinced that Jesus was the key to the Jewish Scriptures. The God who had spoken "in times past through the prophets has in these latter days spoken by his son" (Heb. 1:2). So they searched the ancient record for hints, clues, foreshadowings, and interpretations. One had only to possess eyes that could see. Hence, to retell stories out of the Jewish religious past to illumine a new experience was not to be deceitful, misleading, or false. It was, rather, to illumine the new experience by showing how the past was seen in and fulfilled by the present. The readers of the Gospels who understood this midrashic method of probing Scripture would understand. Only to a generation living hundreds of years later, separated from their Jewish religious roots and clinging to a peculiarly Western mind-set, would the choice appear to be between literal truth and overt lies.

Our twentieth-century world, distorted by religious claims to possess objectivity and literalness, asks, "Did it happen?" The biblical writers deeply involved in the midrash tradition were attempting to answer a quite different question, "What does it mean?" The Gospels, far more than we have thought before, are examples of Christian midrash. In the Gospels, the ancient Jewish story would be shaped, retold, interpreted, and even changed so as to throw proper light on the person of Jesus. There was nothing objective about the Gospel tradition. These were not biographies. They were books designed to inspire faith. The fourth Gospel even suggested, quite overtly, that "these things are written so that you may believe that Jesus is the Christ, the Son of God, and that believing you might have life in his name" (John 20:21). Mark declared he was writing "the gospel of Jesus Christ, the Son of God" (Mark 1:1). Luke asserted that he was writing of those things that are "most assuredly believed among us" (Luke 1:1). To force these narratives into the straitjacket of literal historicity is to violate their intention,

19

their method, and their truth. To see them as expressions of the genre called midrash with a Christian twist is to enter Scripture in a new and perhaps a life-giving way.

Did Jesus physically ascend, or is that a Christian midrash retelling of the Elijah story? Did the Holy Spirit descend with a literal wind and with tongues of fire, or is that a heightened retelling of the promise of Elijah to pour his spirit out on the disciple who sees? Did Judas Iscariot actually go hang himself after the act of betrayal, as Matthew narrates (Matt. 27:3–10), or is that a retelling of the story of Ahithophel, who hanged himself after he had betrayed David, the shepherd King of Israel? (2 Sam. 17:23). Did Judas receive thirty pieces of silver for his act of betrayal, or is that a retelling of the story from the book of Zechariah (Zech. 11:4–14)? Here a prophet was appointed by God as the "shepherd of Israel" but, because of the unwillingness of the people to follow their shepherd, this prophet wanted to resign. At the moment of his resignation he was paid his back wages—thirty pieces of silver. That was the price it cost Israel of old to rid itself of God's appointed shepherd. Was that a parable hidden in the Hebrew Scriptures that really was designed to foreshadow Jesus? That was true to the midrash tradition, and that was the way it would have appeared to the Gospel writers.

Did Jesus feed the multitude with loaves and fishes, or is that a retelling of the story of God feeding the chosen people in the wilderness with manna? Was the raising of the widow's son at Nain (Luke 7:11–17) an event of history or a retelling of the story of Elijah raising the widow's son (1 Kings 17:17–24)? Was that another Elijah hint? Does the fourth Gospel perpetuate the midrash tradition by turning the Lucan parable about Lazarus and the rich man (Luke 16) into a historic narrative that asserted that Lazarus had been raised from the dead (John 11)? Again and again throughout

20

the Gospels we confront the midrash style. One only needs the eyes to see, the mind to understand, and the tradition to enrich.

Perhaps in a form more concentrated than anywhere else in the New Testament the birth narratives are illustrative of Christian midrash. The only obvious historical fact beneath these narratives is that Jesus was born. No one enters this world in any other way, if one is human. The church historically resisted every effort to remove Jesus' humanity from him, although in the common mind he continues to be thought of as a heavenly visitor.

The first building block in constructing the nonhuman Jesus of later Christian mythology is found in the birth narratives of Matthew and Luke. But these need to be seen as midrashic attempts to interpret the power and impact of the adult Jesus. The Bethlehem location, the miraculous conception, the heavenly signs, the gifts of the magi, the visit of the shepherds, the slaughter of the male babies, the flight into Egypt, and perhaps even the names of Zechariah, Elizabeth, Joseph, and Mary are products of midrash. At least these possibilities ought to be entertained and explored.

He was Jesus of Nazareth. His name was a common name in Hebrew society. It was Yeshua, or Joshua. His birth was, in all probability, not noted by anyone other than Mary and whoever attended her. Mary's labor was real. Jesus' birth was human like every other birth. There were contractions, pain, blood, an umbilicus that had to be cut, and the afterbirth with which someone had to deal. As I shall chronicle later, there may even have been a hint of scandal connected with this birth.

Never, however, would these birth narratives have been created had not the experience with the adult Jesus cried out for an explanation. Who is this man? Whence has he come? It took years for the birth stories to be formed. They did not appear in written form until the ninth decade of the Christian era. They reflect the charm of the romantic storyteller who wanted to explain something that the camera or videotape could never capture.

But before we can enter that magical world of virgin births, angelic messengers, heavenly hosts, wandering stars, exotic magi, and hillside shepherds, we need to search for the experience that demanded so elaborate an explanation. That experience, while connected with Jesus, did not originate in the events of his birth but rather in the events of his death. Only slowly did they wander back in history until one could take pen in hand and write, Once upon a time in the village of Bethlehem . . .

3

Born of a Woman—Paul's Witness

Before any Gospel was written, before theological doctrines designed to interpret Jesus came into being, before any
tradition concerning Jesus' birth had been articulated, Paul
had written:

> But when the time had fully come,
> God sent forth his Son,
> born of a woman, born under the law,
> to redeem those who were under the law,
> so that we might receive adoption as sons.
>
> (Galatians 4:4, 5)

These were the first written words to be preserved by the
Christian community describing the birth of Jesus. They
were written by Paul between 49 and 55 c.e., or some nine-
teen to twenty-five years after the events of Calvary and the
experience of Easter and some sixteen to twenty-one years
before the first Gospel was penned. A chapter written on
Paul's understanding of Jesus' origins would be a very brief
chapter indeed, for Paul was unconcerned about these
things. In this Galatian text there is no hint of a miraculous

birth or of supernatural parenting. That issue simply had not yet been raised for Paul, nor was it an interest for this first generation of Christians.

In this same epistle, Paul referred in a matter-of-fact way to James, the Lord's brother (Gal. 1:19). The idea that there might be something strange in the fact that Jesus had a brother was equally inconceivable to this Jewish author. Indeed, James "the Lord's brother" had his position of status and influence in the early church primarily because of his physical kinship with Jesus of Nazareth. Some thirty-five years later, when Luke would write his account in the Book of Acts of the Jerusalem consultation between Paul and Jewish-Christian leaders, the James referred to was no longer identified by the title "the Lord's brother" (Acts 15). However, it is clear that this could only be James the brother of Jesus. Acts earlier had recounted that James the brother of John (and the son of Zebedee) had been slain by the sword of Herod (Acts 12:1, 2). The only other James the Bible knows is James the son of Alphaeus. Could he be the James referred to in Acts 15? That is highly unlikely. When one recognizes the power of James the Lord's brother in the Jerusalem Christian community unequivocally affirmed by Paul in his letter to the church in Galatia, and the absence of any other mention of James the son of Alphaeus in early Christian writings, there is no other valid conclusion. Yet something clearly had occurred in those thirty or so years between Paul and Luke to cause the leadership of the Christian church to suppress the identification of James as the Lord's brother. To this fascinating detail I will return later.

In Paul's letter to the church at Rome, which scholars usually date at 56 to 58 C.E., we have his second and final reference to Jesus' birth. He wrote of "the gospel concerning his Son who was descended from David according to the flesh and designated Son of God in power according to

24

the Spirit of holiness by his resurrection from the dead" (Rom. 1:3, 4). Once again there is no hint of anything unusual about the birth of Jesus. He was a descendant of David "according to the flesh." A Davidid, this would be called. Whether this royal claim came through his maternity or his paternity was not stated, for his descent through the flesh was for Paul of little or no importance. The focus of this text was on the faith affirmation. Jesus "was designated [note the passive verb form] Son of God in power according to the Spirit of holiness by his resurrection from the dead." Who designated him Son of God is clear from reading the rest of Paul. Paul never referred to the resurrection in an active verb tense. For Paul, Jesus never "rises from the dead." Always it is God who raised him (Rom 4:24; 6:9; 10:9; 1 Cor. 15:4, 13, 14, 15, 20; Phil. 2:9). God was one, holy, and sovereign for the Jewish Paul. The idea of a coequal trinity of Persons in the Godhead had not yet been born. Had Paul been alive when that idea did emerge, I suspect he would have resisted it vigorously. Paul was certainly not a Trinitarian, as that concept came to be defined in later Greek-influenced theological discussions. The idea of Incarnation, which also arises out of a Greek dualism, would have been equally incomprehensible to him. The action of resurrection, for Paul, belonged to God alone, who vindicated the righteous Jewish Jesus by raising him. Furthermore, that vindication Paul thought of as the exaltation of Jesus into heaven, not as a physical resuscitation from death back into life. If Paul had narrated that moment, I suspect he would have done so in terms closer to what the church later called the ascension, rather than what the church came to call the resurrection. Paul, however, did not narrate, he proclaimed that God raised Jesus; and he used both the words "exaltation" (Phil. 2:9) and "resurrection" (1 Cor. 15:13) to describe that moment.

25

Paul's clear assumption was that the birth of Jesus was completely normal and completely human. One does not need a supernatural birth to be declared Son of God in a Jewish context. Indeed, delving into or speculating about the origins of a life that was vindicated by God was of no great import to Paul or, presumably, to the early Christian church.

At this moment in primitive Christianity, Paul (who died around 64 C.E.) stood as a witness to a normal human birth process for Jesus. It must be noted that despite his presumption of a natural birth, he nonetheless developed a profound Christology. But it was a Christology that was not dependent on a supernatural origin. For this first great Christian thinker, a nexus existed in Jesus of Nazareth in which the divine and the human had come together. He saw Jesus as God's first creation (Colossians 15). He found a self-emptying divinity in the Jesus of history (Phil. 2:5–11). But no birth story was necessary for Paul to make those assertions. Nor did his understanding of Jesus depend on supernatural intervention at any point prior to the resurrection/exaltation moment. Paul was too much a Jew for that. A pity it is that this Jewish anchor for Jesus did not endure.

Birth traditions do not develop around all people. When they do develop, they constitute a powerful commentary not on the birth of the subject, as people suppose, but on the adult significance of the life whose birth is being described. They reflect the human need to understand the origins of greatness in the person who has so affected and shaped human history. They are akin to the suggestion that the boy George Washington never told a lie, even when he cut down the cherry tree, or to the fascination with the early life of a boy named Abraham Lincoln, who grew up, it was said, in a log cabin on the American frontier. Perhaps birth stories about figures of history are inevitable. When those figures of history are also religious persons of great import to living faith systems, it is almost inevitable that in time a literalizing process will engulf the legendary birth narratives, and adherents of the faith system will begin to suggest that the interpretive birth stories were in fact actual events that took place in history. It was so with both Moses and Muhammad.

For those of us who stand inside the Christian faith system, our task is first to look at the adult power of the Jesus that in time created the tales of his supernatural origins. Jesus himself was once reported to have said, "What do you think of the Christ? Whose Son is he?" (Matt. 22:42). In ingenious ways, the second, not the first, generation of Christians began to address this question with growing legends. This first generation of Christians was concerned to address only the scandal of the cross. How could the messiah be crucified? That was Paul's issue as a member of that first generation. But after the death of Paul of Tarsus, a second generation began to probe Jesus' origins, and when they did, they found it necessary to address what came to be called "the scandal of the manger." To that story we now turn.

4

From the Scandal of the Cross to the Scandal of the Crib

Paul wrote from approximately 47 to 64 C.E. His early letters were midway between the life of Jesus and the First Gospel. His last letters were midway between the life of Jesus and the Fourth Gospel. As these years passed between Jesus' earthly life and the Gospel-writing tradition that sought to explain him, a fascinating theological process occurred. The process moved in a consistent pattern from the Jesus of history to the Christ of faith. It began with a specific human life made of real flesh and blood. He had a particular name, and he came from a particular town. He was known as Jesus of Nazareth (Mark 1:24; Matt. 26:71; Luke 4:34; John 1:45) or as the Nazarene or even as the Galilean.

Jesus was part of a particular family. His mother, brothers, and sisters were identifiable to the people of Nazareth (Mark 6:3). He was known by them as a carpenter (Mark 6:3), though Matthew, writing some fifteen to twenty years later, changed that Marcan reference from his being a carpenter to his being a carpenter's son (Matt. 13:55). It is interesting to note that outside the birth narratives that verse was the only other Matthean reference to Jesus' earthly father. The spouse of Mary was presented in sacred writings of Christians as a shadowy figure, almost a nonpresence, in Jesus' adult life.

In any event, this Jesus in his adult life clearly had an impact on the people of Galilee and Judea. He organized a band of disciples, which in itself was not unusual for a wandering teacher, but the disciples of this Jesus appeared to have little or no social or political influence. They were primarily identified with what might be called the riffraff element of society: fishermen, a tax collector, a zealot,[1] and others somewhat nondescript. Yet tales of power grew up around this Jesus. Stories were heard of healings, exorcisms, nature miracles, and even resuscitations of the dead.

He had a teaching gift. His illustrations were graphic, his stories and parables memorable. They were crafted out of the whole cloth of real life. He spoke of a father who indulged his son and lived to regret it (Luke 15:11–32), of a widow who lost a coin and swept diligently until she found it (Luke 15:8–10), of a man who built the foundation of his house in the shifting sands instead of on the mighty rocks (Matt. 7:24–27), and of a judge who separated the sheep from the goats on the day of judgment (Matt. 25:31–46).

But teachers, even eloquent teachers of renown, were not uncommon in the Jewish tradition. That alone would never have lifted this Jesus out of the obscurity of history. Miracle workers or healers were likewise not unknown, nor were they all flimflam artists or peddlers of snake-oil cures. Beneath the tales that were normally exaggerated, there was usually a kernel of legitimacy, a circumstance that lent wonder or amazement to an event, a measurable result that grew as the tale passed from mouth to mouth. But healers came and went. They certainly did not often inspire legends, nor did they normally drive people to inquire into their origins in order to explain their power.

Somehow this Jesus was different; and when the story of his life was examined, that difference seemed to lie in the events of his last days on earth. This interpretive clue was seen in every Gospel written about him. All the Gospel writers focused on that final one week, devoting 25 to 40 percent of their entire narrative to it.

One modern biblical scholar has suggested that these climactic parts of the Gospel story came into written form first to satisfy liturgical needs.[2] The Jewish people who had become Christians were accustomed to the Scripture readings that accompanied the observance of Passover. In time these first Christians developed the vigil service of Easter at which, in Passover fashion, they read and reenacted the passion narrative of their Lord as they watched through the night in preparation for the resurrection celebration at dawn.

This scholar has also suggested that in time the rest of the Jewish liturgical year was similarly reinterpreted with Christian narratives about Jesus or with Jesus' own remembered words forming the scriptural content. It was for this liturgical purpose primarily, he argues, that Mark, Matthew, and Luke came to be written. To support his argument, he correlates the Gospels with Jewish writings in observance of the Jewish New Year, the Day of Atonement, the Feast of Tabernacles, and the Jewish Pentecost.

It was only because of the experience of Easter, however, that this vigil service was created. That experience alone moved the apostles to reconstitute themselves as a community of faith. At the arrest of Jesus the disciples had fled for their lives. Something had to bring them back together. What that something was and the context in which it occurred formed the crucial interpretive center of the Christian message that we now call the passion narrative. It is no wonder that the first Christian liturgical celebration would be built around the experience that informed that memory. The primary purpose of liturgy has always been to recall and to celebrate saving moments. So the heart of the Christian story is found in the recounting of the events of Jesus' last days with the life-changing moment of Easter forming the climax of the story.

The importance of that moment was also reflected in the way the Christian community structured its life. Since that community had come to see itself as the new Israel it was important that the number twelve be preserved in matters of importance. The twelve tribes of Israel was the organizing principle of the people of the first covenant, so the Christians felt the need to preserve as the organizing principle of the new covenant the structure of the apostolic band as being twelve in number. However, in Judas Iscariot there was a defection in the ranks that reduced the number to eleven, requiring some action of restoration. The book of Acts tells us of the choice of Matthias to take the place of Judas. In that narrative the sole criterion for the selection of this new member of the twelve was that he must have been a witness to the catalytic moment that changed history.

Since that moment also came to be associated with the first day of the week, hardly a holy time in the Jewish tradition, that day quickly got caught up in the Christian drama and became the new Christian holy day. It was called the day of the Lord or the day of the resurrection. The experience of Easter that brought this new faith community into being was building a new content as human beings struggled to put that experience into words.

The meaning of Jesus was to be located in the events of that day which climaxed that crucial week. This was the assertion of each of the canonical Gospels. Something happened that gave his life a new significance, a startling power. Something happened that provided new impetus to the human questions asked time and again in his life: Who is this? What is the meaning of his life? Whence does he come? First, they experienced his power. Second, they sought to understand his power. Third, they attempted to explain the origin of his power. That is a familiar process in human mental meanderings, but it does not occur unless there is a powerful experience that demands an explanation.

Unfortunately, in later history these tales explaining the origin of his life and the source of his power would be literalized. Not every person seems able to distinguish between the levels of human knowledge. Mythology and folklore are means by which one arrives at a rational understanding of an experience that is beyond words. Yet no one doubted that the experience was real, intense, and clear.

Mythology and folklore are not to be identified with the experience. Indeed, mythology and folklore are two steps removed from reality. The experience is always primary, the reflective understanding of the experience is always secondary, and the tales that illumine or explain the understanding are always tertiary. We probe the mythology and folktales to illumine the conclusions people drew that enabled them to talk about their experience. An intense experience ultimately has no form. As soon as it achieves form it is distorted. Yet every human experience has to be processed. The only means we have to do this is by and through the use of words and symbols.

Even the word *God* was, and is, a culturally conditioned construct. The first-century world, and ancient people generally, thought of God after the analogy of a superhuman person. The human image of the highest rank was a king. The king was male, sovereign over a single nation, and the most powerful person in the land. God was pictured as a superking, very much male, with sovereignty over the whole world, with power beyond human comprehension. It was the power of light, darkness, wind, wave, thunder, lightning, flood, drought, life, and death. His throne—for all kings have thrones—was beyond the sky, where he reigned in majestic splendor.

In the face of this divine power, people groveled in fear. They sought to win God's favor with sacrifices, offerings, and words of flattery and praise. They sought to win divine approval with behavior modeled on what they understood to be God's will, God's law. They experienced their own finitude and guilt as alienation and despair, over which they had no control. So they did what all powerless people do: they threw themselves on the divine mercy and pleaded for acceptance and forgiveness. Human beings had no way to climb to heaven, so they prayed for the holy God to come down to earth, to overcome their alienation and impotence, to embrace them with the divine love, to affirm their eternal worth.

These royal images, the gift from an ancient period of our human history, were not questioned so long as kings were kings. Since no one could imagine such things as democracy or the dictatorship of the proletariat, it was assumed that these royal images for God had an eternal, objective, literal truth about them that was beyond question or doubt.

Since God, like earthly kings, was perceived as a mighty warrior, he had to have a mighty weapon of warfare. In those days no one imagined atomic bombs or missiles, jet aircraft, nuclear submarines, or chemical warheads. The most lethal weapon these ancient people could envision was a bow and arrow. So, they reasoned, God must have a gigantic bow, as big as the heavens themselves, one with the resplendent colors of creation. In the story of the great flood, the people had seen, according to the legend, a multicolored mighty bow stretched across the sky. We call that a rainbow today.

They, however, did not understand the nature of color, the prism effect of a ray of light filtered through a drop of water. They saw only a gigantic bow in the realm where they thought God dwelled.

God has laid aside the mighty bow, this divine weapon of war, they reasoned. This means that God will never again destroy the whole earth, they concluded. It was a valid conclusion, given the assumptions of that day, but it was destined not to endure as the explanation of a rainbow. The myths and folk wisdom of a particular day always shape the understanding the people have of their intense experiences. That is why no doctrine created by human beings can finally be unquestioned, no scriptural narrative written by human hands can finally be inerrant, and no human being living at any particular moment of history can finally be infallible.

Folktales, doctrines, dogmas, sacred Scripture, and articulated understandings are, in the last analysis, only doorways through which we walk in our attempt to enter the experience of God that someone else has had. They are valuable to us, but they are not to be literalized. When interpreters feel beckoned to enter the content of the birth narratives of the one called Jesus of Nazareth, they must be cognizant of these realities.

Jesus was interpreted by the early Christians in terms of their assumed and unquestioned concepts of God, modeled after the image of a heavenly king. The focus was on the exalted Jesus seated at the right hand of the heavenly throne. The image reflected the popular mythic understanding of the universe as a kingdom. Human beings were thought of as those loyal subjects who faithfully loved and served their king and who shared in the king's ordering of life so that the will of the deity could be done "on earth as it is in heaven." In various ways, however, so the myth went, fellowship with the divine King had been broken. The good creation had

35

fallen; a wrathful God was primed to punish the human subjects.

Instead, God sent an emissary (son), and through the son's divine sacrifice the justice of God had been satisfied, the vicarious death of the mythic hero had been achieved, and the divine order had been reestablished. The mythic hero suffered and conquered, died and rose again. His work done, he returned to the heavenly throne as the one who had experienced human life, so he made constant intercession to God for weak human beings. Now it was possible once again to live in faithful communion with the Lord of the universe. All one need do was to join the community that acknowledged the mythic hero as Lord and one would receive the gift of salvation that came from on high. There was no other way to achieve salvation, so those committed to this mythology almost inevitably became absolutists and chauvinistic people. The seeds of both religious bigotry and religious imperialism are found here. In terms of this prevailing mythology Jesus of Nazareth was certainly interpreted and God was clearly understood as the heavenly King.

If this interpretive framework had not been attached to Jesus, he may well not have become the central religious figure in Western civilization. A powerful experience has to be interpreted to be passed along. But there is also no doubt that this interpretive framework violated the historical Jesus. Nor was it always easy to attach this interpretive framework to Jesus, because Jesus was so obviously not a divine visitor but a flesh-and-blood human being. He was "born of a woman." An early Christian described him as "tested in every way as we are" (Heb. 4:15); as "beset by weaknesses" (Heb. 5:2); and as one who "in the days of his earthly life offered up prayers and petitions with loud cries and tears" (Heb. 5:7). He did not manifest any power symbols in his life. He had no wealth; indeed, he had no place to lay his head. Even

36

the foxes had holes, and the birds, their nests, but this Jesus was a homeless person (Matt. 8:28). He led no army, held no office, exercised no authority, and, clearly, he had been executed. He died, and that death was real.

This divine-rescuer mythology was basically from the Greek world, and applying it to Jesus was further complicated by the fact that Jesus was a Hebrew Lord. One had to escape the Hebrew context to get to the Greek mythic hero, but even within the Hebrew context the historical facts of Jesus' life did not lend themselves to a mythic interpretation. Among Hebrew people there was a vast messianic expectation that took many forms, but Jesus did not fit any of them. The image of a crucified messiah, hanging limp and dead from a wooden cross, violated Hebrew messianic expectations. Only a man who had committed a crime punishable by death was to be hanged on a tree, said the Torah, and "you shall bury him the same day, for a hanged man is accursed by God" (Deut. 21:22–23). Not only was he executed in a public place, but soldiers rolled dice for his only garment, hurled a spear into his side, and gave him to a petitioning group to be buried in a borrowed tomb. It was not a king-like portrait.

As if that were not bad enough, little else in the life of this Jewish Jesus appealed to the images and hopes of his people. His closest friends certainly did not understand him as a messiah. One of them betrayed him, another denied him, and all forsook him and fled. This ignoble group of disciples had acted in an ignoble manner. Would a real messiah have chosen so benign and lowbrow a group of disciples?

When his words were remembered, he fit neither the mythic hero image nor the messianic image. He claimed no power. Rather he said things like: "Unless you become like little children [powerless children], you will never enter the

37

kingdom of heaven" (Matt. 18:3). He said the "last shall be first" (Mark 10:31). He washed the feet of the disciples (John 13:1–11). "I am among you as one who serves," he stated (Luke 22:27). He exhorted them to decline power images, not to lord it over people as the kings of the Gentiles did (Luke 22:25). He identified his cause with finding the sheep that were lost (Luke 15:4) and welcoming home the prodigal who wasted his father's wealth in a life of debauchery (Luke 14:11ff). His teaching found him using Lazarus, a poor beggar whose sores were licked by the dogs of the street, as the sign of his kingdom rather than Dives, the rich man who dined sumptuously (Luke 16:20ff). He identified his cause with the half-breed Samaritan who went out of his way to alleviate suffering, not with the priest or the Levite who passed by on the other side (Luke 10:29ff). He said his disciples were to turn the other cheek (Matt. 5:39), to go the second mile (Matt. 5:4), and to love their enemies (Matt. 5:44). He placed his cause on the side of the "woman of the city" who washed his feet with her tears and dried them with her hair, not on the side of the morally righteous Simon the Pharisee, in whose home he was guest when that woman arrived (Luke 7:36ff). He was not willing to fight for his rights or his life, to use compulsive power to achieve his objectives. He suggested that his disciples must forgive not once or twice but up to and beyond seventy times seven occasions (Matt. 18:22).

His strength, strangely enough, lay in his willingness to sacrifice himself to his enemies. His life was a call to reverse the standards of the world. In that world, importance was achieved by having power over others; serving others was thought to be demeaning. When this self-giving Jesus was crucified, he refused to defend himself. He accepted the whips and nails of his tormentors, and he died praying for them (Luke 23:34). His life was too vivid to be forgotten, too real to be ignored. He fit neither the messianic role of the Hebrews nor the mythic hero role of the Greeks. Hence Paul called him "folly to those who are perishing" (1 Cor. 1:18) and suggested that Jesus represented a scandal.

How does one take that life and fit it into the expectations of either the Greeks or the Hebrews? Yet how could they deny the power of the experience men and women had with this Jesus? His love was real. His sense of presence was vivid. His magnetic appeal to others was immense. Self-giving, suffering, powerlessness, and self-sacrifice were the marks of his human life. There was an undeniable beauty about this Jesus, who was in fact "a man for others."[3] Conflict between experience and expectation reached a climax on Good Friday. Jesus died, and for his followers the darkness of that moment was almost physical.

Easter broke, I believe, not so much with a supernatural external miracle but with the dawning internal realization that this life of Jesus reflected a new image of God, an image that defied the conventional wisdom, an image that called into question the exalted king as the primary analogy by which God could be understood. This life—selfless, broken, loving, given away, powerless—this life was the very life of God, someone proclaimed in a moment of mind-boggling revelation. To this life could come all who travail and are heavy laden. Here one would find rest and peace, and that was what was meant by God. It was a startling insight. A dead man became the means through which the living God was seen. A weak man, beaten and broken, was the symbol through which the triumphant God was perceived. An executed man became the one who made these disciples aware of the meaning of a divinity to which their eyes had been closed or even blinded.

That life was God's life. The first witnesses to what we now call Easter were invited to embrace the scandal, to

39

transcend the foolishness, to open their eyes in wonder. God was present in that life, was their inescapable conclusion. God was seen not as a king ruling life but as a power within life. God was not to be perceived after the analogy of a distant deity, who was both superhuman and isolated, but rather as a divine essence not separate from and not identical with but incarnate within humanity, emerging from the heart of life in self-giving love and freely offered being. That was the revelation that lay behind the alleluias of that first Easter. That was the meaning of God disclosed in the person of Jesus that somehow challenged the regal images of the past. That essence, consequently, had to be lifted theologically into being the essence and definition of God. The experience of those who perceived demanded it.

But, alas, it was a vision too stunning to endure, and when the attempt was made to lift the essence of this Jesus into the heart of God, the ancient content of the victorious messiah of the Jews and the mythic hero of the Greeks captured, tamed, and refined the essence of Jesus. The experience of self-giving love being elevated into the essence of God was thus interpreted in terms of a mythic king being exalted to a heavenly throne and of a messiah who received God's divine vindication.

It was not long in the folklore of the early Christians before the exaltation of Jesus lost its original meaning. The meaning of Jesus had been lifted into and placed at the heart of God. That was the revelatory experience. But the words began to proclaim God's action in exalting him to the right hand of the heavenly throne. Next it was not even God's exaltation that was primary; it became, rather, Jesus' own triumph over death. So exaltation faded into resurrection, and God's action faded into being Jesus' action. Then the mythic hero role began to fit, and then the scandal of the cross began to be removed by an imaginative and judicious selection of ancient Hebrew texts that seemed to prove that God had intended this from the dawn of creation. Jesus was son of man and suffering servant and vicarious savior.

The cross, far from being the scandal that it in fact was, became the means by which exaltation was to occur in the first place. The cross was transformed even in Christian art into a throne from which not a suffering Jesus but a regal Jesus reigned as the Christus Rex. The twelve apostles were soon transformed from servants to princes of the church, wearing crowns called miters, sitting in chairs called thrones, and receiving the kneeling adoration of their servant people. The shift was no less than 180 degrees. Behind the myth was an experience, but it was not long before the myth captured, shaped, defined, and distorted the experience. The inevitable result was that the humanity of Jesus began to fade.

But he was "born of a woman." That became the Maginot Line designed to preserve at least a vestige of his humanity. With the scandal of the cross removed, however, it was but a matter of time before the scandal of his birth became the focus of the battle to see Jesus in terms of mythic hero, divine savior.

His origins were equally as scandalous as his means of death. He was a nobody, a child of Nazareth out of which nothing good was thought to come. No one seemed to know his father. He might well have been illegitimate. Hints of that are scattered like undetected and unexploded nuggets of dynamite in the landscape of the early Christian tradition. Once again the interpretive task went to work. He was not an illegitimate child, God was his father; he was born of the Holy Spirit. He was not a native of Nazareth, he was born in Bethlehem, the City of David. That Bethlehem birth had been foretold by the prophet Micah. He was not a nobody, he was of the royal house of David. We can trace his genealogy. He was not alienated from his family. His earthly father

41

acknowledged him by conferring a name upon him. His mother kept all these wonders in her heart and pondered them. His birth was not unnoticed. Angels sang of him, shepherds journeyed to his manger, Eastern sages brought gifts that foretold his greatness.

So the battle to save the startling and scandalous insight that God could be seen and experienced in the self-giving love emerging from the life and heart of a betrayed, denied, forsaken, executed man began to shift from the events at the end of Jesus' life to the events at the beginning of Jesus' life. The cross had to be "fixed" before the origins could be addressed. Paul had done his work and died the martyr's death before any of these issues began to be raised. Mark, the first Gospel, wrote his story of Jesus' life with no allusion whatsoever to Jesus' birth or origins. But by the ninth decade of the Christian era, this issue was drawn and addressed in a variety of ways. The birth traditions about Jesus had come into being.

5

The Development of
the Birth Tradition

More than any other part of Holy Scripture, the stories that developed around Jesus' birth have captured the public fancy. Almost every person in Western civilization, whether involved in the church or not, is familiar with the details of this portion of the Christian tradition. Through magnificent art treasures, through best-loved hymns and carols, through the work of a composer like Handel or a poet like W. H. Auden, and through annual pageants, the scenes of Jesus' birth have been riveted to our conscious and subconscious minds.

In the life of the church, Christmas has long since surpassed Easter as the favorite holiday, if not in the minds of the theologians, at least in the minds of the parishioners. Christmas is the season of romance, of candlelight and midnight services. In the celebration of Christmas the promise of peace, the yearning for togetherness, the exchange of gifts, and the family feast all find expression. It celebrates the innocence of childhood by portraying the God who draws near to us in the humility of a powerless infant. All of these elements have served to keep the origins of Christmas part of our tribal memory and to make the content of the birth narratives of the New Testament familiar to everyone who participates in a social order informed by Christianity. These narratives are a treasured part of the folklore of our civilization, and we cling to them with an irrational tenacity not unlike the way we cling to any precious possession.

But these same narratives of our Lord's birth are also a favorite target for criticism by the rationalists. So filled are the birth stories of Jesus with legendary details that their historicity collapses when they are placed under the microscope of modern scholarship. Such items as wandering heavenly stars that led exotic magi to the place of Jesus' birth, divine revelations coming through dreams, angelic choruses populating the heavens, and the miraculous birth of a baby conceived without a human male agent, if seriously believed or literally held, will not escape the kind of critical questions that biblical fundamentalism is loath to face.

Scientists will confront these claims from the disciplines of astrophysics and genetics. Historians analyzing these literalized narratives will identify in them echoes of the past, especially of those traditions that are vital parts of the saga of ancient Israel.

Rational credibility is also stretched when these romantic vignettes of Jesus' infancy are populated by a rich cast of characters who seem quite capable, in a moment's notice, of breaking into song in perfect meter as if they were stars in an operetta. A beloved tradition therefore collides with rationality when citizens of this century begin to read the biblical stories of Christmas as literal history with minds shaped by science and a twentieth-century worldview.

Moreover, no recognized New Testament scholar, Catholic or Protestant, would today seriously defend the historicity of these narratives. This does not mean that the birth stories of our Lord are not loved, valued, or even seen as valid proclamations of the gospel. It does mean, however, that they are not taken literally, nor are they used any longer to undergird such a well-known doctrine as the virgin birth, which is in fact a popular misnomer for what would more accurately be called the doctrine of the virginal conception.

Indeed, the concept of virgin birth itself, if understood in a literal biological fashion, is today quickly dismissed in scholarly circles. Roman Catholics still salute it with lip service, but the best case a Roman Catholic scholar such as Raymond Brown can make for the virginal conception is to suggest that the New Testament evidence does not rule out such a possibility.[1] This is a far cry from the ringing defenses of yesterday. This perception has not yet finished trickling down to either local clergy or the people in the pew, but it will. In time the virgin birth account will join Adam and Eve and the story of the cosmic ascension as clearly recognized mythological elements in our faith tradition whose purpose was not to describe a literal event but to capture the transcendent dimensions of God in the earthbound words and concepts of first-century human beings.

But to assign the birth narratives to mythology is not to dismiss them as untrue. It is rather to force us to see truth in dimensions larger than literal truth, to understand how the language of myth and poetry came to be the language employed by those who sought to describe the divine-human encounter they believed themselves to have experienced.

The accounts of Jesus' birth are not an original part of the earliest known Christian proclamation, called the kerygma.[2] The birth narratives that we now possess may well represent two quite distinct, even divergent, traditions.[3] Their disagreements are absolutely irreconcilable, though the common mind has tended to blend them into a single cohesive

45

narrative—a task that has been accomplished only at the price of ignoring discrepancies and distorting data that was not blendable.

The Gospels according to Matthew and Luke, where we find the only birth narratives, both achieved their final written form late in the first century of the Christian era. The evidence that would suggest that Luke was aware of Matthew is still debated but I perceive that the weight is beginning to shift toward that possibility. Both evangelists appear to have a common source in Mark. Mark, however, began his story with the baptism, an event in the life of the adult Jesus. Both Matthew and Luke, by contrast, responding to issues alive in their day and feeling an incompleteness about Mark's story, added a birth tradition. Those who still deny that Luke had access to Matthew account for their common material by postulating another common source which is called Q, or *Quelle*, the German word for "source." The supposition is that Q was a primitive collection of Jesus' sayings and if this is true it may well constitute the earliest written document of the Christian faith community. No birth tradition, however, emerges out of this primitive source either.[4]

Each gospel writer appears to have had a special and unique source beyond their common material, called the M source for Matthew and the L source for Luke. It is this special source that marks each Gospel story in a particular way. It does appear that each Gospel writer's special source is not a single strand of material but several strands, some written, some perhaps oral. Some may well even represent the creative genius of the evangelist himself. Many of our best-loved parables, such as the good Samaritan and the prodigal son, are recorded for us in Luke alone, while Matthew alone has preserved for us the parable of the last judgment and the account of the divine commission. The important issue for this discussion, however, is to note that the birth material in

46

Matthew and Luke reveals both common themes and wide divergence. The commonality suggests a Lucan dependence on Matthew or at least a common source behind them both. The wide divergence, however, suggests that each author was leaning on a unique source available to him alone, or that the theological agenda of each author was a major shaping influence. The pious suggestion of yesteryear that the differences can be accounted for by the fact that Matthew was writing from Joseph's point of view and Luke from Mary's is simply not supportable. Such an explanation assumes that Mary would not recall the magi or the flight into Egypt and Joseph would not recall the shepherds, the stable, or the journey to Bethlehem to be enrolled.

The first major interpretive task of scholarship, therefore, is to separate the birth narratives of Matthew and Luke. This will enable the reader to grasp the purpose each Gospel writer had in including the birth account and then to see how each part of the birth story serves that larger purpose. The birth narratives then become miniature introductions of larger themes that will be developed in the later chapters for both Matthew and Luke. They also serve to reveal the Matthean and Lucan understanding of the adult Jesus in unique ways. The birth stories address the issue of the origins of the one whom the disciples have come to believe is Messiah and Savior.

To enter this study, the common material just needs to be identified. In both Matthew and Luke the parents of Jesus are named Joseph and Mary, and they are betrothed but have not yet begun to live in married sexual union (Matt. 1:18; Luke 1:27, 34). In both, Joseph is of Davidic descent (Matt. 1:16, 20; Luke 1:27, 32; 2:4). Though the details differ graphically, both contain an angelic announcement about the child who is coming (Matt. 1:20–23; Luke 1:30–35). Both assert that the conception of this child is not through sexual intercourse with Mary's husband (Matt. 1:20, 23, 25; Luke 1:34) but rather is accomplished by an action that in some way involves God's Spirit (Matt. 1:18, 20; Luke 1:35). Although directed to a different person in each, an angelic decree that the child's name is to be Jesus is found in both Gospels (Matt. 1:21; Luke 1:31). There is in both an angelic statement that Jesus is to be savior (Matt. 1:21; Luke 2:11). Both agree that the birth of Jesus occurs after his parents have come to live together (Matt. 1:24–25; Luke 2:5–6) and that the birth of Jesus is related chronologically to the reign of Herod the Great (Matt. 2:1; Luke 1:5). Finally, both concur that Jesus spent his youth in Nazareth (Matt. 2:33; Luke 2:51). That may seem like substantial agreement, perhaps enough to postulate a factual tradition that lies behind both. However, the list of different and even contradictory items that separate the two traditions is even longer and more impressive.[5]

The genealogies included in each of the two Gospels are not only different, they are incompatible. Luke begins with Adam (Luke 3:38); Matthew begins with Abraham (Matt. 1:2). Matthew traces the lineage through the royal line of the house of David (Matt. 1:6ff); Luke goes from David to Nathan (Luke 3:31), not Solomon, and ignores the royal line. Luke has for Jesus' grandfather a man named Eli (Luke 3:23); Matthew asserts that Jesus' grandfather was Jacob (Matt. 1:16). Eusebius of Caesarea, a fourth-century Christian historian, went to great lengths to reconcile these two grandfathers into one person, but his argument was as unconvincing as it was ingenious. He suggested that Jacob and Eli were brothers and that one died without a male heir, so the brother took the widow into his home and produced by her a male child who was thought of as both his son and his brother's son, thereby accounting for the discrepancy in the biblical story.[6] No one today defends Eusebius's thesis.

Following the genealogies, the contradictions multiply. Luke alone relates the Zechariah–Elizabeth–John the Baptist birth story (Luke 1:5–25). Luke uses a census to bring Mary and Joseph to Bethlehem (Luke 2:1, 2), while Matthew assumes that they live in Bethlehem in a specific and known house over which a star can stop (Matt. 2:11). Matthew seems to know nothing about a stable, an angelic chorus, and wandering hillside shepherds; Luke knows nothing of a star in the east, exotic magi who come bringing gifts, and a malevolent King Herod who orders the slaughter of male babies in Bethlehem. Luke's Christmas story is filled with poetry that we still today sing as canticles in church—the Benedictus, the Magnificat, the Nunc Dimittis, and the seeds of the Gloria in Excelsis—none of which was known by Matthew. Matthew, on the other hand, seemed to collect proof texts out of the Hebrew Scriptures to buttress his account of Jesus' birth, a technique and style that Luke seldom employed.

Matthew alone contains the flight into Egypt story, and, because he assumed that Bethlehem was home for the holy family, he told a story to account for the move into Nazareth of Galilee (Matt. 2:21–23). While Matthew was relating this travelogue, Luke had the holy family perform in a calm and unthreatened way the ritual acts of circumcision on the eighth day in Bethlehem and presentation in the temple on the fortieth day in Jerusalem (Luke 2:21ff)—rather impossible if you have fled to Egypt. Luke made the return to Nazareth rather leisurely, for it was Luke's assumption that Nazareth was the home of Joseph and Mary (Luke 2:39–40). Joseph dominates Matthew's story, while Mary dominates Luke's story.

Two narrators of the same historic moment might create variations in detail, but they would never produce diametrically different and even contradictory versions of the events surrounding the same birth. The minimum conclusion is that both versions cannot be historically accurate. The maximum conclusion is that neither version is historic. This latter conclusion is the overwhelming consensus of biblical scholars today. Indeed, it is an almost uncontested conclusion, and to that conclusion I subscribe.

To buttress this conclusion I enter that exciting and revealing period of history between the death of our Lord and the first written records. There I look for hints, clues, fears, threats, myths, legends, assumptions, worldviews that will illumine the process that will finally produce a full-blown written explanation of the origins of Jesus. To explore this terrain is almost as exciting as trying to solve a Sherlock Holmes mystery.

The birth of Christianity was an Easter event, not a Christmas event. Christianity was born in an Easter moment. Prior to whatever Easter was, there was no talk of Jesus' divinity, of incarnational concepts, or of trinitarian formulas. Jesus was a Jew who, after his death, was in some way believed to have been included in the very life of God. The mythological way of saying that was called the exaltation. God had exalted Jesus to God's right hand. It was this understanding of Jesus that produced the story of the exaltation. The ecstatic cry "Jesus is Lord," elicited by the experience of Easter, became the first creed of the Christian church. If one accepts the primacy of the Q material as the first written part of the Gospel tradition, it seems clear that the exaltation of the Jewish Jesus was the original meaning of Easter rather than the later explanation that came to be called resurrection. Edward Schillebeeckx, a Dutch Roman Catholic New Testament scholar, makes this point quite clear in his book *Jesus*.[7]

Also supporting the primacy of exaltation as the original explanation of Easter are the words of praise found in Philippians about the self-emptying God, which many scholars believe to be an earlier Christian hymn that Paul incorporated into his text rather than one he created. That hymn offers corroborating evidence to the earliest kerygma, for the only concept of resurrection it mentions is exaltation: "and being found in human form, he humbled himself and became obedient unto death, even death on a cross. Therefore, God has highly exalted him and bestowed on him the name that is above every name." Note first that God is the source of the action, not Jesus. The second thing to note is that no reference is made at all to resurrection as we have come to think of it. The movement is from death to exaltation into heaven. The righteous Jewish Jesus, who had been put to death by the authorities, had been vindicated by God, who exalted Jesus to the place of honor at God's right hand. The royal image is operative. This adoption of Jesus and all that he meant into God was the first and original form in which divine sonship for Jesus was claimed by Christian people. This is primitive Christianity.

Adoption is an interesting word. Usually it is associated with infancy, not adulthood. The implication of God's adoption is that Jesus becomes God's Son when the adoption, or exaltation, occurred. The divine sonship claim for Jesus appears originally to have been tied to Easter as the moment of exaltation rather than to Jesus' birth, and certainly not to his conception.

When Paul used the word *resurrection*, he was referring to God's action in claiming the meaning of Jesus' life to be the meaning of God. Resurrection for Paul was never a return to life here and now. Paul's message was that Easter meant the moment when Jesus was designated Son of God in power according to the Spirit. For Paul the Spirit made Jesus God's Son, and that occurred not at conception but at Easter (Rom. 1:4).

In a sermon attributed to Paul and recorded in Acts 13, which may also reflect an earlier tradition, the resurrection was again described in symbolic terms as the moment of Jesus' enthronement at God's right hand. The Davidic coronation psalm was applied to this resurrection/ascension event. But the words were the words of a birth: "Thou art my Son, this day I have begotten thee" (Acts 13:33). The same theological order was preserved in a sermon attributed to Peter and recorded in the fifth chapter of Acts. "The God of our fathers raised Jesus," Peter said, "whom you killed by hanging him on a tree. God exalted him at [God's] right hand as Leader and Savior" (Acts 5:30–31). Note once more the movement is from death to God's raising, which was defined primarily as exaltation into heaven rather than resurrection into life.

In the original exaltation language of Easter, God was the active power and Jesus was the passive recipient of that power. God raised the crucified Jesus to the heavenly place. "God raised Jesus from the dead" was originally the language of exaltation, not of resurrection. The raising of Jesus was a demonstration of God's power, not of Jesus' power. The passive tense is clearly original. God raised him up. This means that resurrection/ascension was at the beginning a single event in which the essence is better captured by the word *exaltation*. This understanding constituted the first layer of the rational process of theological thinking about Jesus the Christ. It was already one step removed from the vividness of what might be called the Easter experience of the Christ.

As the exaltation story was told and retold, however, the action of God raising Jesus began to be expressed in the active terms of Jesus himself rising from the grave. Then, almost inevitably, exaltation had to be divided into two events. Jesus rising from the dead in an active sense became the resurrection, and God exalting Jesus into heaven in a passive sense became the ascension. What was once a single proclamation became in time two distinct narratives. We are now two steps removed from the primary Christian experience. As the resurrection was seen more and more as the expression of Jesus' power to rise from the dead, its content was increasingly told in terms of Jesus' return to life rather than in terms of the exaltation of Jesus into heaven. Only at that stage of development do we begin to see the formation of the Easter narratives that focus on both the emptiness of the tomb and the appearances of the resurrected Jesus. Also, only at this point does the claim of physical, bodily resurrection enter the Christian narrative.[8] This tendency in turn forced the creation of a new content into the story of Jesus to account for the exaltation into heaven. So only then do we begin to hear accounts of a cosmic ascension. The unnatural division of exaltation into the components of resurrection and ascension meant that the Gospel writers would have to relate the two now-distinct events to each other. We are at this point three steps removed from the primary experience.

That manner of relating the narratives in fact happened in two ways. In Mark, Matthew, and John, Easter is primarily both resurrection and exaltation. Mark has no resurrection appearance accounts at all, but the clear implication is that it will be the exalted Lord appearing from heaven that the disciples will meet in Galilee (Mark 16:7). The only account of an appearance of the risen Lord to the disciples in Matthew is set on the top of a Galilean mountain, where the exalted Lord came to them out of heaven to give the divine commission (Matt. 28:16–20). In the fourth Gospel the first appearance of the risen Lord was to Mary Magdelene, and Jesus forbade her to touch him, "for I have not yet ascended to my

53

father. But go tell my disciples that I am ascending" (John 20:17). Then later that day it was clearly the ascended exalted Lord who appeared to the disciples and breathed on them so that they received the Holy Spirit (John 20:19–23). In this manner the Gospels give further evidence that the original meaning of Easter was understood in terms of the essence of Jesus' life being incorporated into the very being of God. This was described as God's action exalting Jesus to God's right hand. That is what made Jesus "Lord" and conveyed to the disciples the conviction that Jesus was not only alive again but eternally available to them.

Luke, however, followed a different scheme. Luke separated the resurrection narrative from the ascension narrative by a period of forty days (Luke 24, Acts 1). Luke also used the ascension narrative both to climax or close off the resurrection appearances and to prepare the church for the coming of God's Holy Spirit at Pentecost, which was a third distinct part of Luke's exaltation narrative (Luke 24:50ff; Acts 2). It seems apparent to the world of biblical scholarship that Luke made linear and narrative what had originally been instantaneous and a matter of proclamation.

God had embraced Jesus into the very essence of divinity, to stand at God's right hand. The action of God had vindicated the servant figure and affirmed Jesus' life of love and self-giving. Jesus was therefore God's Son, begotten in a heavenly exaltation that was revealed in the experience of Easter and perceived in the hearts of the believers. That appears to be the original resurrection proclamation underneath the layers of later developed theology and apologia.

Mark, the earliest Gospel, was written thirty-five to forty years after the Easter moment. By the time Mark wrote, much movement had occurred. First, the divine sonship of Jesus, which was hidden from the disciples until the resurrection, was nonetheless announced to the reader in the first verse—"The gospel of Jesus Christ, the Son of God" (Mark 1:1). The supernatural demonic forces were also aware of the true identity of Jesus throughout Mark's story (e.g., 1:24). Second, what the disciples understood at Easter had in fact been conveyed directly to Jesus at the beginning of his ministry. Jesus was declared to be God's Son by the Spirit for Mark, not at the moment of exaltation following his death, as it had been for Paul, but at the moment of baptism, which inaugurated his ministry (Mark 1:11). Jesus' adoption into God had thus begun a journey backward in time. When Mark wrote, that journey had stopped at a way station in the event of the baptism.

Many of the original elements of the exaltation narrative were simply transferred by Mark from Easter to the baptism story. Instead of exaltation into heaven, the heavens now opened not to receive Jesus but to allow heavenly power to descend upon the person of Jesus (Mark 1:10). The Holy Spirit, who in Paul's Letter to the Romans designated Jesus as God's Son at the resurrection (1:4), Mark now identified as the power that designated Jesus as God's Son at the baptism. God's election of Jesus as God's Son by the Holy Spirit had, by the seventieth year of the common era, moved from exaltation into heaven to resurrection into life first and, secondly, now to baptism. As dramatic as that transition was, it would nonetheless not be the final chapter in this expanding faith story.

In human experience a father and mother do not wait until the inauguration of a public adult career to acknowledge the child as their own. It is more appropriate and natural to talk of a begotten son at birth than it is at death, or even at baptism. So the elements of divine sonship, the presence of the Holy Spirit, and even the angelic messengers continued to move from the exaltation into heaven to resurrection into life to the baptism, until finally they came to be associated with birth and conception. Adoption into God faded as an adequate description of the God-Jesus relationship, and a deeper interpretation of the divine beginning at the origin of human life appeared. The stage was thus set for birth narratives to emerge and for accounts of Jesus' divine conception to begin to circulate. And so they did. It was, by this time, at least the ninth decade of the common era.

There were many models for such narratives. In many other religious traditions of the world, the concept of a virgin birth to explain the divine origin of heroic figures was commonplace.

Gautama Buddha, the ninth Avatar of India, was said to have been born of the virgin Maya about 600 B.C.E. The Holy Ghost was also portrayed as descending upon her.

Horus, a god of Egypt, was born of the virgin Isis, it was said, around 1550 B.C.E. Horus also received gifts from three kings in his infancy.

Attis was born of a virgin mother named Nama in Phrygia, before 200 B.C.E.

Quirrnus, a Roman savior, was born of a virgin in the sixth century B.C.E. His death, it was said, was accompanied by universal darkness.

Indra was born of a virgin in Tibet in the eighth century B.C.E. He also was said to have ascended into heaven.

Adonis, a Babylonian deity, was said to have been born of a virgin mother named Ishtar, who was later to be hailed as queen of heaven.

Mithra, a Persian deity, was also said to have been born of a virgin around 600 B.C.E.

Zoroaster likewise made his earthly appearance courtesy of a virgin mother.

Krishna, the eighth Avatar of the Hindu pantheon, was born of the virgin Devaki around 1200 B.C.E.

In popular Greek and Roman mythology Perseus and Romulus were divinely fathered. In Egyptian and classical history such stories grew up around the pharaohs, Alexander the Great, and Caesar Augustus. Even a philosopher like Plato was ultimately explained in terms of a divine origin. These stories would not be unknown to the early Christians, especially after Christianity left the womb of Judaism, which it did increasingly after the destruction of Jerusalem by the Romans in 70 C.E. Of the Gospels, only Mark seems to have been written prior to that destruction. The virgin birth tradition in Christianity did not achieve written form until sometime during the ninth or tenth decades of Christian history and then only in the accounts of two evangelists, Matthew and Luke, both of whom were self-consciously addressing the expanding gentile presence in the church.

There is a possibility that Philo, a Greek-speaking, and in many ways a Greek-thinking, Jewish philosopher who wrote between 45 to 50 C.E., could have had some of his writings interpreted by early Christians in terms of a virginal conception. Philo used allegory to demonstrate that the patriarchs were begotten through the instrumentality of God. "Rebekkah, who is perseverance," he wrote, "became pregnant from God."[9] Paul might have had this in mind when he made a distinction between the two sons of Abraham: Ishmael, who was born according to the flesh, and Isaac, who was born according to the promise of the Spirit (Gal. 4:21ff). However, there is no reason to think that being born "according to the Spirit" for Paul precluded physical intercourse as the means of Isaac's conception. Indeed, originally the idea that the conception of Mary was of the Spirit did not appear to preclude a natural pregnancy—perhaps unusual, but not unnatural.

Miraculous births through various means, though not without known paternity, are not uncommon in the Hebrew

Scriptures. Ishmael, Isaac, Samson, and Samuel come immediately to mind. In each of these instances there is a birth annunciation that follows a regular pattern. First, the appearance of the angel occurs; second, the fear of the recipient is expressed; third, the divine message is given; fourth, the human objection is offered; and finally, a sign is given designed to overcome the objection.[10] Within this general framework the biblical narratives of all special births have been related. In the case of Ishmael, the angelic figure came after the pregnancy, when Hagar was fleeing from a jealous Sarah (Gen. 16:1–15). In Isaac's case, the barrier to be overcome was the age of his parents, both of whom were in their nineties (Gen. 18:9ff and Gen. 21:1ff). As the Book of Genesis says, "It had ceased to be with Sarah after the manner of women" (Gen. 18:11). In the cases of Samson and Samuel, the potential mother was barren (Judg. 13:3; 1 Sam. 1:2). In each of the episodes the child, in his adult life, had a particular destiny to be a saving figure in history, and this adult vocation inspired the tales of his origin.

If these relatively minor biblical figures could be important enough to inspire birth traditions, then surely the one thought of as God's "only begotten Son" could do no less. The designation of Jesus as God's Son had an almost inevitable backward trek in the understanding of the members of the Christian community as they groped to explain their experience with this special life. The earliest Christian tradition appears to have connected the affirmation of Jesus as the Son of God to the adoption of Jesus into heaven by God in the resurrection/exaltation event. Mark announced it to his readers in the first sentence of his Gospel (Mark 1:1), but the first contemporary figure in Mark's story to utter this confession was the centurion who watched Jesus die, who said, "Truly this man was the Son of God" (Mark 15:39). But for Mark, designation of Jesus as "son" had actually occurred at the baptism, when the Spirit descended. As time passed, however, the angels of the resurrection tradition were found present at the announcement of the impending conception, and the Holy Spirit who proclaimed Jesus to be God's Son in power at the resurrection and God's Son in promise at the baptism became the agent for assuring that Jesus was God's Son from conception.

Is there any possibility that the narratives of our Lord's birth are historical? Of course not. Even to raise that question is to betray an ignorance about birth narratives. Origin tales are commentaries on adult meaning. No one waits in a home or a maternity ward for a great person to be born. Royal heirs to ancient thrones might have had their births attended by the people of the realm, but only because they were symbolic of the continuity of the nation.

Jesus was not such an heir to a royal line, despite Matthew's attempt to portray him as the Davidic pretender. Jesus grew up in poverty. The people of Nazareth rejected him. The religious leaders of his nation had him executed. This is not a portrait of royalty. Birth narratives grow up around a person in history only when that adult life becomes significant to the people by whom he or she was produced, or to the world at large. Birth narratives suggest that the moment an important adult was born was an important moment for all human history. Then as the birth narrative grows, the future importance of that life is signaled by the words that are spoken or the heavenly signs that marked the birth or the miraculous events that made that particular birth possible. Such interpretive legendary details have gathered around the births of historically famous people, but in almost all cases not until well after their deaths. Birth narratives are five or six steps removed from the original revelatory moment.

What this means is that the birth narratives of Matthew and Luke finally said nothing factual about the birth of Jesus, but they did say everything necessary about the adult power of the one whose birth was being described. Matthew and Luke each built a narrative to tell the story of Jesus' origin. They built it out of the material available to them. They related their accounts of Jesus' birth in a way that was consistent with their intention in telling the Jesus story in the first place. Attempts to reconcile or to harmonize the differences between Matthew and Luke are based on the false premise that some historical, factual truth lies behind these birth narratives. Since this does not appear to be so, such efforts at harmony will be an exercise in futility. Both nativity stories are powerful and important and worthy of our best scholarship. Both are filled with interpretive clues and insights into the nature of this Jesus whose birth changed the face of human history in a way that no other life has ever done.

So we turn first to the birth narrative of Matthew and then to Luke. We will examine them in detail, explore their hidden treasures, love them, meditate upon them, hear the gospel through them, and in the process, free ourselves from the killing literalism of the past that has distorted these narratives and has hidden from our eyes their wonder, their beauty, and their profundity. Beyond these narratives our focus remains on the one who inspired them, who still holds a magnetic attraction for us, drawing us day after day into mystery, awe, worship, and adoration.

6

Matthew's Story, Part I

For the author of Matthew's Gospel, Immanuel had appeared. He wrote to proclaim his conviction that in Jesus of Nazareth God had been experienced living in human history. This concept was expressed as a promise in the Gospel's opening verses when the angel said to Joseph, "His name shall be called Immanuel, which means 'God with us'" (Matt. 1:23). When Matthew's story was complete, this idea had become a reality and was articulated by Jesus making the Immanuel claim for himself in the Gospel's closing verse: "Lo, I am with you always, to the close of the age" (Matt. 28:20). Within the parenthesis formed by these two phrases, Matthew's story unfolded.

The author of this Gospel, judging from internal sources, was in all probability a Jewish scribe who had become a Christian. He appears to have been schooled in a peculiarly Jewish method of studying the Scriptures. He poured over his sacred Jewish text to find clues, hints, and foreshadowings. His style was that of Haggadic midrash. This was especially evident in those elements of his story where factual details of Jesus' life were shadowy. This author neither suggested nor believed that everything he wrote was factual. His desire was to illumine the presence of the God he met in Jesus, to proclaim how this Jesus had fulfilled the yearnings of the ages, how Jewish hopes, traditions, expectations, and even folklore had found completion in this human life that he had come to acknowledge as Immanuel, Lord, and Christ.

When this Gospel was written, the author could not consult the archives of newspapers or the videotapes of a television network. He could not even peruse a Jewish history of the times. The only objective data available to him was the impact of the life of this Jesus. That impact was so significant that the story of his life had been told and retold from life to life, from heart to heart, from faith to faith.

By the time Matthew wrote, at least fifty years had passed since Jesus' earthly life was concluded. Perhaps as many as eighty-five years had passed since his birth. Modern readers of Matthew's narrative must realize that his work is not history or biography, it is a proclamation of a living faith. It cannot be read as literal history without turning its truth into either nonsense or fantasy.

Since the physical life of this historical figure had come to an end, some difficult events of history had also occurred. A Jewish revolution had taken place against Rome and its political domination of their nation. It was a revolution based more on Jewish emotion than on the reality of Jewish power and was therefore crushed by the Roman legions. The city of Jerusalem was destroyed. The temple was razed, leaving only one wall remaining, which became the "wailing wall," and the Jewish nation ceased to exist.

With the destruction of the Jewish nation came also the destruction of that Jewish center of this Jesus movement. The presence of Jewish people in the Christian movement was greatly weakened, and the Christian church's Jewish ties were loosened. Gentiles began to outnumber Jews among those called "the followers of the way." For the young Christian community, this was a time of great upheaval and anxiety.

So it was that sometime in the early to middle years of the ninth decade of the common era, perhaps ten to fifteen years after the fall of Jerusalem, a Jewish member of the Christian community, probably in Syria, took upon himself the task of writing a story of Jesus. At least one other Gospel, known as *kata Markon* (according to Mark), had already been written, but Mark was simply not adequate to meet the needs that this anonymous person felt. This author felt that Mark was not so much wrong as in need of expansion and perhaps a different emphasis. From time to time he did change and correct Mark, but he was more eager simply to add things to that first Gospel. He did it well, for the common wisdom in the first few centuries of Christian history was that what we now call Matthew was the original and most trustworthy Gospel and that Mark was simply a condensed account—a kind of *Reader's Digest* version of Matthew. This point of view, though all but abandoned by scholars today, accounted for the fact that Matthew was placed first in the canon of the New Testament that was adopted by the church in the second century.

About this author we have almost no personal information. The connection with the tax collecting disciple, called Levi Matthew, is a later and totally unsubstantiated assumption. Nothing about the Gospel suggests that the author was an eyewitness to the events he was describing. From internal sources we know that although he was Jewish, his primary language was Greek. We can presume that he was, in all probability, a Jew of the dispersion. He had certainly been shaped by the heritage of his Jewish worship tradition. He had an enormous respect for the Jewish law, for only in this Gospel is Jesus heard to say, "Think not that I have come to

63

abolish the law and the prophets; I have come not to abolish them but to fulfill them. For truly I say to you, till heaven and earth pass away not an iota, not a dot, will pass from the law until all is accomplished" (Matt. 5:17, 18).

He reflected a deep respect for the authority of the scribes and Pharisees. It is Matthew's Jesus alone who reminded the crowds that "the scribes and Pharisees sit on Moses' seat; so practice and observe whatever they tell you" (Matt. 23:2). His fiercest hostility was directed toward those Jewish religious leaders who had opposed Jesus. They were, in Matthew's words, "hypocrites who shut the kingdom of heaven against people" (Matt. 23:13) and "whitewashed tombs, who obey the letter of the law while ignoring the spirit" (Matt. 23:27). These internal notes make sense only if we assume that the author of Matthew's Gospel was a scribe of the pharisaic party who had come to believe in Jesus. Raymond Brown has even suggested that when the author of this Gospel in chapter 13 praised the scribe, "who has been trained for the kingdom of heaven, who is like a householder who brings out of his treasure what is new and what is old" (Matt. 13:52), he had in fact inserted an autobiographical note into his story.[1]

The presumed date of this Gospel is attached to those events that took place in Jerusalem after its destruction by the Roman army. With freedom gone, with Jerusalem and the temple destroyed, the Jewish people tended more and more to seek solace and security in the law, the Torah, which was for them the only part of their religious heritage that remained. To keep the law became for them the only way they could remember their identity in this period of radical upheaval.

So it was that the Jewish people, led by their religious leaders, began to wrap protective layers of literal authority around the Jewish law. This led directly to the feeling that those members of the Jewish community who had found truth and meaning in the one they believed to be the Jewish Messiah posed a particular threat to Jewish survival. This Jesus had been more concerned about the inner meaning of the Torah than about the external laws. He had challenged the legalistic tradition among the Jews. His movement had destabilized the authority of the literal Scriptures, which had been a tolerable tension prior to the loss of their holy city, their nation, and their temple. Now, however, that tension threatened the sacredness and security of the law, and that was all the Jewish faithful had left to which they might cling. As the trauma of their external history forced the Jewish traditionalists to turn inward, they became increasingly defensive and rigid. They felt acutely the threat brought by those members of their household of faith who did not give to the law and to the traditions of the past the undeviating loyalty that in the orthodox Jewish minds these things deserved. The mood grew tense and even angry. Finally these feelings erupted, and the presence of Jewish Christians inside the structures of Judaism came to be regarded by the Jews as an abomination, a cancer that had to be removed.

By the year 85 this attitude became public and official when a well-known part of the liturgy of the synagogue was reformulated to include a curse on heretics. This curse was obviously and primarily aimed at those Jews who believed in Jesus as the Messiah, and it resulted finally in those Jewish Christians being expelled from the synagogues. This action cut the primary connection that had endured between Judaism and Jewish Christians, which in turn resulted in making these Jewish leaders the chief target of the hostility of the now-excommunicated Jewish Christians.

The author of Matthew's Gospel appears to have been a member of a group of these excommunicated Jewish Christians. He was a Jewish member of a Christian community that included both Jews and Gentiles. He saw the Jewish presence in the Christian church to be declining and the gentile presence to be increasing. He wanted that emerging gentile majority not to forget the Jewish origins of their faith story. He also wanted his Jewish brothers and sisters to escape their narrow understanding of things Jewish that had so violated him and to embrace all that Jesus meant for this writer. Jesus was everything the Jewish tradition expected him to be, and at the same time he was a call beyond that tradition into the inclusiveness of universalism. It was Matthew's goal to say just that in writing in a powerful way. It was an ambitious and worthy task, which helps to explain why Mark's Gospel was simply not considered adequate for his purposes. It also helps to establish the author's angle of vision that in turn illumines what he had to say and why he said it in the way he did.

The Jesus that Matthew's Gospel portrayed was every inch the son of David, the fulfillment of Jewish messianic expectations. But he was also the son of Abraham through whom all of the nations of the world were to be blessed. Finally, and above all for this writer, Jesus was the very Son of God in whom Jew and Greek could find oneness.[2] With a delicate hand and an educated pen, Matthew wove these unifying themes throughout the paragraphs of his story. He used his midrash training to re-create the drama of exodus and exile. He cast Jesus in the familiar terms of Abraham, Samson, Samuel, Balaam, Joseph, and Moses. Yet he broke open every binding Jewish prejudice to show that Israel's fulfillment was ultimately the world's blessing. The Christ figure he portrayed was the Christ figure he needed to affirm the Jewish-Christian community, of which he was a part, at a time when those Jewish Christians had been expelled from the Jewish tradition. He wrote to enable Christians, both Jews and Gentiles, to recognize the primacy of Judaism even as they were being led into the universal embrace of the emerging Christian church.

This author, whom in deference to the tradition of the ages I will call Matthew, divided his work self-consciously into five books, each of which ended with the refrain "and when Jesus had finished these sayings" (Matt. 7:28; 11:1; 13:53; 19:1; 26:1). This work was deliberately designed on the mold of the Torah to be the Christian Pentateuch.[3]

To introduce those five books, he appended the birth narratives, which, not coincidentally, were divided into five episodes: the genealogy, the annunciation, the magi, the flight into Egypt to escape the massacre, and the return from Egypt. Each of these episodes centered around a biblical citation of fulfillment. He closed his story with the passion narrative in which, again not surprisingly, there were five minichapters: the anointing of Jesus for burial at the home of Simon the Pharisee; the Maundy Thursday drama of the Last Supper; Gethsemane and the arrest; the trial and the crucifixion; and the resurrection. His Jewish-Christian audience would know and appreciate his symbols and his skill.[4]

Turning to the narrow focus of the birth narratives of Matthew, we see the major themes of this Gospel writer at work. Jesus as the son of David was implicit in the genealogy and in the angelic revelation to Joseph, who was addressed as son of David. When Joseph, who was said to be a legitimate heir of David, accepted and named Jesus as his son, this theme reached its climax. Jesus was son of David.[5]

The son of Abraham message was seen in the visit of the magi, in the settlement of the holy family in Nazareth, in a province known as "Galilee of the Gentiles," and it echoed in various other parts of the narrative. Matthew was concerned to justify, especially for his Jewish brothers and sisters, the large number of Gentiles entering his Christian community in particular and the whole Christian movement in general. So he said, "Many will come from the east and the west and sit at table with Abraham in the kingdom of heaven" (Matt. 8:11). Matthew's Jesus would also warn the Jews that "God is able from these stones to raise up children to Abraham" (Matt. 3:9). It was through Abraham that all nations would be blessed. Jesus was the son of Abraham.

In the birth narrative Matthew took the biblical themes of son of David and son of Abraham and wove into them his third theme: Jesus was Immanuel. In him God was with us. Jesus was son of God.

Chapter 1 of Matthew's story opens with the genealogy of this Jesus. It is a genealogy neatly divided into three sections, each of which includes fourteen generations. The first section is from Abraham to David. Here Matthew revealed the divine selection process. Isaac was chosen over Ishmael, Jacob over Esau, Judah over Reuben, and with Judah the house of David was selected, for David the Judean was the king who supplanted Saul the Benjaminite.

The second section stretches from David to the exile, touching upon that watershed experience in Hebrew history. The final section carries us from the exile to Jesus, where it culminates, because for Matthew, in Jesus history had reached its final goal.

The genealogy, however, reveals many weaknesses if we are looking for literal truth or historical accuracy. Matthew forced his fourteen-fourteen-fourteen generational pattern sometimes so obviously that questions have been raised even about his ability to count. Actually, the best estimates of scholars would suggest that between Abraham and David there was a span of some 750 years. Between David and the exile the span was some 400 years. Between the exile and Jesus some 600 years elapsed. All of these totals are far too great for the fourteen-generation pattern that Matthew adopted in his genealogy.[6] Beyond that, in his first section of fourteen generations, Matthew presented only thirteen names. In his second section of fourteen generations, he left out four generations and six kings who actually ruled in Jerusalem. That would seriously throw his pattern out of kilter. In his third section he once again named only thirteen generations. In Luke's genealogy (chapter 3), between Abraham and Jesus there are fifty-six generations; Matthew has only forty-one. Surely inerrancy is a virtue ascribed to the Bible only by those who do not bother to read great sections of Holy Writ.

One other fascinating item is buried in the genealogy. Matthew has inserted the names of five women, including Mary, who is identified as "the wife of Joseph of whom Jesus was born" (Matt. 1:16). It was, first of all, unusual in this day to mention women in any genealogy; but, beyond that, these particular women present a special problem. All of them were tainted by some sexual impropriety.

In addition to Mary, the genealogy presents Tamar, who played the prostitute to seduce her father-in-law, Judah (Gen. 38:1ff); Rahab, another prostitute, who assisted the spies in Jericho (Josh. 2:1ff); Ruth, the Moabite lady who, by sleeping in his bed while he was inebriated, forced Boaz to exercise his filial responsibility to marry her (Ruth 3:6ff); and Bathsheba, who was identified in this genealogy not by name but as the wife of Uriah. David had violated this woman and arranged for Uriah's death in battle after being smitten with her charms as he watched her bathing on the rooftop (2 Sam. 11:2ff). The inclusion of these women in this genealogy has intrigued and frustrated interpreters through the ages.[7]

Jerome, one of the early church fathers, suggested that since all the women were sinners, they foreshadowed Jesus as the Savior of men. This bit of logic was typical of Jerome, who was never quite sure that women were fully human. The fact is, however, that in the Jewish piety of Jesus' time these women were highly esteemed and would not have been thought of as sinners by Matthew's readers, so Jerome's argument falters on other grounds.

Luther appears to have been the first to suggest that all these women were foreigners and were included by Matthew to show that the Jewish Messiah was related by ancestry to the Gentiles. Tamar and Rahab were Canaanites, Ruth a Moabite, and Bathsheba presumably was a Hittite. That argument may have some power, given Matthew's desire to uphold universalism. Mary, however, does not fit into this scheme. There is no hint anywhere that Mary was other than Jewish. One of the difficulties that renders this idea not fully supportable is that in Matthew's day these women were regarded by the Jewish tradition not as foreigners but as Jewish proselytes, and this status of proselyte was not the proposed status for the gentile Christians of Matthew's audience. Luther's interpretation, while not without merit, nonetheless has serious weaknesses.

More modern scholars, including Herman Hendrickx, have dared to see in the inclusion of these four women a foreshadowing of Mary's compromised sexual status. Something is highly irregular about the union of each with her sexual partner or husband. Indeed, to the definers of public morality, each would constitute something of a scandal. Yet each stood at a critical moment in the life of the covenant community, and by taking the action she took, each enabled the promise of God not to be thwarted. The line of the Christ came through the violation of Tamar, the prostitution of Rahab, the adultery of Bathsheba, and the grafting of Ruth's half-Moabite son into the sacred history of the Jewish people. This part of the genealogy, therefore, is startling, seldom noted, seldom read, seldom preached on but provocatively included by Matthew as a prelude to his story of Mary, a woman pregnant before marriage by an unknown source

70

that resulted in her betrothed's desire to put her away as "damaged goods." These four women become examples to Matthew of how God could achieve the divine purpose despite the violation of moral norms.

When one sees the impact of the midrash tradition on the birth narrative of Matthew, this conclusion receives additional strengthening. In the midrash these four women not only kept alive the royal line and therefore the messianic hope, but each was said to have done so by submission to the Holy Spirit.[8] In the midrash the clue that linked these women to Mary in Matthew's mind becomes clear and even obvious. Irregular sexual activity initiated by the action of the Spirit has, in the past, enabled the promise of Israel to move forward.[9] Mary's pregnancy, Matthew was admitting, also had about it a bit of scandal that cried out to be understood. To this intriguing note I shall return later.

Jesus' heritage had now been described through the genealogy, Matthew's major themes revolving around Abraham and David had been established therein, and the ground had been laid to develop the Son of God motif. Matthew then turned to telling the story of the birth of Jesus. It took place in this way, he asserted, as he proceeded with his account of the virginal conception.

First, Jesus' parents were introduced. Mary had been betrothed to Joseph. Betrothal in Jewish society had the legal force of marriage and was quite often entered into at age twelve or thirteen, even before puberty. The inauguration of married life as husband and wife might not occur until several years later, perhaps after the onset of puberty. Marital relations in the betrothal period were not absolutely condemned in Judea, but they tended to be condemned in Galilee. In Matthew's narrative, Mary and Joseph lived in Bethlehem and were therefore under the less stringent Judean code that would not have forbidden absolutely what

71

might be called betrothal visiting rights. However, the intense tone of scandal found in Matthew's narrative fits far better the prohibitive Galilean tradition and constitutes another bit of data that casts doubt on the entire Bethlehem location for Jesus' birth.

Matthew did not actually suggest that the Holy Spirit was the father of the child or that the Holy Spirit supplied the male element necessary to conception. When Matthew wrote his Gospel, the Holy Spirit as a distinct person of the Trinity was simply inconceivable. Modern Christians supply that image to Matthew's text when we read the Bible with eyes shaped by centuries of theological development. Some people so literalize these accounts that they have to postulate the somewhat absurd characteristics of an erection of the Spirit, or even spiritual sperm. It is even more complicated when one takes into account the fact that in Hebrew the Spirit is a feminine, not a masculine, word. One of the Gnostic Gospels attacked the literalized birth narratives from this perspective by questioning, "How can a woman give birth to a child by a woman?"[10]

The Spirit in early Christian thinking was an aspect of God, identified with life and breath.[11] The Spirit was the force by which God moved the prophet to speak. The Spirit was the animating principle of Jesus' ministry. The Spirit was the empowering presence of God that came upon the disciples after Jesus' death and caused them to exclaim that Jesus lived. The manner of begetting by the Spirit was creative, not sexual. The Spirit that hovered like a setting hen over the chaos at the dawn of creation to bring forth life now hovered over Mary to bring about in her the new creation. The Spirit of holiness that according to Paul declared Jesus to be God's Son in the resurrection, and which according to Mark adopted Jesus as God's Son at the baptism, was now present to proclaim Jesus as God's Son at conception.

Perhaps there was an early memory that supported the tradition that Jesus was born too soon after Mary and Joseph came together to live as husband and wife. Perhaps people did count the months and came up short. One tradition in Judaism suggested that blasphemers and religious disturbers have their origins examined, for the common wisdom held that illegitimate children tended to create religious problems in their adult lives. They reflected, it was thought, the spirit of the one who had violated the mother. Perhaps the stories of Jesus' miraculous birth were designed to counter this criticism. Perhaps Jesus was illegitimate, perhaps he was even the child of a violated woman, and the early Christians simply could not suppress this truth. Those who entertain this possibility argue that Matthew's story of Joseph debating whether to divorce Mary quietly, in accordance with the prescriptions of the Torah in Deuteronomy (Deut. 22:23–27), could not have been created out of thin air. That Torah passage suggested that "a woman betrothed who was raped in the country where no one could hear her cries for help shall not be put to death." She would, of course, be returned to her family as "damaged goods." If that was done quietly, her disgrace would be minimal. This was Joseph's plan until, as Matthew suggested, the angelic messenger in a dream informed Joseph that the child was holy, that the child was of the Holy Spirit. By placing the four sexually tainted women into his genealogy of Jesus, was Matthew preparing his readers for this possibility? Was he teaching them to listen to the suppressed clues until they could hear the Word underneath the words, a Word that dealt with reality symbolically? I suppose we can never know with certainty, but it makes a fascinating speculation, and it will come up again and again as we wander through the stories of Jesus' origins.

What we do know is that Matthew used this birth tradition to develop the character of Joseph after the pattern of

Joseph the saving patriarch of Israel, and to begin the peculiarly Matthean style of buttressing his account with expectations out of the Jewish Scriptures that find their fulfillment in Jesus. It was a typical approach of midrashic writing. Joseph was a "just man"; that is, a God-fearing righteous Jew. God spoke to this Joseph through dreams, just as God spoke through dreams to Joseph the favorite son of Israel/Jacob many hundreds of years before.

In the Hebrew Scriptures "an angel of the Lord" was a way of describing God's visible presence among men and women. The angel addressed Joseph in the dream as son of David; and, after assuring Joseph that this child was conceived by the Holy Spirit, the angel further declared that the child was to be named Jesus, Yeshua, or Joshua, because this child would be the agent of God's salvation. Joseph was to give the child this name because David's paternity, by way of Joseph, was to be transferred through legal, not biological, means. By naming the child, Joseph in the Hebrew custom was acknowledging him as his own, bestowing upon him all of the heritage of the Jewish father. Once again the hint of illegitimacy is heard. Indeed, it reverberates throughout this passage.

Matthew then introduced his interpretive formula, "All this took place to fulfill what the Lord has spoken by the prophet," citing Isaiah 7:14. The version of Isaiah 7:14 that Matthew quoted is not certain. He clearly was leaning on a Greek text rather than a Hebrew text, and yet the Septuagint was not his source. He deviated from the Septuagint in two interesting places: Matthew said the virgin "will be with child" (*hexei*) when the Septuagint said the virgin "will conceive" (*lēpsetai*). Matthew said "they" (third person plural) will call his name Immanuel, while the Septuagint said "you" (second person singular) will call his name Immanuel. Both Matthew and the Septuagint differ from the Hebrew text, which said "a young woman is with child and she [third person singular] will call his name Immanuel."[12]

Matthew, in this instance as in most of his use of Jewish scriptural sources, was surely shaped by the midrash tradition. Later in Christian history it was assumed that the Hebrew Scriptures used to interpret the Christ were in fact prophetic texts written years before the event to predict quite literal events in Jesus' life. One television evangelist has stated that he was convinced of Christianity's truth by the "fulfilled prophecies" of the Old Testament.[13] Yet once one steps away from the midrash tradition and begins to examine these texts in the light of either their original history or the events to which the evangelists are applying them, they become less than edifying and, indeed, border on the absurd.

This removal from and ignorance of the midrash tradition became commonplace among the early church fathers of the second and third centuries. Not one of them was Jewish. They were not familiar with the midrash tradition. Yet in their polemics against the Jews, they wrenched Jewish Scripture badly out of context and used the literalized text as a weapon. It was a strange and ironic twist of a fateful history to observe gentile Christians beating on Jews with the cudgel of the Jewish person's own holy book. One Jewish scholar arose to protest this misuse of his sacred text. His name was Trypho, and no copies of his work remain intact. We know him only from the response of a Christian teacher named Justin, who wrote a piece called *Dialogue with Trypho*.[14] Today this literalized view of the Old Testament "prophecies about Christ" has been obliterated by modern scholarship. Posthumously, Trypho has finally been declared the winner of the dialogue with Justin, a fact that must come as some surprise to this early Christian martyr.

In some sense Matthew himself began the process of steering the midrash tradition toward a literalized interpretation.

He probably could not have imagined just how far the next centuries' Christian leadership would take this tendency. Perhaps the most flagrant illustration of this tendency in Matthew was his use of the "virgin" text of Isaiah (7:14) to undergird or to create his narrative of Jesus' birth. Because the power of this misused text is still alive in the debates on doctrinal matters within the church today, it is worthy of a serious study and explanation.

When one reads Isaiah 7:14 in the context of Isaiah's history, the first and most obvious fact that must be recorded is that Isaiah was not referring to the virginal conception of Jesus when he wrote this work. Isaiah was concerned with addressing God's challenge to Isaiah's own day, not with predicting the future course of events. Second, and far more damaging to the literalist's view, it must be stated that the concept of virginity existed in this text only in the Greek translation of the Hebrew. Virginity was not present in the Hebrew original. In 1952 when the Revised Standard Version of the Bible was released, its translators rendered Isaiah 7:14 correctly from the Hebrew text to read, "Behold a young woman shall conceive," while they translated Matthew 1:23, "Behold a virgin shall conceive." The translators were not being inconsistent, they were translating accurately the text in front of them—Hebrew in the original text of Isaiah, Greek in the original text of Matthew. The Hebrew word in Isaiah 7:14 is *'almah*. It means "young woman"; she may or may not be married. The Hebrew word for virgin is *betulah*. It is a word used more than fifty times in the Hebrew Scriptures and is the only word used in those Scriptures for virgin. *'Almah* appears nine other times in the Hebrew Scriptures and it never means virgin in any of those appearances. The translators of the Septuagint, however, translated *'almah* with the Greek word *parthenos*, which does mean "virgin." The translators alone placed into this Isaian text the connotation

76

of virginity, and it was this nonoriginal connotation that Matthew made the keystone of his use of this text.

Throughout the years, self-appointed defenders of the faith who came to include the virgin birth as a crucial article of that faith never examined either that element of this text or even the other context of this Isaian passage. Defending the dogma of the virgin birth, which came to be thought of as defending the divinity of Jesus and the doctrine of the Incarnation, forced all other considerations out of sight and consequently out of mind.

The most cursory examination of the seventh chapter of Isaiah would, however, have rendered Matthew's particular use of this text as nothing short of absurd. This is the story behind Isaiah's words:

It was the final three decades of the eighth century B.C.E. The armies of Assyria were on the move. King Ahaz was in Jerusalem on the throne of David. Pekah was the king of Israel reigning in Samaria, and Rezin was the king of Syria reigning in Damascus. Pekah and Rezin entered a mutual defense treaty in an attempt to stave off their common Assyrian foe. They recognized that the military odds were still overwhelmingly against them, so they sent emissaries to Ahaz in Judah asking him to join their mutual-defense pact. Ahaz, who assessed Assyria's armed might far more accurately than his would-be allies, believed, however, that the best chance the kingdom of Judah had for survival lay in accepting the status of a vassal state and paying tribute to Assyria. He refused to join Pekah and Rezin. This refusal so angered the two leaders that they mobilized their forces to march on Jerusalem. It was their intention to defeat Judah, depose Ahaz, and place a more cooperative king on the throne in Jerusalem. A brushfire war broke out, and Ahaz retreated into fortress Jerusalem while Pekah and Rezin took up siege positions around the city. According to Isaiah, the

heart of Ahaz and the hearts of the people of Judah, behold-
ing the armies of Israel and Syria around their city, "shook
as the trees of the forest shake before the wind" (Isa. 7:2).

Isaiah, who served as an unofficial adviser to the kings
of Judah, went out to meet Ahaz. Isaiah took with him his
own son, who bore the prophetic name Shear-yashub, which
meant "a remnant will survive." They met on the battlements
near the city wall, and Isaiah urged Ahaz to "take heed, be
quiet, and do not let your heart faint because of these two
smoldering stumps of firebrands" (Isa. 7:4). It was hardly a
flattering description of Pekah and Rezin. Ahaz, however,
was not consoled. So the Lord, through Isaiah, agreed to give
Ahaz a sign that he and his people would be spared if Ahaz
would but request it. But Ahaz refused to ask for a sign (Isa.
7:12). Perhaps he did not want to be too deeply in Isaiah's
debt, for if Isaiah could produce a sign from God, his power
would be heightened and the power of the king would be
diminished. Whereupon Isaiah, in obvious anger, said,
"Hear this, O house of David! Is it too little for you to weary
men [and women] that you weary my God also? Therefore
[whether you like it or not is the implication] the Lord himself will give you a sign. Behold, a young woman shall conceive and bear a son and she shall call his name Immanuel"
(Isa. 7:13–14). Here Matthew broke off his version of this
text, and many Christians through the ages, convinced that
this was a reference to Jesus, declined to read further. But
Isaiah went on: "He shall eat curds and honey when he
knows how to refuse the evil and choose the good" (Isa.
7:15). Suddenly it does not sound much like Jesus. But that
is not all, for Isaiah continued, "For before the child knows
how to refuse the evil and choose the good [that is, before
this child reaches the age of early decision making], the land
before whose two kings you are in dread will be deserted"
(Isa. 7:16). The siege would soon be lifted, Isaiah was stating,

and with many fearful metaphors he described the devastation that would come with Assyrian hegemony (Isa. 7:18ff).

As history worked itself out, Pekah and Rezin were both destroyed, and Ahaz's decision to seek vassalage in exchange for life proved politically wise, for Israel was overrun by the Assyrian army. Its land was devastated, its people exiled, and the nation of Israel became known as the lost tribes of history. Judah, however, was spared at least for a century, and although bound to the will of Assyria, it was allowed tiny remnants of independence. All of this happened rather quickly, in a space of only two or three years. It would be nonsensical to think that the birth of a child seven hundred years later could have somehow given hope to King Ahaz in that particular moment of crisis. Whatever else the Isaiah text meant, it had literally nothing to do with Jesus.

The birth the prophet referred to was certainly that of a naturally conceived child to be born to a mother who was probably pregnant at that time and who was probably a member of the royal house of David. The birth of such a child would be a sign of the continuity of the people of Judah in this moment of crisis and would be, therefore, a sign of God's providential care. Most scholars today suggest that this text was a reference to the birth of Hezekiah, who was to rule over Judah in the line of royal succession.

By the time Matthew wrote his Gospel, the idea of a miraculous virgin birth for Jesus of Nazareth was already circulating in the early church. It was not, as we have noted, an uncommon idea in the Mediterranean world. Matthew leaped upon this text to buttress that developing tradition. Matthew's misuse of Isaiah 7:14 did not, in my opinion, create the virgin birth tradition, but it did color the expression of that belief and shape the details of that belief for later history. Matthew saw in this text scriptural support for both the Davidic and the divine aspect of Jesus' identity. He gave

79

narrative form to the Pauline proclamation that Jesus was "the son of David, according to the flesh, and was declared Son of God by the Spirit of holiness" (Rom. 1:4). For Matthew it was not at the resurrection, as Paul had suggested, or at the baptism, as Mark had written, but at the conception that this designation became operative.

In this dramatic story Matthew both claimed a divine origin for Jesus and countered those who were suggesting that Jesus was illegitimate. Those critics were thus informed that they were blaspheming against what God had spoken. Even worse, they were blaspheming against the Holy Spirit. Joseph begat him legally but not naturally, said Matthew, and they—a deliberate plural and a deliberate shift in the text he was quoting—they (both the Jew and the Gentile) will call him Immanuel. They will acknowledge him as Savior.

The first word about Jesus in Matthew is Immanuel. God is with us. The last word of Jesus in Matthew is still Immanuel, "Lo I am with you always." The angel of the Lord who announced Jesus' divine origin at birth would reappear at the tomb to announce that the presence of God made known in Jesus was eternally available in an eschatological way through the resurrection. The Spirit that conceived the Christ at the beginning would be the same Spirit that gave birth to the church, which is nothing except another body of Christ. Matthew's story again and again closes the circle.

One additional thing that needs to be noted is that this account of Joseph's dream is Matthew's version of the annunciation. The annunciation of Jesus' birth was for Matthew an annunciation to the father, not to the mother, as it would be in Luke. Such annunciations to the male were not unknown. The angelic visitor that told of Isaac's birth gave the message to Abraham, not Sarah. Michael Goulder argues that Luke transfers the concept of an annunciation to a male in his narrative to the father of John the Baptist.[15] Matthew's narrative reveals, moreover, in at least a general form the steps in the classic biblical annunciation stories: the addressing of the person by name; the expression of fear; the divine message; the allusion to the difficulty; the promise of a sign given to overcome the objection. Because of the context designed to identify Joseph with the Joseph of Genesis, steps two, three, and four are merged.[16] Herman Hendrickx also identifies the pattern of this narrative as "a command-execution" pattern and points out a parallel in Matthew's later narrative of Jesus' entry into Jerusalem.[17]

The angel appeared in a dream. The angel said to Joseph, "Do not fear." The pregnancy and its meaning were revealed, and the child was named. Joseph awoke from his dream, took Mary as his wife, and waited for the child of promise to be born. Abraham's son and David's son form the human side of Jesus, and the claim that Jesus was God's Son constituted the divine side in the dual nature of this child. The human and the divine are set side by side in early Christian preaching. "Whose son is he?" was the question constantly asked by the curious and the hostile. It was deliberately framed to imply scandal and to titillate the gossipers. To defend its Lord against these charges, the church framed its answer: He was Abraham's son and David's son according to the flesh, and he was God's Son according to the spirit. The narrative of Jesus' birth was thus created to give substance and detail to the church's defense of Jesus' origin.

One other Isaian text was also employed in this apologetic. Isaiah wrote, "There shall come forth a shoot from the stump of Jesse, and a branch shall grow out of his roots. And the Spirit of the Lord shall rest upon him, the spirit of wisdom and understanding, the spirit of counsel and might, the spirit of knowledge and the fear of the Lord" (Isa. 11:1, 2). Once again the line of the flesh was intersected by the line of the spirit.

81

Finally, we must acknowledge that in the typical biblical account of an annunciation, the usual obstacle to birth was sterility or age, not virginity. Matthew had taken a pre-Matthean virgin birth tradition and fitted it into the pattern of biblical annunciations. He had recorded a pre-Gospel angelic annunciation of the birth of the Davidic messiah, and now he moved to combine it with a popular narrative in which a story of Joseph and Jesus had been modeled on the adventures of the patriarch Joseph and the infant Moses. That follows in his next chapter.

This author was indeed a scribe "who had been trained for the kingdom of heaven." He was one "who brings out of his treasure what is new and what is old" (Matt. 13:52).

7

Matthew's Story, Part II

A titillating genealogy and the story of a virgin with child constituted the opening part of Matthew's birth narrative. But that was to be just the beginning. Matthew proceeded to weave together a story that focused on a star that appeared in the east and on magi who journeyed in search of the one whose birth that star had heralded. Into his account he drew a wicked king (Herod), gifts of gold, frankincense, and myrrh, another magical dream, an escape into Egypt, and finally, at the proper time, a return not to Bethlehem but to Nazareth. Each episode played its role in his larger story.

Where did Matthew get these vivid images? The literalists of our day insist that this Gospel writer simply told the story as it happened. Their supposition is that these details were orally transmitted with exact accurateness by those especially dedicated to the transmission of a precise tradition, until the time Matthew actually wrote down the story. Because Joseph was the central player in this birth drama, there has even been the hint that Joseph was the original source of the data that appeared in Matthew's story.

That explanation, however, is far too fanciful for a modern person to embrace. Virgins who give birth without a male agent exist for us only in legends and fairy tales. Stars that wander through the sky are not admitted by our knowledge of astronomy and astrophysics. A nonpracticing semi-Jewish king who asked his scribes for a search of the Hebrew Scriptures to tell him where the promised Jewish messiah would be born is too self-contradictory to be believable. Furthermore, a king who took murderous action in a vain attempt to destroy a pretender to his throne who had been brought to this king's attention by three foreign strangers on camels would be laughable if historically real. Yet here it is, opening the New Testament's story of Jesus, and from the second century until the Enlightenment, this narrative was generally assumed to represent literal history and was even called the literal word of God! When literal truth is claimed for Scripture, this assertion guarantees a counterpoint reaction: if not literally true, then it must be false. By going into Matthew's source, I propose to offer another, and I suspect more original, alternative.

The author of Matthew's Gospel, I have suggested, was deeply shaped by the tradition of the Jewish midrash. This fact required that he also be quite familiar with the corpus of the Jewish Scriptures. He wrote as a Jewish Christian utilizing the midrash tradition and interpreting Jesus by seeking to retell stories from that sacred Scripture which he believed presaged or pointed to this Christ. Since Matthew had no actual details of Jesus' birth to work with, he created this birth tradition out of the whole cloth of the interplay between his imagination and the Hebrew Bible. This meant that in order for his narrative to be understood, Matthew was unconsciously dependent upon the religious knowledge and the religious memory of his audience. If the readers of his Gospel ever ceased to be part of the religious heritage of the

Hebrew people, or to have their religious memories shaped by that historic tradition, then misunderstanding and distortion would be inevitable. Without the background required to resonate with the story, literalization would occur, and this in turn would produce the rejection of the literalized story as patently absurd.

When, in the early years of the second century of the Christian era, the church ceased to be primarily Jewish and began the process by which it first became gentile, then Greek, and finally Western, that is exactly what occurred. First, we did not understand, then we literalized, and finally, in this modern world, we rejected. It was not until the world of New Testament scholarship in the early years of the nineteenth century began to recover both the context and the frame of reference in which the Gospel writers wrote their books that a new doorway appeared through which the modern Christian could walk. That scholarship enabled one to escape the dead end of either literalization on one hand or rejection on the other.

The major debate in New Testament circles today is not over whether the events described by Matthew are reflections of things that actually occurred in literal history. The debate is rather over which Hebrew texts actually formed the building blocks that Matthew used to construct his birth narrative. Clearly there are in Matthew's opening chapters both obvious major Old Testament retellings and faint echoes from that sacred text. Sorting out these references, seeking their meaning, understanding why Matthew chose them are all parts of the modern biblical interpretive process.

Matthew was not writing history. These stories are not researched biographical episodes. This entire narrative was a Christian midrash, written to interpret the adult life of Jesus of Nazareth in terms of a rich religious heritage that fed the conviction of first-century Christians that Jesus was the

Messiah who fulfilled the Jewish expectations of the ages. Until this generation stops asking of Scripture the questions of a Western postmodern humanity, the power of the Bible in general and of the birth narratives in particular will be lost.

Lay aside the biases of this modern world and the fears that are born when one's religious tradition insists that its adherents believe the unbelievable and seek with me an entry into the midrash tradition as we explore the biblical roots of these fascinating and familiar narratives. Then perhaps we can succeed in re-creating the experience that transformed the first generations of Christians, an experience that cries out for an explanation. Was it possible that in Jesus God has been met and engaged? That was the Christian claim then, and that remains the Christian claim today.

That experience itself was beyond the capacity of these early Christians to question or to doubt. That was a reality for which they were willing to be persecuted, imprisoned, and even executed. Their task was only to find words, symbols, phrases, and interpretive clues through which they could talk about this reality. So Christian interpreters were driven to the sources of their faith, and in that process they utilized the tradition of midrash.

There are some who believe that the writings of Isaiah, especially the part scholars identify as Second Isaiah (40–66),[1] formed the basis of Matthew's story of the magi. Herman Hendrickx suggests that the story was born when an early Christian preacher used a text from Second Isaiah.[2] This portion of Isaiah, embodying as it does the concept of the innocent suffering servant whom God had acknowledged to be his unique son, was a great favorite of the early Christians and was applied with frequency to the life of Jesus.

· The key text for Hendrickx is "Who stirred up one from the east whom victory meets at every step? He gives up nations before him, so that he tramples kings under foot" (Isa. 41:2). When that text was supplemented, as it surely was in the early days of the church, by other references from that part of Isaiah, the case is strengthened. "Kings shall see and arise; princes, and they shall prostrate themselves" (Isa. 49:7). This verse came shortly after Isaiah had written, "The Lord called me from the womb, from the body of my mother he named my name" (Isa. 49:1). The imagination could easily have been stimulated to think of Jesus' birth when poring over this text.

Isaiah went on to write: "And nations shall come to your light and kings to the brightness of your rising. . . . A multitude of camels shall cover you, the young camels of Midian and Ephah; all those from Sheba shall come. They shall bring gold and frankincense, and shall proclaim the praise of the Lord" (Isa. 60:3, 6). This comes right after Isaiah has exclaimed, "Arise, shine; for your light has come, and the glory of the Lord has risen upon you" (Isa. 60:1).

Suddenly the elements come into focus. A rising light becomes a star rising in the east. Kings come, they journey from the east to do homage. They bring gifts of gold and frankincense. It does not take a vivid imagination to leap from this data to Matthew's story, especially if you are a child of this method of viewing Scripture.

While not minimizing the contributions that these Isaian texts made to Matthew's narrative, Raymond Brown suggests a quite different primary source of influence. For him the key to the magi story in Matthew is found in the story of Balaam and Balak in the Book of Numbers (22–24). Under the probing of his skillful mind, the parallels of that passage begin to be apparent.[3] Balaam was a seer from the east, a Gentile who saw the star of David rise and who was led to acknowledge the greatness of Israel's ruler. Surprisingly, the Balaam account is not a very familiar story to most people.

If anything is remembered about Balaam, it is the suggestion that God somehow spoke through Balaam's donkey. Here are the narrative details:

The children of Israel were in the wilderness between the exodus from Egypt and the entry into their promised land. Balak, the king of Moab, saw this wandering nomadic host and feared Israel greatly, so he sought a means to destroy this marauding nation. Hence he summoned the famous seer Balaam to put a curse on Israel. Balaam was a non-Israelite, an occult visionary, a practicer of enchantment who was called a magus by the popular Jewish writer Philo. Balaam was thought to be both good and evil. His goodness was displayed in that instead of cursing Israel as Balak had hoped, Balaam blessed Israel. His evil was seen in that after this episode the men of Israel were seduced into idolatry by the women of Moab, and the biblical tradition blamed Balaam for this. This hostile view of Balaam found its way into other Christian writings, indicating a midrashic use of this narrative by early Christians. The Book of Revelation states, "But I have a few things against you: you have some there who hold the teaching of Balaam, who taught Balak to put a stumbling block before the sons of Israel, that they might eat food sacrificed to idols and practice immorality" (Rev. 2:14). The Epistle of Jude records, "Woe to them! For they walk in the way of Cain, and abandon themselves for the sake of gain to Balaam's error, and perish in Korah's rebellion" (Jude 11). Second Peter declares, "Forsaking the right way they have gone astray; they have followed the way of Balaam, the son of Be'or, who loved gain from wrongdoing, but was rebuked for his own transgression; a dumb ass spoke with human voice and restrained the prophet's madness" (2 Pet. 2:15, 16).

But each of these books was probably written after Matthew's work was complete. Matthew appears to have leaned on the primary narrative of Balaam in the Book of Numbers, in which Balaam is good. Philo says Balaam was filled with the authentic spirit of a prophet.[4] In the Numbers account, Balaam came from the east, accompanied by two servants, and foiled the hostile plans of King Balak by uttering oracles that foretold the future greatness of Israel and the rise of a royal ruler. A wicked king tried to use a foreign magus whose name was Balaam to destroy those he perceived to be his rivals and his enemies. That is the story of Balaam that Raymond Brown believes provided the backdrop to Matthew's story of the magi.

Still another candidate for primary influence in shaping the magi story of Matthew is the visit of the queen of Sheba to Solomon (1 Kings 10:1–13). The queen had heard of Solomon's wisdom and had come to test him with hard questions. She brought with her gold, spices (perhaps myrrh), and precious stones. In Matthew's story the magi came and confronted Solomon's successor, Herod, with hard questions: "Where is he who has been born King of the Jews, for we have seen his star in the east and have come to worship him" (Matt. 2:2). Herod, however, as an unworthy successor to Solomon, revealed only ignorance of this central event in Israel's history and turned to the scribes for an answer.

The Jewish midrash further developed this narrative by incorporating a star into the visit of the queen of Sheba, "As the Queen of Sheba approached the holy city reclining in her litter, she saw at a distance a wondrous rose growing at the edge of a lake. But when she came near she saw to her astonishment the rose suddenly transformed into a flashing star. The closer she came the more dazzling was its light."[5]

I hope that my earlier suggestion is now apparent that the argument among biblical scholars today is over which narrative in the Hebrew tradition was primary in helping Matthew develop his magi tradition. No one I know in New

Testament circles is debating whether or not the magi were actual people living in history. The universal assumption is that they were not. Matthew was clearly writing Christian midrash.

As we get more and more deeply into Matthew's account, we begin to see other themes out of the Hebrew past woven into this narrative. The patriarch Joseph in the Book of Genesis (37–50) took his family to Egypt in order that they might escape death from starvation. In this manner Joseph enabled God's promise to Abraham to be kept alive. This theme is certainly echoed in Matthew's account of his Joseph taking the family of Mary and Jesus to Egypt also, to escape death this time at the hand of Herod (Matt. 2:13–16).

The mention of Egypt and the backdrop of a birth serve to remind the author of Matthew of the story of Moses and the pharaoh's attempt to end the life of that one born to be the deliverer of Israel by killing all the Jewish male babies in Egypt (Exod. 1:15ff). Obviously that story forms the backdrop to Matthew's account of Herod's murder of the Jewish male babies in Bethlehem (Matt. 2:16ff) in his attempt to destroy another deliverer who is perceived by Herod as his rival for the throne.

Later Jewish midrash often used the star device to announce the birth of a heroic Jewish figure. Astrologers were said to have told the wicked King Nimrod, when Abraham was born, that a son had been born to Terah, for they had seen a rising star in the heavens. The exact date of this legend, however, cannot be fixed, so we are left to wonder whether this story influenced Matthew or he influenced this story.[6]

The midrash mentions another star at the time of Moses' birth and still another when Isaac, the child of promise, was born to the elderly Abraham and Sarah. When this star tradition is coupled with the story from the Hebrew Scriptures about the pillar of fire that led the children of Israel through the wilderness by night (Exod. 13:21), one begins to see how the announcing star might be transformed into a guiding star under the skillful pen of someone like Matthew. A heavenly light that would guide the world to the birthplace of the Jewish Messiah would have met almost all of Matthew's major literary motifs.

Still other events probably known to the author of Matthew may have shaped his narrative. Some of these took place in the secular arena. Perhaps some natural phenomena had occurred in the heavens and entered the records of the astronomers of that day and thus found their way into the folklore of the people. A study of the movement of heavenly bodies fascinated ancient people. The popularity of astrology and the signs of the zodiac today indicates that this fascination has not yet died. Perhaps when the story of Jesus' birth began to be told by Christians, someone conducted a search into the astronomical records of the ages for corroborative data.

Two heavenly signs were, in fact, recorded about the time of Jesus' birth. The first occurred in 12–11 B.C.E., when what we now call Halley's comet was visible in the earth's atmosphere during the winter. This comet constituted the only wandering light in the heavens we know even today. In pre-scientific days, Halley's comet was identified both as a star and as a sign of things to come. Halley's comet came from the east, streaked across the heavens, faded while overhead, and then reappeared before it set in the west. This well-remembered heavenly event could have given some credibility to the story of a star that wandered through the heavens, disappeared, then appeared again. Interestingly enough, that comet would have risen in the astrological charts in the realm of Gemini with its head toward Leo. Leo was associated in ancient times with the lion of Judah.[7]

The second heavenly sign that might have been associated with the time of Jesus' birth was a rare juxtaposition of three planets—Jupiter, Saturn, and Mars, which together would have created a bright glow occurring only once in a great span of time. This heavenly phenomenon, featured in the Christmas show of many planetariums in the Western world, occurred in the year 8 B.C.E. and might well have entered the folklore of the early church. When Christians, who stood on the other side of Easter, tried to imagine the moment when Jesus was born, both Halley's comet and the planetary juxtaposition could have been drawn into the interpretive framework.

Josephus wrote about foreign ambassadors journeying to Jerusalem to hail King Herod on the occasion of the completion of the palace in Caesarea, which occurred in 9 B.C.E. This too may have served as background for Matthew's story.[8] In the 66th year of the common era, another event occurred that captured the imagination of people throughout the empire and was recorded by Cassius Dio.[9] The king of Armenia, a man named Tiradates, came to Italy with the sons of three Parthian rulers. They too journeyed from the east in a triumphal procession. Rome was decorated to bid them welcome. People crowded the streets and rooftops to glimpse the royal visitor as Tiradates went forward to pay homage to Nero.[10] This king also did not return by the route he had come but departed via another way. The Roman historian Pliny, who also mentioned this event, referred to this Armenian king and his entourage as magi.[11] Matthew, writing some twenty years later, may have been influenced in part by this well-remembered moment of Roman history. If magi from the east could come to pay homage to the Emperor Nero, how much more might they have come to pay homage to the King of Kings, the son of David, the son of Abraham, the Son of God.

These are some of the details that lie behind Matthew's story of the events accompanying Jesus' birth. How well this Jewish-Christian scribe has woven together symbols out of the treasure house of the new and the old to introduce the one whom he regarded as the Savior of the world. Later interpreters read other elements into Matthew's narrative that were consistent with their faith in this Messiah and added to both the charm and power of Matthew's tale, even though they may or may not have been part of Matthew's intention.

First, nowhere in the Matthean narrative is the number three specifically associated with the magi. Yet the Epiphany carol "We Three Kings" has placed into the corporate memory the image of three magi become kings. Later tradition has identified the three as representatives of the three races of humanity—Caucasian, black, and oriental. This is an accurate if not literal extension of Matthew's suggestion that a universal sign in the sky would draw all the world to the place of Jesus' birth to worship the one who has risen out of the seed of David. The promise given to Abraham was that he would be the agent through whom all the nations of the world would be blessed. Matthew described the fulfillment of that promise as Jew and Gentile alike come to acknowledge this life and to find unity through their common worship of this Jewish Messiah. Matthew's narrative was a powerful story that continues even today to create its own interpretive mythology.

Second, the gifts of gold, frankincense, and myrrh have also been brought into an interpretive framework, theologically and especially homiletically. Gold and frankincense are part of Isaiah's contribution to this narrative (Isa. 60:6), but the origin of myrrh is more difficult to locate, though I have suggested it may have arisen from the spices brought by the queen of Sheba. Nonetheless, the folklore of the church has taken those gifts and interpreted them. Gold was the traditional gift that one brought to a king. Jesus, Matthew asserted, was the son of David, and was therefore the heir to the Jewish throne. Frankincense was used in the worship of the temple and was an appropriate offering to God. So the divinity of this child as one to whom prayers were addressed that rose to heaven like incense was affirmed. Myrrh is a yellowish to reddish-brown aromatic gum resin obtained from a tree in East Africa and the Middle East. It has a bitter, slightly pungent taste and was a spice associated with embalming and therefore with death. Hence it has been thought to presage in Matthew's Gospel the story of Jesus' suffering and death. It has come to be seen as the first shadow of the cross to fall across the life of Jesus.

Once the visit of the wise men had been completed, Matthew continued his dramatic story, still weaving together familiar elements out of the well-known heritage of the Jewish nation. Jesus was taken to Egypt so that, like Israel of old, God could call forth the divine Son out of Egypt. The slaughter of the innocent children brought to mind, for Matthew, the picture drawn by Jeremiah of Rachel weeping in Ramah for her children who were no more (Matt. 2:18), which evoked for his readers images of the exile.[12]

Finally, Matthew arrived at what was perhaps the climax of this birth story. Jesus, in his earthly life, was clearly identified with the village of Nazareth in Galilee. That fact constituted a problem for the Christian church to explain. Nazareth was not to be the place of origin for the messiah. How then did the Christ come to be identified with that place? "Can anything good come out of Nazareth?" (John 1:46). So Matthew carried his reader from Bethlehem, the City of David, to Egypt, the land of oppression, to Ramah with its echo of the exile, and then to Nazareth. It was a fascinating theological, not geographical, journey.

An angel spoke to Joseph in a dream and gave him verbatim the words of the Lord to Moses about Pharaoh's death: "Those who sought the child's life are dead," said the angel to Joseph (Matt. 2:20). "Those who sought your life are dead," said the Lord to Moses (Exod. 4:19). The death of Pharaoh freed Moses to begin his mission of return to the promised land. So also Herod's death led Jesus to the starting place of his ministry. Joseph was specifically told to take Jesus to the land of Israel. He complied. Then the angel warned him not to go to Judea, for Archelaus, Herod's son, reigned there. Instead Joseph was directed to Galilee. Joseph again complied. Finally Joseph chose out of all of Galilee the city of Nazareth to be Jesus' home. That was done, said Matthew, in fulfillment of the prophetic word that "he shall be called a Nazarene" (Matt. 2:23).

Once again Matthew's dominant and unifying themes are heard: Go to Israel for you are the son of David. Go to Galilee of the Gentiles for you are the son of Abraham through whom all nations will be blessed. Go to Nazareth for you are Son of God set aside to be holy as were the Nazarenes.[13]

So Nazareth was to be Jesus' home. Recall that Luke assumed that Nazareth was always his home and hence used a census or enrollment to explain why Jesus' birth took place in Bethlehem. Luke then had Jesus return to Nazareth after the rites of circumcision and presentation. Matthew, on the other hand, found it necessary to explain why Jesus happened to come from Nazareth. In part this was a Matthean polemic against those Jewish people who stoutly maintained that the messiah could not come out of Galilee. Matthew took the name of Nazareth and filled it with other clever nuances so that the town, pejoratively mentioned by Jesus' Jewish critics, now elicited and evoked far more than just the name of a place. Matthew wanted to dangle before his readers the other meanings to the title *Nazarene*. It served well his literary purpose. In the Hebrew Scriptures a Nazirite was a holy person, selected and set aside for God's service (e.g. Num. 6:2). Samson and Samuel were both Nazirites and both, not coincidentally, had annunciation stories and birth stories told about them in the Hebrew Scriptures (Judges 13). To associate a Nazirite with the town of Nazareth was the kind of data a scribe, trained in the tradition of midrash, would employ.

The title *Nazarene* also reminded Matthew's audience that Jesus was the messianic branch. The Hebrew word for branch is *neser*. The annunciation story in Matthew's Gospel closed when Joseph named the child Jesus. The entire birth narrative, for Matthew, closed when Joseph brought the child Jesus to Nazareth so that all might call him Nazarene, one special to God, holy and set apart. Matthew was suggesting that this fulfilled a prophetic word, "He shall be called a Nazarene," but scholars are not certain where in the Hebrew Scriptures such a prophetic word is spoken. The best guess is a text in Isaiah (4:3) that says, "He will be called holy." The Hebrew word rendered in the Greek as both holy and Nazirite is *nazir*. Since Jesus was for Matthew the holy one of God, Matthew could have read Isaiah 4:3 to say, "He will be called a Nazirite."[14] The spelling was different from the town of Nazareth but it was close and Matthew was not disturbed by literal discrepancies.

In the Book of Judges (13:5) an angel appeared to the mother of Samson in an annunciation and stated that the child to be conceived in her barren womb "shall be a Nazirite to God from birth and he shall deliver Israel from the hand of the Philistines." In Matthew the angel said of Jesus, "He will save his people from their sins" (Matt. 1:21). Matthew took the name of Jesus' home, Nazareth, a town scorned and criticized by those Jews who wished to dismiss Jesus and opened it to the meanings of the past. *Neser,* the branch that shall come forth from Jesse; *nazir,* the Hebrew word for holy, *Nazirite* the Hebrew term for one set apart by God for a special purpose—all become part of Matthew's affirmation of the one who happened to hail from Nazareth and who was believed by this Jewish scribe to be son of David, son of Abraham, and Son of God. For the modern mind these references would represent an enormous stretch in logic. For a student of Jewish midrash, this was all in a day's work of probing and teasing the Scriptures to make them reveal their true message.

For Matthew, the Hebrew Scriptures and the Christian gospel met in the infancy narrative. He attached the Caesarea Philippi confession, "You are the Christ, the son of the living God," to the conception of Jesus. He held the birth narrative together through his creation of the character of Joseph, whom he described as a Jew who was upright, scrupulously faithful to the law, and who protected Jesus time after time from the hostile authorities. Joseph, of the house of David, acknowledged Jesus as his son by naming him in Bethlehem. Joseph enabled Jesus to repeat the life cycle of Israel by taking him down to Egypt in order to save Jesus' life, and thereby God's promise, from death. Joseph was the patriarch who, like Israel, was called by God out of Egypt; and Jesus, like Moses, was enabled to begin the work of deliverance when the wicked king who sought his life died. Joseph took Jesus to Nazareth, a town in Galilee of the Gentiles. He was a faithful Jew who brought Gentiles to Jesus to fulfill the law and the prophets. Faithful Jews, the author was saying, were those who saw in Jesus the fulfillment of the Jewish Scriptures and an opening of the Jewish tradition that would enable the Gentiles to participate in Jesus, who was, and is, the Jewish gift to the world. Jesus was the means through which the promise given to Abraham that all the world will be blessed through Abraham's seed was to find fulfillment. It is not surprising that Jesus' final words in Matthew's Gospel were what we call the divine commission: "Go preach to all people, baptize all people" (Matt. 28:20). The Jewish Jesus had become the universal Christ, who bound Jew and Gentile together in a holy community. This was the life whose birth was marked, said Matthew, by such symbols as a virginal conception, heavenly lights, exotic magi, wicked kings, a flight to Egypt, and life in Nazareth.

It is a beautiful, powerful story, not literal but true, opening to all of us in every generation the opportunity to follow our stars to the place and the moment where the divine and the human meet. There, kneeling in homage, we may present our gifts and see this life as son of David, son of Abraham, and Son of God. This vision of Jesus and of his birth we possess today because there was a Jewish scribe who wrote the Gospel we call Matthew and who placed into that Gospel one autobiographical reference when he praised those scribes who had been trained for the kingdom of heaven. They are "like a householder," he said, "who brings out of his treasure what is new and what is old." For that is obviously what the author of Matthew has done for us.

8

Behind Luke—An Original Pageant?

Whoever authored the Gospel we call Luke had the ability to write in beautiful and grammatically perfect Greek. It was clearly his native tongue. He was, by his own admission (Luke 1:2), not an eyewitness to the events he described. He was rather a second-generation convert to Christianity and in all probability a Gentile. Indeed, he appears to be the only Gentile who authored part of what we now acknowledge as Holy Scripture. His was not a minor contribution, for his work included not only what is called Luke but also the Book of Acts. His two-part story consisted of fifty-two chapters and makes up more than 20 percent of the canonical Christian Scriptures.

Who this author was has never been established with certainty. Before the end of the second century, however, the name of Luke was firmly connected to this corpus. The internal clue that led to this designation was found in the "we" passages from the Book of Acts that read like a diary. It was as if the author had joined the missionary team, and the pronoun of the narrative shifted from "they" to "we." When the traveling companions of Paul were analyzed, the most obvious one to be designated the author was Luke, whom Paul called a physician (Col. 4:14). Thus the figure of Luke, the beloved physician, entered the tradition of the Christian church and has inspired romantic tales and fanciful folklore for almost two thousand years.

Recently, however, New Testament scholars have begun to raise questions about Lucan authorship of both books. The lack of harmony between Paul's experience as revealed through the Pauline epistles and Luke's accounts of Paul's ministry in the Book of Acts has been cited to rule out the possibility that Acts was written by one of Paul's companions (Gal. 1:16–17 vs. Acts 9:19–29, e.g.). Ernst Haenchen, one of the world's leading Christian scholars on the Book of Acts, argues powerfully against Luke's authorship for either.[1] Paul certainly occupied a prominent role in Acts, and yet Paul's claim to have been an eyewitness to the resurrection, which validated his apostolic authority, was challenged by the Book of Acts. Luke used the story of the ascension to climax the resurrection appearances and to announce that resurrection appearances had ceased. Paul's conversion was placed well after the account of the ascension in the Book of Acts and was presented not as an appearance story but as a vision not substantially different from Peter's vision of the great sheet let down from heaven (Acts 10:9–16). Paul had said that his experience of Jesus' resurrection differed from the others in no way save that his was last (1 Cor. 15:8). The Book of Acts was also careful to limit the apostles to twelve; and Matthias, not Paul, was the twelfth member to complete the authentic apostolic band (Acts 1:26).

Yet whoever was the author of the Luke-Acts corpus believed, like Paul, that the mission of the Christian church to the Gentiles was God's preordained plan. The mission to Israel had been short-circuited, in his opinion, by the hardness of the hearts of the Jewish people. His story line passed from

100

Jerusalem of the Jews to Rome of the Gentiles. The Gospel part of that story, however, only prepared for the launch among the Gentiles.

The third Gospel, which for lack of any better title I shall call Luke, is actually framed by the scenes involving the Jewish temple. It opens with Zechariah's vision in the temple (1:8) and concludes with the postresurrection scene of the disciples, who returned with great joy to Jerusalem, where they were continually in the temple blessing God (24:53). At the beginning of Luke's story, the mute Zechariah is incapable of blessing the people. At the conclusion, the resurrected Jesus in the moment before his cosmic ascension lifts his hands and performs the high-priestly blessing even as he is parted from them. Luke had a sense of drama and wholeness. He too closed the circle with regularity.[2]

Luke said in his preface that since "many have undertaken to compile a narrative of the things which have been accomplished among us," he had decided to set the various narratives in order. What were the many narratives to which Luke referred? Two are certainly obvious. Luke, at least in the final rendition of his Gospel, leaned heavily on Mark. He used Mark, however, in a rather different way from Matthew. Matthew simply expanded Mark, correcting and changing him wherever either his convictions or the sensitivities of his readers might require. Luke, on the other hand, inserted great chunks of Mark into his narrative. The fact that Luke still reads cohesively even when the Marcan material is removed has led some scholars to suggest what is called the proto-Luke theory. This maintains that Luke wrote his story in more than one version and that the original did not include material from Mark. Those who hold this theory also assert that the entire birth narrative of Luke 1 and 2 was part of a later addition. The elaborate dating process that begins chapter 3 (3:1–3) and the inclusion of a genealogy in the

101

strange, indeed unheard of, place after, rather than before, the birth story are evidence for some that Luke's story at least at one point in its literary career started with chapter 3 rather than chapter 1.

The second narrative that Luke appears to have had access to was either Matthew or the Q material, to which I have referred earlier. The material, common to both Matthew and Luke but not to Mark, requires either the postulation of an earlier source, Q, on which both were dependent or the dependency of one on the other. That Luke was dependent on Matthew has been suggested and even defended vigorously by English scholar Michael Goulder.[3] The possibility that Matthew was dependent on Luke is not thought to be conceivable.

Luke's third narrative source, though easily identified, is more highly speculative but perhaps even more important. It is referred to in New Testament circles as L and is identified as Luke's special source. It includes everything that cannot be assigned to the Books of Mark and Matthew or to the Q document. But once that generalization is made, it becomes obvious that the L source is more than a single source. The speeches of Peter and Paul in the Book of Acts, the canticles of Zechariah, Mary, and Simeon in Luke's birth narrative, the Lucan genealogy, many of the unique parables, and major parts of the birth narratives—each might represent a different source that Luke collected before he started his Gospel. Some of this material might have been written, some of it was surely oral, and some of it Luke himself may well have created. At the very least he would be the first person who had put this particular part of the oral tradition into written form. But the fact remains that Luke wove all of these sources into his own narrative, making each part serve the needs of the whole and revealing in a consistent way Luke's themes. On any of these once-separate sources Luke's editorial genius cannot be denied.

The basic outline of the very familiar Christmas story that now opens the Gospel of Luke in all probability had some kind of independent life before Luke made it his own. Language and stylistic differences divide the birth story from the rest of the Gospel. Chapters 1 and 2, for example, are filled with Semitisms that would not have been natural parts of the vocabulary of this Greek-speaking gentile writer: "You will call his name John," "In the days of Herod King of Judea," "and her name was called Elizabeth," "You have found favor with God," "I do not know a man," "The child to be born will be called holy" are all Semitisms that the Greek language accommodated only with difficulty. The frequency of these Semitisms in the first two chapters of Luke points, I think, to an original source independent of the author of the balance of the Gospel. I am not persuaded by the (oral) argument of Jeffrey John of Oxford that Luke's dependence on the Septuagint accounts for these Semitic phrases.

Within the birth story there are other fascinating clues to what might have been their original setting. A regular formula was employed again and again to change the scenery. It was the device of a departure or a returning that allowed the scene to shift. The vision scene of Zechariah in the temple was concluded with the words, "And when his time of service was ended he went straight to his home" (1:23). The annunciation to Mary scene ends with the words "And the angel departed from her" (1:38). Mary's visit to Elizabeth concludes with the words "And Mary remained with her about three months and returned to her home" (1:56). John the Baptist's birth scene was concluded by moving John from center stage, "And he was in the wilderness till the day of his manifestation to Israel" (1:80). The vignette describing the annunciation to the hillside shepherds was closed by declaring that "the angels went away from them into heaven" (2:15). The scene in which the shepherds found the child in Bethlehem ends with the words "and the shepherds returned." The temple presentation drama concludes as they (Mary, Joseph, and Jesus) "returned into Galilee" (2:39). Finally, the entire birth drama comes to an end with the words that Jesus "increased in wisdom and in stature, and in favor with God and man." Although not a word of moving or returning, it is a statement announcing the completion of the infancy story, which in turn sets the stage for the adult story to begin. These transition points have the effect of framing each scene into a dramatic whole in which their power can be experienced and their ever-increasing dramatic impact can be noted.

While Matthew's wise men are more vivid than Luke's shepherds, it remains a fact that Luke's infancy story is far better known than Matthew's infancy story. In the common mind of the masses of Christian people, the biblical narrative of Christmas consists of Luke's story with the magi of Matthew tacked on as the concluding episode. This is true, I am convinced, because the Lucan Christmas story has, from the very beginning, been communicated to people not through either reading or preaching but through its being acted out. The Lucan material is familiar to most all of us because we have, at some point in our lives, been a shepherd or Mary or Joseph or the innkeeper in a Christmas pageant. If not a part of the pageant, then at least we have watched others in these roles as a regular feature of our Christmas observance. When the final scene of these traditional holiday pageants presents Matthew's magi kneeling with the shepherds at the manger to present their gifts, it is clear that the single scene from Matthew has simply been grafted onto Luke's schema with no attention whatsoever paid to the data that makes such a Matthean grafting inappropriate.

But what was the original context of Luke's familiar Christmas story? How did Luke come upon it? What was its original form before Luke's adaptive genius and creative pen molded it into his very own? The clue to the answer might lie in the material's suitability to dramatization. We find it easy to stage as a pageant because it was in fact originally just that—a pageant.

Imagine, if you will, a stage. Place yourself in the audience. Shrink the time span so that these events take place in the present as you view them. The curtain rises and you are introduced to Zechariah. You learn that he is an elderly righteous Jewish priest and Levite, whose wife Elizabeth is barren. Then you are told that this Zechariah has won, by lot, the incredible honor of entering the temple of the Lord to burn the ceremonial incense. It is an opportunity that comes to a priest only once in a lifetime. But there in the sacred temple a vision takes place during which the angel Gabriel proclaims that Elizabeth's barrenness will be overcome by the gracious God and that these two elderly persons will produce a son whose name will be John. The role of John is then described in great detail. Zechariah, doubting this vision, is struck deaf and mute. He comes out of the temple but is not able to perform the ceremonial act of blessing the people, so he walks off the stage to return home. The power of the divine-human confrontation has been experienced. Thus ends the first scene.

Scene two is the annunciation to Mary. The stage is clear, so Mary enters from one side and Gabriel from the other. The stage is thus set for a second meeting between the divine and the human. This episode brings us knowledge about the birth of Jesus, who will be conceived by the action of the

Holy Spirit overshadowing the young virgin. This is to be understood as a moment not of divine sexual activity but of divine creative activity. The sign to validate the details of this annunciation is the angelic message revealing to Mary the pregnancy of her kinswoman Elizabeth. Then the scene concludes as the angel makes an exit.

Mary, alone on the stage, makes a symbolic journey to the other side that is identified to the audience as the hill country of Judah, where she enters Elizabeth's home to inaugurate scene three. There another dramatic confrontation takes place between the two women and their unborn fetuses, whose lives are to be critically related as adults. Once again the divine and the human intersect. In the process, more clues in this developing narrative are disclosed. The supremacy of Jesus over John the Baptist is asserted, and all the involved parties acknowledge that supremacy. Then the scene closes as Mary departs.

Elizabeth now remains on the stage alone. It is the ninth month of her pregnancy. A Semitism, "Now the time came for Elizabeth to be delivered," opens the scene. People crowd onto the stage to celebrate this incredible birth to Elizabeth and Zechariah, together with the circumcision and the naming of John. It is accomplished with such marvels that people ask the question, What role will this child play in the drama of life? The scene closes as John is located in the wilderness, from whence he will reemerge (in Luke's chapter 3). The curtain comes down on act one.

Act two opens with another stage-setting explanation. An elaborate dating process is utilized. A worldwide enrollment for taxation purposes is recalled to explain why Joseph and his wife are on a journey to Bethlehem. They enter the stage from the left. The audience is informed that they have come from Nazareth and that Mary is at the point of delivery. In the words of Elizabethan English, "She was great with child." Jesus is born, swaddled in cloths by his mother and placed in a manger, because, we are told, there was no available space in the inn.

In scene two of act two, the attention of the audience, and later of the reader, is then directed to the opposite side of the stage, perhaps through the means of extinguishing lamps or candles on one side and lighting them on the other. There a vignette on a hillside in nearby Judea is dramatized. Shepherds are in the field, watching their flocks. It is night. Suddenly the sky is aglow with a heavenly light. Perhaps all in the scene turn their oil lamps to their maximum capacity. An angel appears to announce glad tidings and good news: a savior, the Messiah, the Lord, has been born in the city of David. The interpretive sign given the shepherds to enable them to identify this holy child is that he is swaddled and lying in a manger. The clear implication is that the shepherds must go, seek, and find.

The shepherds talk animatedly among themselves until the decision is made to go to Bethlehem and to see this thing that has been revealed to them by the divine messenger. The shepherds then walk across the stage as the lights are once more lit where Joseph and Mary have been waiting. The shepherds thus enter the life of the holy family and become the first witnesses to the Savior's birth. They share with the parents the story of their hillside vision, creating great wonder and raising the implicit question that had also been raised at the birth of John the Baptist, What will this child be? It is to answer this question, concerning both John and Jesus, that the entire Gospel that follows was written. Mary alone seems to comprehend, for she files all these memories for pondering, and the shepherds exit to their familiar pastures.

The final scene in this nativity drama is the naming, circumcision, and presentation of the newborn child, Jesus. It serves as the author's literary device to move the drama from Bethlehem to Jerusalem, and from the stable to the temple. It also provides a means to introduce an old man, Simeon, and an old woman, Anna, who continue to acquaint the audience with the meaning of this child, including a hint of the passion—"A sword shall pierce through your own soul" (Luke 2:35). Finally the holy family returns to Nazareth, where the child grows and where he lives until his manifestation to Israel. Here the curtain falls on act two of the original drama.

Is it not possible that the original setting, the kernel of this lovely birth story—so powerfully dramatic, so neatly divided into scenes, so complete with stage directions for the exiting of one set of actors to make ready for the next, and so connected by the movement of one set of characters into the presence of another—was at its very beginning a pageant written for and performed by a Jewish-Christian community? Did Luke discover it, view it, expand it, or at the very least borrow it for his narrative? Surely the pageant format is present even in his expanded version. My thesis is that the original pageant contained only four scenes, and they revolved around the parallel but not equal narratives that placed Jesus and John the Baptist into relationship with each other; a relationship in which John pointed consistently to Jesus. The original scenes, I believe, were these:

1. The annunciation about John the Baptist, which caught up the themes of the ancient story of Abraham and Sarah and the child of promise, Isaac;
2. The annunciation about Jesus, which caught up the themes from the ancient story of Hannah, including divine intervention;
3. The birth, circumcision, and naming of John the Baptist;
4. The birth, circumcision, and naming of Jesus.

108

To this core Luke has, I believe, added his genius. He connected the two narratives with Mary's visit to Elizabeth. He suggested a physical kinship between John and Jesus by calling Elizabeth Mary's kinswoman. He added the two temple stories—one at forty days, the other at twelve years. But he kept the dramatic form of the pageant. Luke saw this narrative presented as a pageant, I believe, and having been charmed by it, he incorporated it into the introduction of his story of Jesus. That would be my speculation.

If this hypothesis can be supported, it is still quite conceivable that Luke shaped even the core of the pageant that he incorporated. The canticles, I believe, were not part of the original narrative. Luke got them from another source and added them to this drama. They served the vital purpose of enabling his characters to speak when in the original drama there was no dialogue. The pageant seems to have been originally done in a kind of pantomime with only scene-introducing and scene-connecting narration. I am confident that Luke edited this pageant, as he did all of his sources, making it reflect his theology and his understanding of Jesus. In this manner, it became Lucan in substance as well as in form. He did not, however, edit out its Semitic origins and phrases, nor did he always understand the Jewish ceremonies he sought to leave intact. The presentation and the purification stories, for example, are hopelessly confused. Luke also added the boy-in-the-temple story, which really does not fit the narrative at all. This addition forced him to duplicate his scene-ending words, so that after the return to Nazareth, Luke wrote, "And the child grew and became strong, filled with wisdom; and the favor of God was upon him" (2:39, 40). Following the boy-in-the-temple account, Luke once again had to conclude his narrative, and he did so with the repetitive words "And Jesus increased in wisdom and in stature, and in favor with God and man" (2:52).

109

Did the first viewers of this pageant treat its content literally, or did they see it as a pageant that contained a beautiful interpretive drama? Did Luke adopt and adapt this pageant because he was convinced of this explanation as to the literal origin of Jesus' power? I am convinced that the original audience at this pageant, and its original authors as well, viewed it as a play that attempted to explain the source of Jesus' adult meaning. They were simply adopting a familiar piece of folklore whereby adult significance was foreshadowed dramatically in the birth events. They were also leaning on material familiar to those in touch with the tradition of Jewish and Christian midrash. I do not believe that Luke's birth story changed the content of his Gospel nearly so much as Luke's Gospel shaped the content of these birth stories.

For example, only in the first act of this ancient Christmas pageant is there any reference to an abnormal or unusual birth for Jesus. If chapter 1 of Luke's gospel were to be removed, the assumption that Jesus was the child of Mary and Joseph would be easy to make, or at least the difficulty of that conclusion would rest on something other than the birth narrative. It would also be obvious that through these narratives surrounding Jesus' birth and his boyhood, Luke was interpreting a theological movement that was growing in the church. Who was this Jesus? Whence comes his meaning? What was his origin? Luke, like Matthew, now focused this discussion on Jesus' conception. But it will not remain there. Some ten to fifteen years later the fourth Gospel will appear, identifying Jesus with the divine Logos who was with God from the beginning of time and by whom God created all things. This eternal divine Logos, stated the fourth Gospel, was essentially identified with God and was incarnated in human form in the birth of Jesus. It was yet another stage in the developing Christology of the early church.

But did Luke intend for the message of this infancy pageant to be literalized into those dogmatic theological doctrines as a means of proving Jesus' divinity? I do not believe so. Yet that is exactly what occurred. From the second century of the Christian era until the nineteenth century, the church viewed the literal virgin as an undoubted fact of history. Anyone who questioned it was presumed to be questioning nothing less than the divinity of Jesus. Biology and theology were inextricably bound up together. That is no longer so today.

Luke perceived in the infancy narrative a story that would allow the covenant relationship between God and God's people to enter a period of transition that would move the covenant from Israel to the followers of Jesus. He used those stories as a vehicle through which to introduce the major themes of his Gospel. Luke accepted, I believe, the creative genius of the one who stood behind the original pageant, who in midrash fashion had patterned the characters presented in the infancy of Jesus on the figures of Hebrew Scriptures. Luke undoubtedly heightened and added to this to meet his own theological point of view. People like Abraham, Sarah, Isaac, Eli, Hannah, Samuel, Samson, Judith, and Micah all provide background and echoes in this segment of Luke's Gospel. Even Simeon and Anna are portrayed as the final representatives of the traditional piety of Israel in its last beautiful flowering. Everything in Hebrew Scripture was presumed by the Christians of this time to undergird and portray Jesus as both the glory of Israel and the light that will lighten the Gentiles.[4]

Finally, Luke used the figure of Mary to be the first one to whom the secret of Jesus was revealed. Thus she alone bridged, for Luke, the world of the Hebrew Scriptures and the world of the Christian church. Mary heard and understood, she pondered and stored things in her heart, and she was identified by Luke as present with the disciples at Pentecost. On the person of Mary the old covenant pivoted and the new covenant was established. Was that a deliberate attempt to defend her honor? Jane Schaberg argues this case, suggesting that it was a subtlety that bordered on deception.[5] This note we will explore later in detail. I pose it now as an issue not to be ignored.

Freed from the straitjacket of literalism, we can discover in the infancy narrative of Luke's Gospel treasures beyond our most fanciful imagination. The original pageant was shaped, formed, edited, and added to by the brilliant author Luke, but its identifying structure and its Jewish-Christian origin were not abridged. Through Luke this pageant that once played to limited audiences in a Jewish-Christian community has now played to countless millions of people of every ethnic background the world over. With images drawn primarily from Luke's birth story we sing "O Little Town of Bethlehem," "It Came upon a Midnight Clear," "While Shepherds Watched Their Flocks by Night," and "Silent Night, Holy Night," and we too are drawn to that stable where time and eternity meet and where humanity and divinity interact, and we still invite that child, born amid the wonders of a heavenly chorus, to be born again, but this time in us so that we too might be incarnations of God's presence in our world.

9

Luke's Story, Part I

Many themes are heard in the birth narrative of Luke. The mood is celebratory: barriers are overcome, music is omnipresent. The images are mysterious: an overshadowing spirit, a brightened, angel-filled sky, a swaddled infant. Luke crafts a parallel narrative that places John the Baptist and Jesus of Nazareth in an intense relationship. Indeed, the doorway into Luke's story appears to be the sorting out and the defining of these two figures as they impact each other.

In Palestine in the late second or early third decade of the common era there appear to have been two figures, each proclaiming the imminence of God's kingdom. Each died the death of a martyr. The two figures shared some contact with each other, but the extent of that contact cannot be stated with certainty. The one who appears to be the earlier figure was named John, or Yohanon, a common name in Judea and Galilee. This charismatic religious leader inaugurated a movement whose principle sign of identity was the action of baptism for repentance. He thus became known as John the baptizer, or John the Baptist. The other figure was named Jesus, Joshua or Yeshua, also a fairly common Jewish name.

All the evidence points to the fact that this Jesus was baptized by John the Baptist, so he was, at one time at least, a member of the Baptist's movement. Jesus wandered into the wilderness after that baptism, debating the various possibilities that might be open to him. When John the Baptist was arrested, Jesus emerged into a public ministry, but with a distinctly different style. He went to Galilee as a liberator, healer, and savior. Citing this action style, he said that he hoped John the Baptist would not be offended (Matt. 11:6; Luke 7:53).[1] When the two movements became separate, their common origin was not lost, for baptism also became a mark of the Jesus movement (Matt. 3:13; 28:19; 1 Cor. 1:16), and some of the disciples of John the Baptist became disciples of Jesus (John 1:35ff).

In early Christianity there was no sense of rivalry between these two figures. As the Jesus movement grew, there appeared to be no effort to excise the memory of John the Baptist. However, a clear need to subordinate that movement to Jesus did appear as the years went by. John the Baptist more and more frequently was referred to as the forerunner, the voice in the wilderness who prepared the way for Jesus. This was quite obviously a Christian adaptation. John the Baptist was, for Christians, one who prepared the way for God's dawning presence that they believed was achieved only in Jesus.

As the christological debate in the early church focused on the divine nature of Jesus, the work of John the Baptist fitted nicely into its budding theological thought. Some of these early Christians went so far as to portray John in the role of Elijah, whose role was to herald the coming of the messiah, whom they had now identified with Jesus. Not all the early Christians were happy with this identification of John the Baptist with the founder of Jewish prophecy. The author of the third Gospel, called Luke, was one of these. He was not at all sure he wanted to assign the Elijah role to John. A good part of his story focused on Jesus as the new and greater Elijah.[2] Luke went so far as to suggest that John the Baptist played the role of the one who prepared the way without either knowing he was doing it or understanding it. This Gospel alone had the Baptist send emissaries to Jesus to inquire, "Are you the one who is to come, or shall we look for another?" (Luke 7:19). Luke further implied that John the Baptist was blessed because he took no offense at Jesus (Luke 7:23). Yet at some point in history, representatives of the former disciples of John the Baptist must have turned hostile to the Jesus movement, or John's movement must have constituted in later Christian history a potential rival, for the need to ensure the subordinate position for John seemed to grow.[3]

A John the Baptist movement appeared to be alive still when the Book of Acts was written about 90–95 C.E. (Acts 19:3–4). Jesus was recorded by Luke as having said, "Among those born of woman none is greater than John; yet he who is least in the kingdom of God [that is, anyone who has been born of the Spirit] is greater than he." John is the last of the old dispensation. He is not even the least in the new dispensation.

In John's Gospel (95–100 C.E.), this containment of John the Baptist in a subordinate place grew even stronger. The fourth Gospel's prologue said of John the Baptist, "He was not the light," his purpose was rather "to bear witness to the light" (John 1:8). It went on to have the Baptist state, "I am not the Christ." Indeed, this Gospel even had the Baptist deny that he was Elijah (John 1:20).

Still later, the fourth Gospel had John say quite firmly, "He must increase but I must decrease" (John 3:30). When one movement has to portray the leader of another movement in such a stance, acquiescing in every detail and extolling the virtues of the head of the rival movement, one may be sure that tension either had been or was now present.

The Christians admitted the fact that the movement centering on the Baptist was the older of the two movements by assigning to it the role of preparation for Jesus. In Mark, Jesus' baptism by John the Baptist was the moment in which the Spirit descended upon him. But in the fourth Gospel the inauguration of Jesus' ministry was moved back to the Incarnation of the preexistent Word. So the fourth Gospel had John the Baptist prepare the way for the Incarnation (John 1:6–9, 14). It was, as Raymond Brown suggests, "absurd chronology but very perceptive from the viewpoint of salvation history."[4]

In the opening scene of the birth narrative, Luke set the time and then introduced the cast of characters. This birth occurred during the days of Herod, king of Judea, Luke began. He was referring to the Herod known in history as Herod the Great. He had been given the title king of Judea by the Roman senate in 40 B.C.E., after Mark Antony had come to his support militarily to offset a rebellion led by a powerful political alliance that included the Hasmonean Jews. This combination had succeeded in driving Herod's military forces from the land, but, aided by troops under the command of Antony, he had been able to return in triumph and reclaim his kingdom. His reestablished rule lasted until his death in 4 B.C.E. The word *Judea* used in this text probably should be understood simply as the land of the Jews, for the political subdivision of the land of the Jews into Galilee, Samaria, and Judea did not occur until well after Jesus' birth. It was in place, however, at the time of the crucifixion and played a role in that narrative in the interplay between Pilate and another Herod over who had jurisdiction in regard to the one who claimed to be king of the Jews.

Zechariah was introduced next. He was a priest, married to a woman named Elizabeth, who was identified as a daughter of Aaron. This couple, though righteous and obedient in keeping all the commandments and ordinances, were nonetheless childless, a status widely believed to be a sign of God's disfavor. This patriarchal age explained childlessness in terms of the barrenness of the wife. It was an irrevocable situation in the mind of Zechariah, for they were both now well advanced in years. This is the only source we know of in which the names of John the Baptist's parents are given. Is this accurate data? If so, how did Luke or his source come by it? Or were these names chosen like the other details of this story, to root it in the Jewish past? What interpretive clues might be revealed in the names of these two persons?

The name Zechariah was a priestly/Levite name that can be found seven times in the Book of the Chronicles. The most famous Zechariah was a sixth-century B.C.E. prophet whose name was attached to the next to last book of the minor prophets. This Zechariah was a contemporary of the prophet Haggai, who shared his zeal for a rebuilt temple, a purified community, and the coming of the messianic age. He employed a style of writing that included visions and dialogues with God, interpreted by an angel. He drew images of a messianic prince of peace and a good shepherd, smitten for his flock. The book was best known for its portrait of the king who came to Jerusalem humble and riding on a donkey and the foal of a donkey. That narrative was quoted in the story of Jesus' triumphant entry into Jerusalem, which we still relive on Palm Sunday. Whether or not this Book of Zechariah nuanced the character or provided the name of John the Baptist's father is an interesting speculation.

That speculation is helped by the fact that Zechariah immediately precedes Malachi in the books of the minor prophets.[5] Malachi was not in fact the name of the author of

117

the last book of the Bible. *Malachi* is a Hebrew word that means "my messenger." The anonymous author of this book pictured himself in a manner similar to the way Christians came to picture John the Baptist. He was but a voice whose principle message was, "Behold, I send my messenger to prepare the way before me" (Mal. 3:1ff). The juxtaposition of Malachi the messenger to Zechariah his immediate predecessor might well have suggested to Luke, or the author from whom Luke was borrowing, that Zechariah was an appropriate name for the father of the messenger John the Baptist.

The only Elizabeth mentioned in the Hebrew Scriptures was Elisheba, the wife of the first high priest, Aaron, the brother of Moses (Exod. 6:23). Luke's only identification of Elizabeth was that she was a daughter of Aaron. Aaron and Moses had a sister named Miriam, a name that is the Hebrew form of the word Mary. Luke was the only Gospel writer who suggested a blood kinship between Jesus and John the Baptist. This idea is certainly challenged by the fourth Gospel, which goes so far as to have John the Baptist say of Jesus, "I myself did not know him" (John 1:31). But Luke did not know John's Gospel, and inter-Gospel contradictions bother only the biblical literalists. A tradition that seems to have begun with John Wycliffe called Jesus and John cousins, though the only possible biblical support for that conclusion lies in this Lucan reference that calls Elizabeth Mary's kinswoman. If the pattern being employed by Luke or the original playwright was modeled on the name of Aaron's wife Elisheba and Aaron's sister Miriam, that would make Elisheba and Miriam sisters-in-law and would in fact make their offspring first cousins. It would also give the visit by Mary to Elizabeth some credibility, and that is an important element in Luke's story. The choice of the relatively remote name of Elizabeth or Elisheba to be the name for Zechariah's

118

wife and John the Baptist's mother does, however, lend weight to that speculation.

There were other details in Luke's narrative that revealed a familiarity with the traditions of the Jerusalem priests. Luke identified Zechariah as a member of the order of Abijah. That was the eighth of twenty-four priestly courses set out in 1 Chronicles 24. The ninth priestly course was the Hebrew name for Jesus.[6] Is this a coincidence? Or is it a Lucan creation and therefore a clue for the discerning reader? The note that Zechariah and Elizabeth lived in the hill country outside Jerusalem may be an accurate detail, or it may be the author's way of saving the Bethlehem/Jerusalem setting to be the birthplace of Jesus, not the birthplace of the forerunner. Some scholars have suggested that stories about John the Baptist were collected by his followers, and that these accounts may well have found their way into the Jewish-Christian pageant and later into Luke's hands. But that is not a majority conclusion.

Perhaps there were two quite different messianic expectations in pre-Christian Judaism. Perhaps one focused on a son of Aaron, the perfect priest, and the other focused on the son of David, the political savior. Perhaps it was the competition between these two messianic models that gave substance to the tensions that divided the two movements and forced a later subordination of the declining John the Baptist tradition to the dominant Jesus tradition. Penetrating the veil of darkness and ignorance that hangs over Judaism before 30 C.E. can only at this point be done by raising questions, but worthy questions they certainly are. In any event, the time was set, the principle characters were introduced, and the drama moved on.

In Luke's narrative Zechariah was chosen by lot to enter the temple and to offer the incense. Luke undoubtedly meant for the reader to assume that the lot fell on Zechariah by divine intention. Luke used the same device to tell of the choice of Matthias to take the place of Judas Iscariot (Acts 1:26). Being chosen by lot was an incredible honor, Zechariah being only one among some eighteen thousand priests and Levites in Jerusalem during the time of Jesus. This mountain-top privilege would occur only once in a lifetime for any particular priest. It was in this context of the awe-evoking holy place surrounded by the incense of prayer that the vision to Zechariah occurred. In the salvation history that Luke was developing, this was the first annunciation story, and it came, we need to note, to the prospective father. The promise of Isaac's birth had also been given to the father (Abraham) and by divine messenger (Gen. 18:10).

In the temple, the angel Gabriel appeared to a troubled and fearful Zechariah. After urging him not to be afraid, Gabriel informed him that his prayer had been heard, that a son would be conceived, that the barrenness of his wife and the obstacle of their age would be overcome, and that the child would be named John. The angel described the coming child as one who would not drink "wine or strong drink" but would be filled by the Holy Spirit "from his mother's womb." He would turn many people in Israel to the Lord. This new life, if not to be identified with Elijah, would at the least, said Luke, go before God in the spirit and power of Elijah. That description was shaped by the words of Malachi. John the Baptist would "make ready for the Lord a people prepared" (Luke 1:14–17). Zechariah responded in wonder. "How can this be?" he asked. Age and his barren wife precluded such things. For his doubt Zechariah was given the punishment of muteness, which appeared to include both an inability to hear and to speak. They did not seem to understand that for one who became profoundly deaf in his adult life, the ability to speak was not lost. But Luke was not concerned about such literal details. Zechariah was thus rendered speechless until all these things were fulfilled.

The vision over, Zechariah came out of the holy place stunned and mute. He departed for his home, leaving the unblessed crowd, one can imagine, wild with speculation. In many ways this annunciation to Zechariah was a typical biblical annunciation story: the messenger appeared, the response was fear, the assurance was given, various obstacles were mentioned, a sign that the obstacles would be overcome was offered. But into that familiar pattern the author placed some striking content.

First, the angel was identified as Gabriel. This angelic messenger appeared previously in the Bible only once, and that was in the Book of Daniel (Dan. 8:16ff and 9:21ff). It is obvious that the Daniel narrative shaped this story.[7] Midrash once again was working.

Both Luke and Daniel called the appearance of Gabriel a vision. The verb translated vision was *ōphthē*. This verb was used by Luke later to describe the Pentecost manifestation of the Spirit as a tongue of fire. It was also used by Luke to describe the vision of Jesus to Paul on the road to Damascus (Acts 9:1ff). John's father alone saw Gabriel. The people waited outside (Luke 1:10). Daniel alone saw his vision. The men with him did not see (Dan. 10:7). Gabriel came to both Daniel and Zechariah at a time of liturgical prayer as God's message bearer. To that corporate liturgy Daniel and Zechariah both had added their own personal prayers rising out of their human distress. Finally, in both narratives, the receiver of the visitor was told not to fear, but upon hearing the prophecy, both were struck mute. Such points of connection are too consistent to be accidental.[8]

Other themes that Luke would employ later in his developing story were first signaled in this scene. The angel said

John would be great. Jesus confirmed this in their adult lives, said Luke, by asserting, "There are none greater than John the Baptist" (Luke 7:28). The angel said John would not drink wine or strong drink, a phrase that connected his birth in Jewish minds with the birth of Samson in the Book of Judges, where a similar vow was made. Once again this motif found corroboration later in Luke's Gospel, when Jesus said, "John the Baptist has come eating no bread and drinking no wine; and you say, 'He has a demon'" (Luke 7:33). The angel said John would be filled with the Holy Spirit from his mother's womb. That was accomplished in Luke's narrative when Elizabeth was filled with the Holy Spirit as a consequence of the visit of the messiah-bearing Mary. Yet the disciples of John the Baptist were portrayed in Acts (19:3, 4) as not having heard of the Holy Spirit, and John said of himself in Luke's Gospel, "I baptize you with water; but he who . . . is coming . . . will baptize you with the Holy Spirit" (Luke 3:15–16). John was a recipient of the Holy Spirit through his mother as the result of Mary's visit. He was not, however, a channel for the Holy Spirit. That function was reserved for Jesus. From conception to adulthood, in every conceivable way, John was portrayed as being subordinate to Jesus.

This theme was apparent once more as the scene shifted abruptly from Zechariah to Mary, and the second and obviously more powerful annunciation story began. Once again Luke set the stage by giving us time, place, and characters. It was six months later. The place was Nazareth, a city in Galilee. The characters included a person named Mary, identified twice as a virgin, betrothed to a man named Joseph but not yet taken into her husband's home. Joseph was described as one who had descended from the house of David. The already introduced Gabriel, who once again was sent by God, completed the actors in this phase of the drama.

The angel's greeting, "Hail, O favored one," in Greek is

Kecharitomenē, which virtually translates the Hebrew meaning of the name Hannah, which is "favored one."[9] The phrase "full of grace," so popular in many traditions of the church, was not in fact in the annunciation story at all. Indeed, the only place in the New Testament that the phrase "full of grace" is found is in the Book of Acts where Luke is describing Stephen the martyr. I doubt if that insight, however, will have any effect on those who say the Rosary.

Just as the Daniel story seems to lie behind the annunciation to Zechariah, so the Hannah story provided the backdrop to the account of the annunciation to Mary. Hannah was the barren woman to whom the child Samuel was born by God's promise and intervention. Once again the regular features of biblical annunciation stories were incorporated here. Mary was afraid. The divine messenger overcame that fear. Mary offered obstacles. The divine messenger overcame those obstacles. Inside this single episode in Luke, and only with this episode, the idea of virgin birth or virginal conception entered Luke's Gospel.

Why did the virgin birth tradition arise, or why did Luke take it seriously? It was certainly not essential to his story. Nothing about the corpus of Luke, apart from the birth narratives, assumed a miraculous birth for Jesus. Without the birth narrative, Luke's Gospel remains powerful, compelling, intact, and whole. If Luke did indeed begin his original story at chapter 3, as some scholars have concluded,[10] then at best the birth tradition is a nonessential afterthought. But why did it arise, grow, gain power, and eventually dominate Christian thinking?

Raymond Brown has argued that the conception of Jesus by the Holy Spirit was a step increase in a conscious parallelism between John the Baptist and Jesus.[11] The birth of John the Baptist was achieved by having an elderly childless woman become an expectant mother. Jesus' birth had to top that in wonder. Both were acts of God, but virginal conception is a greater miracle than ending barrenness. In this manner, quite consistent with other details in the birth narrative, the superiority of Jesus over John was proclaimed. Although Professor Brown is, in my estimation, the world's leading New Testament scholar, he does not draw the inescapable conclusion required by his scholarly probing that the virgin birth is nothing but Luke's theological invention. As a Roman Catholic he must constantly discipline his scholarship in the service of the official teaching and dogma of his tradition. That makes it difficult for him to follow his scholarship if it leads to ecclesiastically unacceptable conclusions, or to raise critical questions that seem to point in a contrary direction. But the ground on which the doctrines of his church depend has been, nonetheless, eroded by the demands of his scholarship. Brown certainly must know this, and if he doesn't, other scholars, like Jane Schaberg and Michael Goulder, delight in pointing it out.[12]

We are also now aware that critical speculation existed in the primitive church about Jesus' origins. It arose from the enemies of Christianity. For years this data was considered too sacrilegious to be considered. Jane Schaberg quotes Raymond Brown as calling it "a very unpleasant alternative."[13] In recent years, however, these possibilities have grown in power. The enemies of the Christians, which included leaders of the Jerusalem Jewish hierarchy, saw their faith and their tradition threatened to the point of extinction by the rise of Christianity. Their hostility eventuated rather quickly into persecution. It was led at one point by no less a person than Saul of Tarsus. Certainly these critics attacked the credibility of the Easter story, and that attack finally lodged in the Gospel of Matthew (28:14, 15). When the critical moment of divine revelation for the Christian story began to shift from the resurrection—first to the baptism and then to the conception of Jesus—it is quite likely that these attacks also shifted. So a defense at the origins of Jesus became an important part of the apologetic task of the early Christian community. Both Matthew and Luke felt the need to offer such a defense. Neither, however, obliterated the substance of the attack, and both left ample clues as to the nature of the charges. The birth narratives attempted to interpret the data. They did not create the data. Was the data true or false? I doubt if that can ever be determined. But this is the data:

Christian writers made no attempt to hide the generally held assumption that Mary was pregnant in that period between betrothal and home-taking that marked the two stages of Jewish marriage. Was she pregnant by Joseph? That would have been a violation of custom but not a cause for scandal. Commitment was achieved at betrothal. The woman was the possession of her husband from that moment on. To be pregnant by one's husband in the period between betrothal and home-taking was not a terribly serious breach in the moral code. It would not have created much of a stir. She would not have been the first young bride to have a baby early. Certainly that circumstance would not have created the tremendous need to defend Mary's character with elaborate, miraculous birth traditions.

Yet in the narratives, great pain was taken to deny Joseph's paternity. Matthew had Joseph reluctant to complete the wedding ceremony and desiring to "put her away quietly." Luke specifically had Mary state, "How can this be since I have no husband" (1:34). Yet in verse 27 he had stated that she was a "virgin betrothed to a man whose name was Joseph." In chapter 2, Joseph and Mary were portrayed as traveling together. Mary was pregnant though still identified as "his betrothed" (verse 5). In chapter 3, before the Lucan genealogy of Jesus was given, the now-adult John the Baptist was engaged in a conversation with his Jewish detractors on the meaning of one's origins. "Do not begin to say to your-selves, 'We have Abraham as our father,'" John admonished. He went on to say that God did not need Jewish paternity to raise up children to Abraham. God could achieve that, if desired, via these stones, he asserted.

It was important to these early Christians to broaden the sense of those who were to be included in God's family. Was the background to that lingering tradition the possibility that Jesus himself was not legitimately a part of God's people? When Luke did the genealogy, he added the words "as was supposed" as a parenthetical note to the statement that Jesus was the son of Joseph. Was it so well known that Jesus was not Joseph's son that the Christians never had that defense line to which they might cling in the controversy about his origins? Was his origin more scandalous than the violation of a betrothal relationship? Was it so scandalous in fact that it could be countered only by the creation of a supernatural birth tradition? Was Jesus the child of adultery, the product of seduction? Was Mary a violated woman, the victim of rape? Is it possible to accept Raymond Brown's analysis that the comparison of Luke's account of John's birth with Jesus' birth is specifically designed to affirm Jesus' superiority to John without seeing Jesus' birth as requiring virginal concep-tion to achieve superiority over conception despite barren-ness? Could the Holy Spirit be perceived as validating a child conceived in either rape or seduction as a life chosen by God for the accomplishment of God's will? Given the status of women and the moral climate of the first century, would not that kind of birth and that kind of affirmation be perceived as a miracle far more stunning than a conception beyond menopause in a woman assumed to be barren?

Since the Holy Spirit in early Christian literature was not assumed to have played the male role literally in the concep-tion of Jesus, do we have to be locked into sexual images or even sexual explanations? Do we need to debate things like parthenogenesis, or postulate a spirit with sexual organs and fluids? Must we speculate, as some later Christians did, that conception occurred through Mary's ear so that her virginity could be preserved? Is it possible that Mary was a violated person and that people referred to her as "the virgin" who had been raped so that Mary the Virgin became the way people thought of her and the name by which they called her?

With these possibilities now raised to consciousness, we read Luke's annunciation story and discover these hidden hints there that we did not see before. When Mary said, "How can this be since I have no husband" (Luke 1:34), what did she mean? She was betrothed, and betrothal provided her with the legal protection of a husband. But under Jewish law if she was violated, the husband might remove her from his protection, and she would become a vulnerable woman in a patriarchal society. That had been the fate of each of Matthew's four women in his genealogy. They had no husbands, and that meant no protection in a patriarchal world. Tamar was removed from Judah's protection and returned to her family when her husband died and his brothers refused to take her to themselves. That was the fate of Rehab, who lived by selling her body as a prostitute. It was the fate of Ruth, who, as a widow, had no man to protect her until Boaz spread his blanket over her (Ruth 3:9) and took her under his protective arm. It was the fate of Bathsheba, who, as a widow, was left outside male protection until David made her his wife.

Mary had a husband but no husband to protect her is the implication of this text. Was this so because she was pregnant by someone other than her husband? To Mary's question the angel responded that the Holy Spirit would come upon her and the power of the Most High would overshadow her. Therefore the child to be born would be called holy, the Son of God (Luke 1:35). When that passage is read in the light of our questions, it can be understood in a fresh way as God doing for Mary in Luke's account what Joseph did for Mary in Matthew's account. God took the vulnerable Mary under the divine protection. God claimed her child as God's own, just as Joseph did in Matthew by acknowledging and naming the child. The image of the Holy Spirit overshadowing Mary carried with it the same protective note found when Boaz spread his blanket/skirt over the vulnerable Ruth to bring her under his protective arms.

These clues are given further credibility when one examines the words of the Magnificat. We will later analyze the sources of the canticles, but for now the task before us is to isolate the context. Why did Luke place this canticle on Mary's lips? This canticle fits Mary's circumstances so poorly that some scholars have even suggested that originally the magnificat was a song not of Mary but of Elizabeth. What, for example, was the low estate (*tapeinōsis*) of Mary about which the Magnificat spoke? That Greek word usually means "humiliated." In what way did Mary experience humiliation? She was not barren. Virginity was not a scandalous state. Indeed, the pregnancy of a betrothed girl by her betrothed was more positive than negative, for it was thought to guarantee children and to ensure the male line. The absence of virginity in a betrothed woman would be scandalous only if the sexual act had not involved her intended. Why did Luke see Mary in the context of the community of Jewish Christians who were numbered among the poor and downtrodden? Only an illegitimate pregnancy could make sense out of that designation, and only an illegitimate child and its mother who were fully incorporated into Israel could sing of future generations who would call a humiliated woman blessed, who would acknowledge the great things God had done for her,

128

who would know what it meant to be exalted when one was of low degree. Perhaps God's overcoming of Mary's humiliation was a greater step than God's overcoming of Elizabeth's barrenness, and the theme of the step parallelism of John and Jesus could be preserved without requiring the miraculous event of a fatherless conception. These questions and speculations were first opened to me by Jane Schaberg, a feminist Bible scholar and theologian.[14] The viability of these suggestions has haunted me and intrigued me ever since. Their persuasiveness has also grown in me, not to the point of conviction but to the place where I now believe the church should face and openly debate these possibilities.

Regardless of the original apologetic and interpretive purpose, however, by the time the narrative achieved written form in Luke, the virginal conception had become a most important consideration. Luke seemed eager to assert that virginity was essential to his message. Since conception in Luke's account presumably had not yet occurred, Mary could have assumed that conception would occur when she entered Joseph's house to complete the second stage of her marriage process. After all, she was betrothed. But Luke did not encourage this assumption. Indeed, the text pushed the reader to understand both Jesus' identity, "He will be called the Son of the most high" (Luke 1:32), and his origin, "The Holy Spirit will come upon you, and the power of the Most High will overshadow you; therefore the child to be born will be called holy, the Son of God" (Luke 1:35).

There are many Hebraic echoes in these words. The prophet referred to Solomon at his birth as "The beloved of the Lord" (2 Sam. 12:25). The royal psalms used language like "You are my Son. Today I have begotten you" (Ps. 2:7) and "I will establish his line forever and his throne as the days of the heaven" (Ps. 89:29). We can be certain that the expected messiah, about whom the psalmist wrote, had been identified with this Jesus at some pre-Lucan point, and the texts from the Hebrew Scriptures had been gathered to support that claim all the way back to the moment of his conception. It had happened about the cross, which was scandalous. It would surely happen about the birth, which may also have been scandalous.

This virgin birth as Luke portrayed it had the connotation of an act of creation itself. The image of the Spirit overshadowing Mary was not significantly different from that found in the first chapter of Genesis, where the Spirit brooded over the waters of chaos to bring forth the first creation. Jesus, the new creation, was to be produced by the same Spirit that now brooded over Mary's womb. The Spirit would create again ex nihilo the new Adam, the herald of the new age of the reign of God. The initiative in this creation, like in the first creation, was vested solely in God. Mary's womb became the new tabernacle where God could dwell in the midst of God's people.

The term *virgin* also needs to be traced in the Hebrew tradition to discern its meaning for Luke. The word *virgin* is not unknown in Jewish writings. Though there are no other virgin birth stories in the Bible, Israel was called virgin Israel in Amos (5:2) and in Jeremiah (18:15). There was the virgin daughter of Zion in Isaiah (37:32) and "the virgin daughter of my people" in Jeremiah (14:17). The ravaging of nations by foreigners was compared in Hebrew Scripture to the rape of a virgin. However, references to virgin Israel in Hebrew Scriptures generally portrayed the nation as being in a state of oppression or waywardness, lusting after foreign lovers and untrue to God. Israel was a faithless daughter being called to return to her status as virgin Israel. Mary, who was totally faithful and obedient, might well have been portrayed as symbolic of that virgin Israel to which the prophets called their people.[15]

130

Mary played a unique role in Luke, quite different from her role in any other Gospel. The changes Luke made in Mark's portrait of Mary were striking. In Mark, Jesus' mother and brothers came during his adult life, asking for him. They wanted to seize him, Mark suggested, because they suspected that he was mad. Jesus rebuked them and claimed that those who did the will of God were his mothers and his brothers. In Mark's Gospel it was a story with a harsh edge (Mark 3:31ff). Luke, however, modified this story dramatically (Luke 8:19–20). He omitted the first part, so there was no hint that Jesus' family thought ill of him. In Luke, Jesus' mother and brothers came to see him. He was told of their presence. He responded by saying, "My mother and my brothers are those who hear God's word and do it." He was stating that his mother and brothers were disciples. In Acts (1:14) Luke reported that Jesus' mother and brothers were in the believing community. Mary was thus among those who heard the word and did it. This concept shaped Mary's response in Luke's annunciation scene. Mary heard the word of God through Gabriel and responded, "Let it happen to me according to your word." Mary closed this scene by calling herself the handmaiden of the Lord. It was a term Hannah had used upon learning from Eli that she was to be Samuel's mother. The song Mary would soon sing was also patterned after the song that Hannah sang (1 Samuel 2).

Now the drama brought the two annunciation stories together. Mary had become pregnant, though Luke did not document the moment. The verifying sign Mary had been given was that Elizabeth her kinswoman was also pregnant. This postmenopausal pregnancy was as yet known by no one else save Zechariah, for Elizabeth had hidden herself. Mary's knowledge was secret knowledge, divinely revealed knowledge. Mary arose and journeyed from Nazareth of Galilee to the hill country of Judah to visit with Zechariah and

Elizabeth. Mary greeted them, and the baby leapt in Elizabeth's womb. Elizabeth was filled with the Holy Spirit and exclaimed, "Blessed are you among women, and blessed is the fruit of your womb! And why is this granted me that the mother of my Lord should come to me? For behold, when the voice of your greeting came to my ears, the babe in my womb leaped for joy. And blessed is she who believed that there would be a fulfillment of what was spoken to her from the Lord" (Luke 1:42–45). Mary responded with the Magnificat. Elizabeth, in the presence of the unborn Jesus, was filled with the Holy Spirit, and from the womb John the Baptist was made to hail the messianic age. It was hardly a literal story.

Both Elizabeth and Mary sang canticles of praise for what God had done for Mary in the conception of the Messiah. My first realization many years ago that the birth narratives were not history and were not intended to be taken literally came when I finally grasped this scene. Here were two expectant Jewish mothers, and both of them were praising only one of their yet-to-be-born children. No Jewish mother I have ever known would acknowledge before her child's birth that her child would be second to someone else's.

Elizabeth's canticle found an echo in Deborah's song, "Blessed be Jael among women" (Judg. 5:24), and in the woman of the crowd who shouted, "Blessed is the womb that bore you" (Luke 11:27). The action of John in her womb revealed to Elizabeth that Mary was the mother of her Lord. This was John's first opportunity to prepare the way of the Lord.

Did Mary then break into song and sing the Magnificat? Hardly. Luke incorporated the canticles, making them the messages of his characters. There is debate as to whether or not Luke was the author of any of the canticles that adorn

132

the birth narratives. If he was not their creator, certainly he was their adapter. I have indicated earlier my conviction that these canticles were not part of the original pageant. Yet the canticles are very Jewish. They stress Israel, David, and "our Father." The canticles served to give voice to the characters who once acted in pantomime, or with the reading of a narrator. In the coming together of the two mothers, the text said Mary greeted Elizabeth, but no words were given. Later we are told Zechariah ended his muteness by speaking, but once again no words were given. Still later we are told that Simeon the priest blessed Mary, but once again no words of blessing were provided. In each case the canticles, Magnificat, Benedictus, and Nunc Dimittis supplied the words. A pantomime had been turned into an operetta.

In many ways, some of which we already have observed, the canticles did not fit the context to which they were assigned. We have seen how the words of the Magnificat raised questions about Mary, but now look at the questions they raised about Jesus. How did Jesus "scatter the proud" and "put down the mighty," for example? The birth of John the Baptist did not constitute salvation "from our enemies and the hand of those who hate us." No words or concepts in the canticles absolutely required a Christian context. These canticles, rather, focused on a concept of Jewish salvation. Many scholars, like Raymond Brown, believe these canticles were originally the products of the Qumran Jewish Christian community known as the Anawim and were borrowed by Luke to flesh out his birth story. The Anawim were people who emphasized the idea of the remnant. They conceived of themselves as poor, defenseless ones who needed God's protection. They held all their goods in common. It may have been the Jewish-Christian Anawim that provided Luke with his image of the early Christian community described later in Acts (2:43–47; 4:32–37) and in the story of Ananias and Sapphira (Acts 5:1–11). Luke became aware of these hymns, Raymond Brown suggests, then adapted them to his purposes and inserted them into this narrative.[16] This idea is stoutly refuted by Michael Goulder.[17] Yet both agree that the material of the canticles comes from Hebrew sources. The Magnificat is based on Hannah's song (1 Sam. 2:1–10), and the Benedictus on the song of David (1 Kings 1:48ff), though clearly other references in each canticle can be discovered with a careful gleaning.

Mary remained with Elizabeth for three months, said the narrative, or up to the moment of Elizabeth's delivery, at which time Mary returned to her home. Her journey provided the transition necessary to inform the audience that a new episode was about to begin.

The next scene gives the details of John's birth, his naming, and his father Zechariah's prophecy. It opens with another almost untranslatable Semitism. Literally the words say, "Now the days of Elizabeth's bearing were fulfilled." They are similar to the words used in Genesis to describe Rebecca's delivery (Gen. 25:24). They would be repeated when Mary's story was complete. The two annunciation stories were now going to be completed with the paralleling of the two birth stories.

Wonders that elicited awe from all the neighbors accompanied John's birth. Elizabeth, for example, picked the name of John, given by the angel to Zechariah but not shared by him with her, since he was mute. Zechariah confirmed this name in writing for the first time. In Isaiah 8 the prophet was ordered to write on a tablet the name of the child to be born. The tradition of midrash was still at work. Then suddenly Zechariah's tongue was loosed and he was able to speak, and he blessed God. All of these events created fear and wonder and caused them to ask, "What then will this child be?" (Luke 1:66). It was in response to this question that Zechariah sang the words of prophecy that we have come to call the Benedictus. "A prophet of the Most High who will go before the Lord to prepare the way," answered Zechariah. In Luke's scheme, only one who was filled with the Holy Spirit could discern that future role. Zechariah had, by foresight, entered into the kingdom. The main reason for praising God was found in the fact that in Jesus, God had visited and redeemed the people. The canticle concluded with the note of the light of God coming to those in darkness. These words would later be echoed in another canticle called the Nunc Dimittis. John, said the Benedictus, would be a prophet of the most high. Later Jesus was to say of John, "He was a prophet and more than a prophet" (Luke 7:26). The adult portrait of John the Baptist was signaled again and again in the story of his birth.

No, it was not history. It was never meant to be. It cannot be literalized. It is so filled with literal inconsistencies as to be nonsensical. It deals with rumor, charges, gossip, innuendo, and the response of Christians who searched for clues in the sacred texts of the Jewish people. But this narrative points its readers inevitably toward that which was believed to be both real and true. Its content was, I believe, first an interpretive pageant that charmed audiences long before Luke's Gospel was written. It was created out of the memory of the adult power of both John and Jesus. It had been made to serve the need in the Christian community to subordinate John to Jesus. Luke turned it into a narrative that introduced the corpus of his work. That corpus would describe John the

Baptist preparing the way for Jesus as an adult. We will meet this shadowy figure, clothed by Luke with the sense of a desert prophet emerging from the wilderness to call Israel to repentance and to prepare the way for the Christ.

The curtain has come down on the first act of the birth drama. We now await the birth of the one for whom John was but a forerunner.

10

Luke's Story, Part II

Luke, like Matthew, was deeply influenced by the style of Jewish midrash. In this tradition the Scriptures of antiquity could be teased, reinterpreted, and even reused until God's revelation in the present was made consistent with God's revelation in the past. More important, yesterday's understanding of Scripture was thought to illumine today's experience and, therefore, today's truth.

Because the Christian enterprise had its beginning in a Jewish context, this Jewish way of searching the Scriptures for clues that would interpret present events became the Christian habit. Perhaps no other activity consumed the first Christians so completely as did their persistent and thorough search for pointers in holy writ to which they could turn to understand and thus to defend their experience with Jesus. Key passages of the Jewish Bible were collected quickly and used perhaps initially in a polemical defense against non-believing Jews. It was an interesting ploy to make Jewish holy writ serve an increasingly anti-Jewish bias.

The first Christians, who were in fact also Jews, claimed the Jewish Scriptures as their own interpretive source of authority. With these Scriptures they proved the role of "authentic Jewish Messiah" for their Jewish Jesus. Certain passages were crucial to this enterprise. The role of the servant from Isaiah 40–55; the Twenty-second Psalm, which came to be read only in terms of the crucifixion; and the passage from Zechariah that lay behind the Palm Sunday celebration were, from the beginning, among the Christian favorites.

In time these passages were used not only to interpret the remembered events of Jesus' life but also actually to shape those events. The stories about Jesus were bent and twisted to match the interpretive passages of Scripture applied to them. The notes of Psalm 22 about parting his garments and casting lots were written into the story of the crucifixion. The words from the servant songs of Isaiah marked both Jesus' baptism and his trial. The Micah reference to Bethlehem as the anticipated place of origin for the hoped-for messiah in all probability created the Bethlehem tradition in the birth narratives of Jesus. Far from "fulfilling the Scriptures," as the Christians once claimed, the ancient Scriptures actually determined the way people told what they thought they remembered. So it was that history and interpretation merged in practice even before being written down in the Gospels.

So far removed are the average pew-sitters of our churches from this understanding that these suggestions come as revolutionary and even hostile to those who think of themselves as simple believers. They find these thoughts both incredible and faith threatening. An enormous gulf separates the world of biblical scholarship and the understanding of the Bible present among the average churchgoers.

Yes, there are raging debates in the circles of New Testament scholarship. Were the canticles in Luke's birth narratives originally Jewish songs or Christian songs? Do they have a Hebrew original form? Did Luke create them, or take them over and edit them to suit his purposes? There is a wide divergence of opinion on such questions. No one, however, will even suggest that the canticles found in Luke represent history or that any of the characters in Luke's birth drama actually spoke or sang the canticles. To put it bluntly, Mary did not utter the Magnificat, Zechariah did not speak the Benedictus, Simeon did not sing the Nunc Dimittis.

Scholars will debate the sources from which Matthew created or derived his wise men, and Luke, his shepherds. They will seek to understand whether there were two different traditions, both of which succeeded in making it into the written Christian narrative, or whether Luke, out of his antipathy toward those he thought of as "magus," expressed in the Book of Acts (8:9ff; 13:6–8), transformed Matthew's kingly wise men into humble shepherds. That debate is vigorous. No scholar that I know of, however, would argue for the historicity of either the magi or the shepherds.

There is enormous debate over how and why Matthew and Luke crafted their stories of the virginal conception. Did they reflect the influence of Greek mythology? Were these narratives simply an attempt to apply the "virgin" text from Isaiah? Were they an apologetic to counter the Jewish contention that Jesus was illegitimate? Was it some combination of these, coupled with other elements too complex to mention in the space available to me in this volume?

These are the issues that are argued among the scholars. No one in scholarly circles that I know of, however, is willing to defend the historicity or the literalness of the virgin birth story! Continued belief in a literal, biological virgin birth for Jesus of Nazareth is based only on a faith or a dogmatic commitment. It cannot rest on the evidence. Such a belief is

139

no longer defended on the basis of Scripture, not even by Roman Catholic scholars, who have much more invested theologically in this possibility than Protestant Christians do.

The fact that these ideas are commonplace among the biblical scholars of our world and yet are all but unknown among the average worshipers in either church or synagogue is, in my opinion, scandalous. It cannot help but be a reflection of the ecclesiastical hierarchy's fear that such knowledge, if broadly shared, would render the faithful faithless. Conservative bishops and priests content themselves by asserting that biblical scholarship is an ever-changing, inexact science that cannot be counted on for final answers. They argue that we must, therefore, trust the church's historic teaching authority. It is a weak and almost pathetic argument.

Biblical scholarship certainly is changing and inexact. From my attempt to read the field to prepare to write this volume, I can attest to the debate, the challenges, the criticisms that one scholar presents to another, sometimes on the most minute points. Does Phanuel, listed as the father of Anna the prophetess (Luke 2:36ff), relate to the place of Penuel in Genesis 32:30, where Jacob said there he "saw God face to face"?[1] I suspect few of the faithful will ever know about this point, while scholars are busy choosing up sides in the debate.

Yet amid the changes and the arguments in the world of New Testament scholarship there is a consensus that cannot be denied. The stories of Jesus' birth are not literal. They are not biographical. They were created out of the interpretative process of midrash. They are attached to external events that might be remembered rather imprecisely. They attest to the faith of the community that created them, not to the literal details of their telling. My readers must enter this understanding, stand inside this tradition, ask the right questions, and make the proper assumptions. Only then will the birth

140

narratives of the New Testament begin to communicate the truth that they contain.

In this chapter I turn my attention to what is probably the best-known portion of the Bible. It portrays Mary and Joseph's journey to Bethlehem in response to the orders of the Roman government. It tells of a stable, a crib, swaddling cloths, and a newborn baby. It introduces to us hillside shepherds and angelic hosts, who announce from the heavens the birth of Jesus and invite the shepherds to go in search of this wonder. It describes that meeting and forever transforms that stable into a place of intense romance, which in time produces tales of a "little drummer boy" who plays his drum for this child and a shepherd who speaks to a lamb to inquire, "Do you see what I see?"

The drama moves on from Bethlehem to Jerusalem and from the stable to the temple. The text introduces us to an old priest and an elderly prophetess, both of whom are waiting for all that this baby has come to signify to the Christian world. The birth narrative of Luke then concludes with the story of the boy Jesus in the temple. In this final episode not only did this Jesus confound the scribes, but he claimed the temple and was lost for three days. Each of those was a note that would be struck again before Luke had completed his narrative. When we see these connections, we wonder why we have never seen them before, for they become so obvious. Forewarned, we now turn to the second act of Luke's drama.

Luke opened this act in a now-familiar way. He set the stage with time and place and then introduced the principals. The time was during the reign of Caesar Augustus, when Quirinius was governor of Syria and an enrollment, or census, was ordered. It was the first enrollment under Quirinius, Luke added. This census required each male person to go to his native city to be counted.

Luke's facts here seem to be confused. Herod died in 4 B.C.E. Quirinius was not made legate in Syria until 6 C.E., a decade later. There is no record of any census in which people had to return to their ancestral home, nor would one's wife have had to make such a journey. Wives neither voted nor paid taxes, for this was a man's world.[2] Josephus did record a census under Quirinius that took place in 6–7 C.E., but it covered only Galilee, not Judea.[3] There is no corroborative evidence in secular records anywhere of a worldwide census ordered by the Roman emperor. Luke was not a careful historian. The census that Luke seemed to be confused about is referred to a second time in the Book of Acts (5:36–37). The census ordered by Quirinius in 6–7 C.E. provoked a rebellion by Judas the Galilean, the founder of the Zealots. That Judas led this uprising was mentioned in Gamaliel's speech as one of the messianic possibilities that came to nothing.[4]

Luke was aware, as the early Christians all seemed to be aware, that Jesus was a child of Nazareth in Galilee. Yet the need for the early Christians to portray Jesus as the heir of David and the fulfillment of all the expectations of the Hebrew Scriptures required that his early origins be Judean, and even more specifically, that he had to be born in the city of David, which was Bethlehem. Luke needed a literary device to get Joseph and Mary into Bethlehem before the birth of Jesus could be told. His sources and the tradition of which he was aware did not allow him to assume, as Matthew did, that Jesus lived in Bethlehem in a house with his parents. The census and the ancestral home story, which Luke himself may have created, served his literary purpose. Recall that Matthew had to develop a narrative to explain how the holy family came to live in Nazareth, and this occasioned another dream vision for Joseph (Matt. 2:22, 23). In both Gospels the Bethlehem tradition is tenuous at best. It appears to have been created under the influence of the Book of Micah to meet apologetic needs. The Nazareth connection has about it the ring of authenticity.

There was a second reason to which Luke also seems responsive. Everything about the birth of Jesus had to reveal a status higher than that ascribed to John the Baptist. John was, for Luke, a Jewish figure born during the reign of Herod. Jesus was a world figure whose birth was dated from a decree from Caesar. John's birthplace was anonymous. Jesus was born in the city of David to which he was brought by Scripture and divine guidance.[5] So Luke took a census, of which he was vaguely aware, that had occurred, he thought, sometime near the time of the birth of Jesus, and he used it to accomplish his literary purposes. Is it literally probable that any first-century man would have put his near-term pregnant wife on a donkey and forced her to ride sidesaddle for approximately one hundred miles from Nazareth to Bethlehem? As one feminist scholar observed after reading this narrative, "Only a man who had never had a baby could have written that account."[6]

He would also use this narrative to underline again one of his central themes. Luke wanted his Roman friends, and most particularly "Most excellent Theophilus," to whom this Gospel was addressed, to know that Christianity was not a movement of political rebellion, and Rome should therefore offer to Christians the full protection of the law. Luke would strike this note once more in the passion narrative, where he had the Roman procurator Pontius Pilate assert three times that Jesus was innocent of the charges against him (Luke 23).

Jesus was not a promoter of the rebellion against Rome that led to the destruction of the temple in 70 C.E., Luke was asserting. He was not part of the rebellion that began when Judas, the zealot of Galilee, refused to be obedient to the taxation demanded by Caesar's delegate Quirinius. The

Galilean parents of Jesus, in contrast to this Judas, were obedient to the decree ordering a tax enrollment. They journeyed to their ancestral home. In God's scheme this set of circumstances allowed the Davidic savior to be born in the city of the Jewish royal family, Bethlehem, because Joseph was of the house and lineage of David.[7] It was a fascinating use of material. One thing further needs to be noted. Only in chapter 2 of Luke's Gospel is Joseph named. He was not a major figure in Luke's story of Jesus.

How long Joseph and Mary were in Bethlehem before the child was born is uncertain and not important to the author. The important detail and the focus in Luke's birth story was where they laid the baby. This baby when born was to be swaddled and then placed in a manger because of the lack of space in the lodgings. The manger was mentioned three times (Luke 2:8, 12, 16). The emphasis was not on the innkeeper. Indeed, there is no innkeeper in this narrative. The innkeeper is a product of homiletical zeal wedded to biblical literalism. Sermons excoriating the innkeeper for inhospitality or praising the innkeeper for sensitivity to a woman in labor and putting her into private, if nonetheless humble, space are unworthy of Luke's genius. But alas, faithful churchgoers are probably condemned to the fate of hearing innkeeper sermons for generations yet to come.

The manger did not symbolize poverty but a peculiarity of location caused by circumstances. The lack of lodging was the means Luke employed to explain the use of the manger. Perhaps there is, as Hendrickx suggests, an allusion here to Jeremiah (14:8), where the prophet complained that when God visited the chosen people, God did not stay with those who were God's people but lodged in an inn, as a foreign traveler would do. The child Jesus, as an expression of God's new disposition toward the people, should not stay in an inn but should tabernacle with the people.[8] The key to this concept is in the meaning of the word *manger*.

Isaiah had written many years before, "The ox knows his owner and the ass its master's crib; but Israel does not know, my people do not understand" (Isa. 1:3). "Master's crib" is translated in the Septuagint by the same word that Luke used here for manger. By placing the Savior in a manger, by making that the place where the shepherds were to find him, Luke was saying that God's people were finally beginning to know the one who created and chose them.[9] They would know their owner and their owner's manger. This theme was solidified in the double use of the phrase "swaddling cloths" in verse 7 and again in verse 12. In the apocryphal Book of Wisdom, Solomon, Judah's wealthiest king, said, "I was carefully swaddled and nursed, for no king has any other way to begin at birth" (Wisd. of Sol. 7:4, 5). To be wrapped in swaddling cloths (not clothes) was a sign that Israel's Messiah, its real King, was not an outcast among his people but was properly received and was one to whom proper care was given. Perhaps here again there was a veiled allusion to the rumors about Jesus' illegitimate status, for an illegitimate child would remain an outcast in Israel. But God had covered this scandal with the overpowering presence of the Holy Spirit. The baby Jesus was wrapped in swaddling cloths, for, as Solomon suggested, this was the way every king began at birth. He was placed and found in the manger because he knew the God to whom he belonged.

The last note in this opening segment was the assertion that Jesus was Mary's firstborn (*prototokos*) son. This phrase assumed that there were other children and made no sense apart from that assumption. In Luke's time there was no tradition of Jesus being the only child or of the perpetual virginity of Mary. Those ideas would emerge much later and would be in the service of a totally different theological agenda, to which we shall shortly turn. But here Luke simply meant that there was no child before Jesus, so he could enjoy the status of the firstborn. This piece of data was mentioned here to make sensible the offering for the male child who first opened the woman's womb, about which Luke would tell his readers later in this chapter (2:22–24). The first scene was now complete, and the attention of the audience was directed to another part of the stage where the next scene commenced at once.

A revelation of God must be received or it ceases to be revelatory. The revelation of God in Jesus was thought by the author of this narrative to have been the crucial moment in human history. Attention must therefore be paid to those he chose to be the recipients of that revelation. In the early Christian proclamation, as reflected in both Paul and Mark, the christological moment of revelation was the resurrection. Those who were the recipients of that revelation were the disciples, who were thus charged with the responsibility to be witnesses and apostles to the world. Luke, however, had moved that christological moment back to conception, about which only Mary, Elizabeth, and presumably Joseph and Zechariah, knew. When this life was born, somehow the world needed to respond. Matthew addressed that need with the magi. Luke did it with shepherds. The response to the revelation of God in Christ was always twofold. There was both acceptance/praise and rejection/persecution. Matthew hinted at this in the gifts of the wise men. Luke included the acceptance/praise motif in the response of the shepherds and the rejection/persecution motif in the prophetic warning issued by the old priest Simeon when Jesus was presented in the temple.

So the Lucan spotlight was now turned to another part of the stage, where it captured a group of shepherds tending

146

their flocks in the open country somewhere outside the little town of Bethlehem. Records indicate that tending the flocks outside at night was done only from May to November, though dating the birth of Jesus that specifically did not appear to be important to Luke.

What was the meaning of the shepherds? A study of comparative religions reveals that shepherds were present in the birth narrative of the god Mithra and in the infancy story of the god Osiris. But neither seems to be a source for Luke's shepherd story. There was also in Jewish writings a negativity toward shepherds. "A father does not train his son to be a herdsman," said a midrash, "for that is the craft of robbers."[10] Perhaps Luke wanted to say that even at his birth Jesus lived among outcasts, but of that we cannot be certain.

What we do know is that Luke's attention was focused on Bethlehem. Mary and Joseph had to go to Bethlehem (Luke 2:4). The shepherds following their heavenly vision said, "Let us go now even to Bethlehem" (Luke 2:15). Luke has thus informed us on two occasions that Bethlehem was the city of David (Luke 2: 4, 11). David was the shepherd boy called by God when still a child, young and ruddy, to be king of Israel (1 Sam. 16:10ff). David left his flocks to respond to this call from God. On two occasions the Hebrew Scriptures referred to something called the Migdal Eder, which means the tower of the flocks. That tower on both occasions was located at or near Bethlehem (Gen. 35:16–21; Mic. 4:8–51). In the Genesis account, the Tower of Eder was also associated with childbirth. Rachel, dying in childbirth when Benjamin was born, was buried in Bethlehem, and her grieving husband, Jacob/Israel, journeyed just beyond Bethlehem and spread his tent beyond the tower of the flocks. Bethlehem was crucial to the birth narrative, and shepherds seemed to be crucial to the meaning of Bethlehem. The birth of Jesus in Bethlehem was certainly an important part of the

147

Christian story and is even mentioned in the fourth Gospel. John had Jesus' detractors arguing about his origin and saying, "Has not the scripture said that the Christ is descended from David and comes from Bethlehem, the village where David was?" (John 7:42). The Hebrew text that lay behind the Bethlehem tradition was found in the Book of Micah. Raymond Brown believes that Luke's story in chapter 2 is shaped by and may even be a commentary on Micah 4 and 5. To that passage, therefore, our attention must be directed.[11]

The picture in that segment of the Book of Micah is one of Jerusalem being threatened by the armies of Assyria. Many nations were saying that Zion was finished. But they did not know the thoughts of the Lord, said Micah. The suffering of Zion was not, and would not be, terminal. It was rather to be likened to a woman in labor, writhing in pain, but the final result would not be captivity in Assyria but rescue and redemption by the Lord. Then people would know that Zion was the mountain of the Lord. Jerusalem was the Migdal Eder, the tower of the flocks to whom the kingdom would be restored. The agent of that restoration would be a ruler who rose up from David's place of origin, Bethlehem. Then those who asked, "Why do you cry aloud?" "Is there no king in you?" (Mic. 4:9), would see the crying replaced with joy and the assertion being made that indeed the King of kings was present in Bethlehem. People the world over would flow to Jerusalem.

As Luke's story opened, people were flowing toward Jerusalem/Bethlehem in response to the call for a census, bringing Joseph and Mary in particular to the city of David. Later, he once again portrayed the people flowing toward Jerusalem in the triumphant entry that preceded the last events in Jesus' life. Twice in Micah there was mention of a woman in birth pangs (Mic. 4:9, 10; 5:2, 3). The words of the angels "this day" became a fulfillment of the words of Micah that God would give up his people until the time "when she who is in travail shall bring forth" (Mic. 5:3). "Then the rest of his brethren shall return to the people of Israel," and the new Bethlehem-born ruler "shall stand and feed his flock in the strength of the Lord, in the majesty of the name of the Lord his God" (Mic. 5:4). Micah focused on the triumph that would occur in Jerusalem/Zion through the Bethlehem-born ruler, while Luke shifted his total attention to Bethlehem. It was to Bethlehem that one went to see the Lord. The tower of the flocks was in Bethlehem. Bethlehem, not Jerusalem, was for Luke the city of David. It was a powerful theological connection but not necessarily a historical connection.

Luke's story of the angels' annunciation to the shepherds followed a modified outline of all the biblical annunciation stories. The angels appeared, the shepherds were filled with fear, the angels asked them not to be afraid and delivered the birth announcement. This announcement was modeled on Isaiah 9:5–6, "To us a child is born, a son is given." In Isaiah this child was heir of David, so royal titles followed. The child would be called "Wonderful Counselor, Mighty God, Everlasting Father, Prince of Peace." Luke substituted for these royal words the titles for Jesus used in the early Christian proclamation—Savior, Messiah, Lord (Luke 2:11). No one asked, "How shall this be?" as was customary in annunciation narratives. But this was not a customary annunciation. It was not about something yet to occur but something that had already occurred. A sign was given. "This will be a sign for you: you will find the babe wrapped in swaddling cloths and lying in a manger" (Luke 2:12). Then the heavens were aglow with the spirits who dwelt in God's presence and who sang God's praise. Only in this single biblical episode was the canticle of praise not sung by the receiver of the revelation. The angelic song carried with it a distinct echo of Isaiah 52:7, where good tidings, peace, and the reign of God were proclaimed.

In this revelatory moment the divine glory shone all around them. It was the same glory that brightened Moses' countenance after his face-to-face meeting with God. It was the same glory that marked the overshadowing presence of God in the story of the transfiguration.

"Peace in heaven and glory in the highest," words highly reminiscent of the song of the angels, were the words that greeted Jesus on the first Palm Sunday in Luke's story (Luke 19:37, 38). But Luke in this narrative moved that moment of revelation from the resurrection to Jesus' birth, hence suggesting that God's angels recognized at birth what the disciples came to see after Jesus' death. The one who was King, Savior, and Messiah had come in the name of the Lord.

The shepherds, like Mary and Joseph earlier, now went to Bethlehem. By a simple stroll across the stage, the two scenes of this drama came together. Mary swaddled him with cloths and placed him in a manger. The shepherds came to find the one so swaddled and lying in a manger. Israel was at last coming to know the manger of the Lord (Isa. 1:3). The response of all who heard the tale of the shepherds was wonder and astonishment. In the heart of Mary the angelic song found roots in the fertile soil of belief.

Mary alone, for Luke, would interpret these signs correctly after Jesus was exalted to the heavenly place, for Luke would portray her as part of the gathered community, the second body, on whom the Holy Spirit would be poured at Pentecost (Acts 2). In that community she would hear Jesus glorified as Lord, Savior, Messiah (Acts 2:36; 5:31). The message of the angels to the shepherds and of the shepherds to Mary would finally become the message to the world.

This scene closed with the departure of the shepherds glorifying and praising God. The narrative now moved on to the episode of circumcising and naming this child. In this scene the parents were not mentioned. This segment of Luke's Gospel used the phrase "the time came" to indicate a carefully planned schema, almost an inexorable process. "The time came" for Mary's delivery, for the circumcision and naming and for the presentation in the temple. The ritualistic acts performed in obedience to the law were as mandated as the birth process itself. Jesus, Yeshua, Joshua, was obedient in every detail to the law of the Jewish people.

The presentation in the temple is a fascinating episode because the purification rite indicated a natural birth. As I mentioned previously, the virgin birth did not appear to be assumed anywhere else, either in this chapter or in the remainder of Luke's story. The dialogue between Mary and the angel was the sole place where virgin birth appears to have been written into Luke's text. It was certainly not an essential element in his story.

Before this drama moved too far afield, Luke paused to introduce us to two additional receivers of the revelation of Jesus, Simeon and Anna, an old priest and a prophetess. The setting had shifted. Bethlehem had been left, Jerusalem had been entered. Originally the rite of purification and the rite of presentation were two separate and distinct rites, but Luke confused them totally. The first rite was the consecration of the child to the Lord. It was based on two texts in the Book of Exodus. The first text said, "The Lord said to Moses, 'Consecrate to me all the first-born; Whatever is first to open the womb among the people of Israel . . . is mine'" (Exod. 13:1). The second text said, "And when the Lord brings you into the land of the Canaanites, as he swore to you and your fathers, and shall give it to you, you shall set apart to the

151

Lord all that first opens the womb" (Exod. 13:11). No one was concerned at that point in Christian history with such questions as whether Mary's womb had actually been opened or whether her perpetual virginity had been kept intact. That would come, but not yet.

The custom of dedicating the firstborn came out of the Passover tradition of Israel. Recall that in the Passover moment, all the firstborn were slain except the firstborn of the house of Israel, who were all spared (Exod. 2:29ff). So the lives of the firstborn were to be lived in thanksgiving, or in *eucharistia*. Later, the role of the firstborn dedicated to God was taken over by the Levites, who assumed the role of those people of Israel who were especially consecrated to the service of God (Num. 8:15, 16). With the Levites in the role of God's consecrated ones, all others of the Jewish firstborn could purchase their lives back from God's service for the sum of five shekels. This sum was paid at the sanctuary in the temple at a formal presentation ceremony. If it was paid, there was no obligation for the parents to bring the child in for redemption. That was the liturgical practice that lay behind what Luke called the presentation.

The second liturgical act was the purification of the mother after childbirth. It was required by the Book of Leviticus. "The Lord said to Moses, 'Say to the people of Israel, If a woman conceives, and bears a male child, then she shall be unclean seven days; as at the time of her menstruation, she shall be unclean. And on the eighth day the flesh of his foreskin shall be circumcised. Then she shall continue for thirty-three days in the blood of her purifying; she shall not touch any hallowed thing, nor come into the sanctuary, until the days of her purifying are completed'" (Lev. 12:1–4). The text continued to say that if the firstborn was a female, the mother should be unclean for two weeks, and sixty-six days would be required for her purifying. The low value of a woman was everywhere assigned in the Bible. When the woman did come for purification, the offering of a lamb was required. If a lamb could not be afforded, two turtle doves or pigeons might be substituted. Then the priest should make atonement for the woman, and she should be declared clean.[12]

Luke, or his source, blended the two ceremonies and at the same time gave us an indication of the absence of wealth in this family by mention of the turtle doves offered instead of the lamb. He had also omitted the payment of the five shekels to redeem the firstborn male from God's service. Perhaps that was purposefully omitted as a way of saying that Jesus remained in God's service his entire life.[13]

Behind this narrative was the Hebrew story of the presentation of Samuel. In both stories the child of promise was presented to an old priest in the temple, Samuel to Eli, Jesus to Simeon. Eli blessed Samuel's parents as Simeon blessed Jesus' parents. The Samuel story made a reference to the women who ministered at the gates of the city with whom the sons of Eli were improperly related. The Jesus story referred to Anna, a woman who never left the temple and who lived in her virginity for a lifetime. She worshiped, prayed, and fasted daily. The birth drama of John the Baptist began with a description of an upright, law-observant man and woman named Zechariah and Elizabeth. Now it closed with the account of an upright, law-observant man and woman named Simeon and Anna.

Simeon greeted the child Jesus and uttered the words of prophecy. The future greatness of Jesus would be made possible first by his obedience to the law and second by the power of the Spirit. Simeon, now inspired by that same Spirit, uttered the canticle we call Nunc Dimittis. Whether Luke got this canticle from the Anawim community, as Raymond Brown contends, or created it out of Hebrew references, as Michael Goulder argues, makes little difference. Its primary purpose was quite simply to explore the meaning of Jesus. The canticle contains an echo of the words of Jacob at the time of his death, when, through God's providence, his son Joseph had been found (Gen. 46:30). Peace came because God had completed God's word.[14] The angelic chorus had promised peace to those in whom God was well pleased. Simeon was one of those favored ones. References to Second Isaiah also abound in this canticle. Seeing salvation in the presence of all the people was reflected in Isaiah 59:10. "A light to the Gentiles" is a phrase used in both Isaiah 49:6 and Isaiah 42:6. "Glory for Israel" was recorded in Isaiah 40:5 as well as Isaiah 46:13. The canticle did serve to enhance Luke's call to universalism.

Simeon was vocalizing the understanding of the place the Gentiles would occupy in the kingdom that would later be associated with Peter and Paul in the Book of Acts. Peter would tell how God visited the Gentiles to make of them a people for his name. Israel, "a chosen people out of all the nations," had been reinterpreted to include the Gentiles (Acts 15:14ff). This action proclaimed by Peter was concluded in the closing verses of Acts when Paul said, "Let it be known to you then that the salvation of God has been sent to the Gentiles" (Acts 28:28).

Simeon's second oracle concerned "the fall and rising of many in Israel" (Luke 2:34) and then referred to an image of a sword piercing the heart of Mary (Luke 2:35). Simeon was given the insight of a seer, who could see the twin responses of salvation for Israel and the Gentiles alike on one hand, and rejection and catastrophe on the other. To Mary he spoke the words that conveyed his vision. Later in Luke's Gospel Jesus would talk of the division he would bring, father against son, mother against daughter (12:51–53). Simeon incorporated that into the second oracle. Jesus was sent for the purpose of judgment. Some would rise, and some would fall.

He would be for some a stumbling stone and to others a cornerstone (Luke 20:17, 18). This popular theme in the early church found expression in Romans (9:32) and in I Peter (2:6). Jesus, when rejected by the Jews, would be offered to and embraced by the Gentiles. The movement would go from Jerusalem of the Jews to Rome of the Gentiles. Luke had placed into the mouth of Simeon not just the shadow of the cross but the story that would unfold in the Book of Acts. Mary could not be spared the sword of pain, but she would decide positively and would be part of the community of the Holy Spirit, in which all the language barriers of all the nations would fade as the Gentiles came to the light.[15]

Then the prophetess Anna greeted the child. Her widowhood, devoted to worship, prayer, and fasting, expressed the ideals of the Anawim community. This life opened her to the spirit of prophecy and enabled her to recognize Jesus. More than any other Gospel writer, Luke mentioned widows. A Christian widow was described in the First Epistle to Timothy (5:3–16) as being over sixty years old, married only once, one who continued in prayer day and night, someone much like Anna. The virtues extolled in widowhood seemed important to the Jewish people and thus to the early Christians. In the days of the Apocrypha, Judith was a widow of the tribe of Simeon who delivered Judah from peril. Judith also spent her days observing the law and fasting. After delivering her people, she gave thanks to God in a canticle of praise and lived to be 105 years old. This was the age that Luke seemed to attribute to Anna in this vignette, according to Raymond Brown. If this is an accurate reading it would hardly be a coincidence, I would wager.[16]

The birth narrative is now drawn to a close. Mary and Joseph had performed everything according to the law of the Lord, so they returned to Galilee, to "their own city, Nazareth" (Luke 2:39). John the Baptist was said to have grown strong in spirit. Jesus was said to have grown, become strong, "filled with wisdom; and the favor of God was upon him" (Luke 2:40). Since Jesus was conceived by the Spirit, he could not grow in the Spirit.[17] The narrative seemed to be over. I suspect that the original Christmas pageant did conclude here. John and Jesus had both been taken through annunciation, birth, circumcision, and naming experiences. At every point the superiority of Jesus to John had been asserted. It had been a dramatic pageant, but Luke had one further story he wanted to add, and so he did, even though it created editorial awkwardness.

The story is quite different from the birth material, leaving scholars to debate whether it was independent or part of Luke's creative genius.[18] In this narrative Joseph was called Jesus' father, and Mary was astonished at her son, an astonishment that seemed strange so soon after the annunciation. This story also contains fewer Semitisms than found in the remainder of the birth narrative. It marks a shift from a revelation about Jesus to a revelation from Jesus. It is the only story in any Gospel that purports to penetrate that period of Jesus' life between birth and baptism, unless John's account of the wedding in Cana is put into this category.[19] Many such stories occur in the noncanonical Gospels. They all seem to be illustrative of the christological moment coming at an earlier and earlier time in Jesus' life.

The visit of the boy Jesus to Jerusalem was presented as an illustration of the piety of Mary and Joseph. They went up "every year" to celebrate the greatest of all Jewish festivals. They had been obedient to the law in circumcision, purification, presentation, and now in the observance in Jerusalem of the Passover. Could the note that Jesus was twelve also indicate that it was a trip designed to celebrate the maturing process, which came to be called bar mitzvah? Or was it a midrash tale based on a story from the Book of

Susanna that tells of Daniel at age twelve receiving the spirit of understanding? In any event, this episode suggested that the christological awareness occurred when Jesus was old enough to express himself; it did not wait until the heavenly voice adopted him at baptism. All that voice really did was to reveal publicly what he already was. As a boy he was capable of creating wonder and awe. Stories that purported to reveal startling knowledge in childhood were also part of the tradition surrounding Buddha, Osiris, Cyrus the king of the Persians, Alexander the Great, and Caesar Augustus. The Jewish historian Josephus suggested that Moses' growth in understanding far outdistanced his growth in years.[20] So, Luke attested, at age twelve Jesus would reveal that he was aware of his origins.[21]

Luke began his Gospel in the temple with the vision of Zechariah. He would end his Gospel with the disciples "continually in the temple blessing God" (Luke 24:53). The adult Jesus would claim the temple as "my Father's house," as the first act following the Palm Sunday parade. In this episode Jesus would claim that temple in his boyhood.

Luke's birth story was now complete. Here we have the account of the origin of the one recognized as Messiah and proclaimed as Lord in the exaltation of Easter. This narrative would also serve the church well as it sought to protect the reputation of Mary from the taunts of those who would suggest that Jesus was baseborn. But it was above all else an exercise in Christian midrash, an interpretation based on familiar texts of the past. It was never intended to be a biography.

Is it true? If that question is an inquiry into the literal historical truth of this narrative, the answer is, of course, no! Indeed, as I hope is clear by now, that is not even a proper question to ask. There was no biologically literal virgin birth, no miraculous overcoming of barrenness in the birth of John the Baptist, no angel Gabriel who appeared to Zechariah or to Mary, no deaf muteness, no angelic chorus that peopled the heavens to announce Jesus' birth to hillside shepherds, no journey to Bethlehem, no presentation or purification in Jerusalem, and no childhood temple story. Indeed, in all probability Jesus was born in Nazareth in a very normal way either as the child of Mary and Joseph, or else he was an illegitimate child that Joseph validated by acknowledging him as Joseph's son. All that can be stated definitely is that the echoes of the status of illegitimacy appear to be far stronger in the text than the suggestion that Jesus was Mary's child by Joseph.

But if by asking "Is it true?" one intends to inquire into the meaning of Jesus' life that accepts symbols, myths, and romantic imagination, that breaks the limitation of human words when employed to make rational sense out of the mystery of the divine, then the answer is yes. Yes, these narratives capture truth to the eyes of faith; truth that mere prose cannot capture. This truth touches the hearts of men and women in every generation with the power of its insight.

In this alien and sometimes hostile universe, when fragile human beings stare into the vastness of space wondering whether they are alone, the message of these narratives comes to proclaim that beyond our finitude there is the infinity of a God who embraces us, and that this God has drawn near to us in the person of Jesus. Through that divine life, human beings have received the ultimate validation of their worth. Heaven and earth have come together in a babe born in Bethlehem. We are not alone. We are not just an accident of a mindless physical process of evolution. We are special folk, the recipients of the love of God. Our humanity has been judged a worthy vehicle in which the love of God can dwell. The Holy Spirit hovers over each of us to assist in the process of the Christ being born in us. So we too can sing glory to God in the highest, and we too can journey to those places that become Bethlehem for us, the places where God is experienced as dwelling in our midst and inviting us to come, worship, and adore.

11

Birth Hints from Mark and John

Although only Matthew and Luke recorded a birth tradition, illuminating hints about Jesus' origins can be found elsewhere in the Christian Scriptures. We have already examined what Paul seems to say on this subject, slight and negligible as it is. But before completing this biblical survey, I want to scan the other two Gospels, Mark and John, for clues.

Mark, being the earlier work (65 to 70 C.E.), though devoid of a birth tradition is not devoid of a tradition about Jesus and his family in their adulthood. The image of Jesus' relationship to his family in Mark is a hostile one. Jesus had been in the region of Capernaum, Tyre, and Sidon. He had created a bit of a stir. He had challenged the rule on fasting. He had violated the Sabbath by picking, and allowing his disciples to eat, grain from the fields through which they were walking (2:23ff). He had announced that the Sabbath was made for man (2:27, 28) and had proceeded to demonstrate this in a synagogue on the Sabbath day by healing a man's withered hand (3:1–6). Then, withdrawing with his disciples, he chose the twelve to launch his movement that would be known among some as the New Israel.

Then Jesus went home to Nazareth (verse 19), where first a crowd pressed upon him and then his family sought to seize him (verse 21). People were saying, "He is beside himself" (verse 21). That was the common way of saying he was crazy. To be beside oneself was to be out of one's mind, to be schizophrenic. The scribes who came down from Jerusalem confirmed this diagnosis by suggesting that he was possessed of the devil. Jesus defended himself against those charges by suggesting that Satan could not cast out Satan. Then he added, "A house divided against itself will not stand" (verse 25). His house, that is, his family, certainly appeared to be divided. Then he added that "no one can enter a strong man's house and plunder his goods unless he first binds the strong man. Then indeed he may plunder his house" (verse 27). Could this be an autobiographical note that his family would understand? Was Joseph the strong man who once was bound while his goods, including his betrothed, were plundered? Why the placement of this vignette immediately after the note that his family came to take him away? It is an interesting question.

Then, to make the argument even stronger, Jesus went on to talk about sin against the Holy Spirit. All sins were to be forgiven, he asserted, except the sin against the Holy Spirit. "'Whoever blasphemes against the Holy Spirit never has forgiveness, but is guilty of an eternal sin'—for they had said, 'He has an unclean spirit'" (Mark 3:29, 30). An illegitimate child born out of wedlock was to be cursed. He would possess the evil spirit of the violator. But the Holy Spirit had spread the divine protective cover over the violated one, pronouncing this child to be holy, to be of God. The scandal of the conception had been absorbed by Mary, who responded to God, "Be it unto me according to your word" (Luke 1:36).

The scandal of the cross had been absorbed by the child of Mary's womb, who said, "Not my will but thine be done" (Luke 22:44). In both cases the presence of God in the person of an angel had brought the life threatened by the scandal of rejection under its protection. A crucified one was proclaimed to be God's son by the heavenly messenger at the resurrection. Could it be that a child of fornication or rape was proclaimed to be God's son by another heavenly messenger at his birth? Was Mark's message placed on Jesus' lips to assert that anyone not seeing in Jesus' life the validation of the Spirit of God was committing the unforgivable sin? Surely these are questions and hints worthy of both historical and theological consideration.

Mark's narrative continues. His mother and his brothers were standing outside the crowd and calling him to come to them. His family, who had perhaps rejected him and his membership in their divided household because of his questionable origins, was now rejected by him. "Who are my mother and my brothers?" Jesus responded. Then, looking around on those who sat about him, he said, "Here are my mother and my brothers! Whoever does the will of God is my brother, and sister, and mother" (3:32–35). It was a remarkable passage, perhaps more revealing of the circumstances of Jesus' birth than the church had yet been able to admit or entertain.

Later, in the sixth chapter, Mark further emphasized the distance between Jesus and his family. They were clearly nonsupportive, not members of the family of disciples. The people of Nazareth were pictured as wondering about his origins. They were astonished at his teaching. Whence came his wisdom and his mighty works? "'Is not this the carpenter, the son of Mary and brother of James and Joses and Judas and Simon, and are not his sisters here with us?' And they took offense at him" (Mark 6:3). Jesus responded, "A prophet is not without honor, except in his own country, *and among his own kin,* and *in his own house*" (verse 4, emphasis added). Then he called to him the twelve (verse 7).

Previously Jesus had claimed that kinship was not based on bloodlines and that physical descent made no difference when it came to entry into the kingdom of God (Mark 3:32ff). Was he now also saying that illegitimacy does not matter? To designate Jesus "son of Mary," as this Marcan text did, was quite unusual. Mark never mentioned Joseph. This could be an allusion to the possibility, or even the probability, that Jesus was known in Nazareth to be an illegitimate child. A later Jewish legal principle considered a man illegitimate when called by his mother's name,[1] though there is no proof that this principle was operative in the first century.

This text clearly bothered the early church, for it was changed substantially when Matthew incorporated this part of Mark's Gospel into his own (Matt. 13:53ff). Would that deliberate and overt change have been made without some reason? Was it, in fact, an obvious slur on the character of Jesus? Was his father unmentioned because his father was unknown or known not to be Mary's husband? No matter how one answers these questions, the fact remains that to call Jesus the son of Mary in a Gospel that does not have a birth narrative was shocking. There is no virgin birth tradition in Mark's background of his narrative to soften this text. Is it a charge of illegitimacy that Mark alone has the courage to incorporate into his story? If so, Mark met this charge of illegitimacy by dismissing not it but Jesus' mother and brothers. Only Mark listed Jesus' own kin as being those among whom a prophet had no honor. Mark was the first Gospel by some fifteen to twenty years. The possibly scandalous nature of Jesus' birth was certainly not obliterated from the earliest Gospel record.

Again and again Mark had Jesus assert that the eschatological family was not to be identified with the biological
family. When Mark had Jesus describe the family that a disciple shall receive for leaving all and following Jesus, it still
had no father. They will receive "houses and brothers and
sisters and mothers and children and lands, with persecu-
tions, and in the age to come eternal life. But many that are
first will be last" (Mark 10:30, 31). Human fatherlessness, a
sign of illegitimacy, is transformed into eschatological fatherlessness of those whose real father is God. This is the conclusion to which Jane Schaberg comes when she examines
this data.[2] The gap of fatherlessness in Jesus' family and later
in the Christian spiritual family is filled by the Father God.
Was this Mark's way of saying that Jesus was born under the
validating protection of God, who spread the Spirit over
Mary to remove the scandal of this birth and to designate
this life as God's life, produced by God's Spirit? That theme
is overt in Luke. Is it covert here in Mark? Perhaps the Jesus
who had experienced rejection from his own family based
upon the circumstances of his birth had, because of that reality, come to see the loss of natural family as one more mark
of the kingdom (Luke 18:28–30). The Christian convert was
grafted into a new set of relationships.

James, the Lord's brother, did seem to be the power in
the Jerusalem church. He did appear in Galatians to be a
critical rival to Paul (Gal. 2:12). Perhaps the antifamily references in Mark come out of that same tension. That possibility
needs to be acknowledged. Behind these texts there may be
echoes that need to be heard in our search for light in seeking Jesus' origins. Mark, I submit, is not so silent on this
subject as the church would like to believe.

Turning now to the fourth Gospel, aware of these possibilities, the plot only thickens. There can be little doubt that

by the time the fourth Gospel was completed (ca. 95–100 C.E.), the birth traditions were widely known. Yet this Gospel writer chose not to include them. Instead, a prologue introduced the Gospel of John, in which the inadequacy of conception as the moment in which the divine entered the human was asserted.

To review briefly: in the writings of Paul, who died in 64 C.E., Jesus was "designated Son of God in power according to the Spirit of holiness *by his resurrection from the dead*" (Rom. 1:4, emphasis added). When Mark wrote the first Gospel in 65–70 C.E., the Spirit of God descended on Jesus at the moment of baptism. In both Matthew and Luke (written between 80 and the early 90s C.E.) the Spirit was in some mysterious way the agent of conception. From the moment of conception Jesus was always God's Son, those Gospels proclaimed.

Now along comes John, and the Christ was identified with the preexistent and eternal Logos, who was incarnated into human life via birth. "The Word [logos] became flesh and dwelt among us, full of grace and truth" (John 1:14). There was no mention of Mary or Joseph or conception. Was the author aware that people were already literalizing these narratives and treating them as biological truth? Time and again in this Gospel, John seems to ridicule literalism. Nicodemus heard the words on being born again and wondered how he could return to his mother's womb (John 3:4). He could not escape the need or the desire to literalize. The woman by the well wanted to know where she could go to draw the living water of which Jesus spoke (John 4:12). Because she was thinking in literal terms, Jesus' words were nonsensical. When Jesus said, "I have food of which you do not know" (John 4:32), his disciples wondered who had brought him this food. When Jesus talked about the eating of his flesh and the drinking of his blood, the literalizing

166

disciples responded by saying, "This is a hard saying, who can listen to it?" (6:60). More than any other biblical writer, the author of the fourth Gospel seems to warn against, inveigh against, and show the absurdity of that all-too-human tendency to seek to capture divine mystery in literalized propositional statements.

It is therefore conceivable to me that John, offended by the literalism overtaking the birth tradition, substituted in his prologue a theological understanding that would resist literalism. Ironically the result in history was just the opposite. John's prologue was read into the birth tradition of Matthew and Luke so that it soon became the incarnate Word and the preexistent Lord who was born to the virgin Mary by the impregnation of the Holy Spirit. Traditions that were mutually exclusive and antithetical were in fact merged by that incredible blending capacity that has always marked the life of the typical believer. The result of this process was the steadily weakening grip that the Christ of the church had on his own humanity. In time this tradition also fed the gradual dehumanization of Mary, whose virginity became a bulwark behind which the divine nature of Jesus was defended. Mary moved in history from virgin birth to perpetual virgin to virgin even in and through childbirth to her own immaculate conception to Mother of God (*theotokos*) to bodily assumption and finally to a place in the expanded Trinity. That cannot all be attributed to the fourth Gospel, but this author did unwittingly, I believe, contribute mightily to that process, even though I am convinced he sought to do exactly the opposite.

When the Gospel of John is isolated and read separately, however, other data emerge. This Gospel made the case that physical and spiritual birth were two separate realities and were not to be confused. Indeed, John asserted that the first has no bearing on the second. Unless one was "born from above" (John 3:4), that person could not see the kingdom of God, John argued. When Nicodemus questioned this, Jesus replied that this birth must be "of water and the spirit" (3:5). "That which is born of the flesh is flesh, but that which is born of the Spirit is Spirit" (3:6). This paradox in the fourth Gospel would seem to argue that one could be born both of God's Spirit and through normal human conception, without the two being contradictory. Indeed, one seemed to demand the other if Jesus' paradox was to be consistent.

Jesus' mother made her entry into the fourth Gospel in the story of the wedding in Cana of Galilee. Not once in that narrative was she called by name. When she presented to Jesus the problem of a wine shortage, Jesus responded, "Woman, what have you to do with me? My hour has not yet come" (John 2:4). Despite this rebuke, she ordered the servants to do whatever he commanded and disappeared from the scene, indeed, from the Gospel, save for an appearance at the foot of the cross, where Jesus commended her to the care of the beloved disciple (John 19:26–27). Jesus' brothers made only one appearance in John's Gospel, and it was without names (John 7:3). It was a mocking reference, concluded with the statement, "for even his brothers did not believe in him" (John 7:5). The separation of Jesus from his family seems to be reflected in this Gospel as it is in Mark.

But the crucial text in the fourth Gospel, I believe, is chapter 8, where a debate on origins and the meaning of authentic sonship ensues between Jesus and the Pharisees. It is a striking debate, to which my eyes were not opened until I began my study of the birth narratives and until Jane Schaberg raised for me the possibility that a not-too-well-suppressed tradition of Jesus' illegitimacy can still be discovered in Holy Scripture, if one is willing to look.[3]

The narrative begins in chapter 7, just following the episode with his brothers. Chapters and verses were imposed on the biblical text long after each book was written. Sometimes this arbitrary imposition has caused the reader to separate accounts that the author did not intend to be separated. Following his brothers' rebuke, and in spite of it, Jesus went up to Jerusalem for the Feast of Tabernacles. He went privately, for there was a great public dispute about him, much of it centering on the question "Who is this?"—the same question that the birth narratives were designed to answer.

"He is a good man."

"He is leading the people astray."

"How is it that this man has learning when he has never studied?"

"Can it be that the authorities really know that this is the Christ?"

This last question was dismissed on the basis of Jesus' known origins. "We know where this man comes from, and when Christ appears no one will know where he comes from" (John 7:27). Jesus asked them if they really knew him and whence he had come, implying that he was from God (John 7:29).

The argument continued. Jesus invited the thirsty "to come to him and drink" (John 7:37), with the text explaining to the reader that he was talking of the Spirit that believers were to receive after he was glorified (John 7:39). This only intensified the debate. A prophet? The Christ? Is the Christ to come from Galilee? Is not the Christ to be descended from David and born in Bethlehem? When Nicodemus tried to defend Jesus (John 7:51), they scoffed at him, suggesting that he too must be from Galilee. They invited Nicodemus to "search [presumably the Scriptures] and you will see that no prophet is to rise from Galilee" (John 7:52).

That is the background, the context in which the debate in chapter 8 occurs. The chapter opens with the story of the woman taken in adultery. A note in the Revised Standard

169

Version, however, informs us that most ancient authorities do not contain this episode. It appears to be an authentic incident in Jesus' ministry, though not belonging originally to John's Gospel or to this place in John's Gospel. At some point it was placed here by some scribe. Why here? Why, in the midst of a long debate between Jesus and the Pharisees about Jesus' origin, was an episode attached about a woman taken in adultery whom Jesus refused to condemn? Jesus called her simply "woman," the same word he used to address his mother in the wedding feast account. "Neither do I condemn you" is the climax of the narrative. Was this an autobiographical story? Did it dredge up the experience or memory and family tradition of an illegitimate child and a violated virgin whom God did not condemn? Farfetched? Perhaps, but read on.

The hostile dialogue between Jesus and the Pharisees continued. Jesus claimed to be "the light of the world" (John 8:12). He said, "I know whence I have come" (John 8:14), "but you do not know." "You judge according to the flesh" (8:15). "I judge no one. When I do judge, I do not do so alone, for the Father who sent me bears witness to me" (8:18). The word *Father* changed the debate to a new level of intensity. "Where is your Father?" (8:19), they inquired. Jesus responded that if they knew him, they would know his Father. It was not a direct answer.

The debate continued, growing angrier by the verse. Jesus talked of going to a place where they could not come. They did not understand. Jesus insisted that their origin was from below, while his was from above (John 8:23). "You are of this world, I am not of this world." "Who are you?" they continued to ask. Then Jesus spoke to those identified in the text as "Jews who had believed in him" (John 8:31). "If you continue in my word, . . . you will know the truth, and the truth will make you free" (8:32). Somehow these words triggered their Jewish pride. They responded, "We are descendants of Abraham, and have never been in bondage to anyone. [How quickly they forgot Egypt and Babylon.] How is it that you say, 'You will be made free'?" (8:33).

Jesus responded, "I know that you are descendants of Abraham; yet . . . my word finds no place in you. I speak of what I have seen with my Father, and you do what you have heard from your father" (John 8:37–38). The Jews insisted that Abraham was their father, and then they turned on Jesus with the assertion, "We were not born of fornication" (John 8:41). Is the implication here that Jesus was? The conversation descended even further. Jesus suggested that their father was the devil. His Jewish antagonists responded by calling him a Samaritan, a half-breed, one who had a demon (John 8:45). Could that also mean that he was born of violence, of rape, of adultery; that as a child of sin he bore the curse of illegitimacy? Is there a hint here that the suspected father was not Jewish? A later Jewish tradition suggested that a Roman soldier was the responsible man. This strange episode concluded with the story of the man born blind, and the disciples inquired of Jesus whether the man himself sinned or his parents, that he was born blind. Neither, Jesus asserted, but that the works of God might be manifest in him.

Jesus had just claimed that the works of God were manifest in himself. Perhaps this too was a hidden allusion to the difficult circumstances of his own birth. They were circumstances over which he had no control, but circumstances which must obviously have shaped his life and his sense of his own identity.

I am aware that there are many levels of communication at work here. There had been a schism in the synagogue. Jews who acknowledged Jesus had been expelled. Anger and pain abounded, and that surely found expression in this text. Johannine Christology was also being expressed, calling for

171

a very specific identity between the Father and the Word that was made flesh in Jesus. "I and the Father are one" (John 10:30) is the Johannine credo. The Christ who spoke the great "I am" words (bread, water, resurrection, way, truth, light) made a claim to be related uniquely to the "I am who I am," Yahweh of the burning bush (Exod. 1–14).[4] But behind this text, I would argue, lay also a memory and a debate about the origins of Jesus. This was a battle fought by the early Christians on many levels. "Can anything good come out of Nazareth? No prophet is to rise from Galilee" (John 7:52). "We were not born of fornication" (John 8:41).

The church dealt openly with the scandal of the cross, transforming the instrument of execution into a symbol of life. But, I submit, they dealt less openly with the scandal of Jesus' birth, creating legends to cover a possible source of shame. Perhaps, given the prejudice toward women, the attitude toward sex, and the patriarchal mind-set, they could do no less. But I wonder if Jesus is less the Christ of God, the Son of God, the Incarnate Word, if his birth was natural? If Joseph was his father? If he was illegitimate? The child of adultery or rape? I think not. Would it not be fascinating to discover on the day of the great awakening that God made the divine power of God's life known in human life through a human being who was born of the flesh, broken and sinful, but who was also born of the Spirit, life-giving and whole, and that one of these births did not violate or negate the other.

If God can be seen in the least of these, our brothers and sisters, as Jesus suggested, could not God also be seen in the infant of a violated woman who needed the protection of a man in order to survive in a patriarchal world? Dare we take seriously the baptismal vow to seek Christ in all persons and to respect the dignity of every human being? Is that scandalous? Or is it Godlike?

172

12

Facing the Implications of Scripture

"He was conceived by the Holy Spirit and born of the
Virgin Mary." This phrase is in the heart of the historic
creeds of the Christian church. Like all theological statements, the creeds are filled with symbolic words and time-
distorted meanings. Creedal phrases always look backward
to their origins as well as forward beyond their limits. Behind
the words is always an experience that cries out for a rational
explanation. Beyond the words is always a realm of truth
that can never really by reduced to words. Even the most
important word—God—central in every religious tradition,
is finally nothing more than a symbol, growing out of an
experience and pointing to a truth that must be beyond all
of its time-honored definitions. It is probably inevitable that
the common minds of men and women will always literalize
the symbols of their religious heritage. The very abstractions
of theological language can be so difficult as to be emotion-
ally draining. But this also means that these very literalized
symbols will inevitably have to die in the passage of time.
The only way to keep symbols alive forever is to crack them
open periodically so that they can be filled with new meanings.

No symbol can ever remain as a timeless truth, inerrant or infallible.

If this analysis is correct, then, despite the furor traditional religious folk raise against those who insist on opening the symbols, the fact remains that only those who are aware that symbols must always be changing can in fact be "defenders of the faith" of the past. These people alone will ensure the transmission in time of the truth that always lies beyond the symbols. The real enemies of a faith system are not the tradition benders but the tradition freezers, who by not being able to change and grow, turn symbols into mummies and make it impossible for those who live in a changing world to remain inside that household of faith with integrity. What the institutional church needs to recognize is that for every literalizing fundamentalist or traditionalist there is the counterpoint of those who have simply chosen to walk away from the life of that church where the literalized message has become too unbelievable to be embraced. These dropouts become the members of the church alumni association and they take up citizenship in the secular city. One cannot defend the faith of the past unless that faith is open to change, open to growth, and open to new meaning. The literalists of religious life fail to comprehend that literalized symbols are doomed symbols. So is the faith system whose adherents have attempted to retain its truth inside the set forms of the past.

This battle has been fought inside the Christian church for two thousand years, and it has been ever the same. The symbols of our faith story are always literalized. Time moves on and knowledge expands until the literalized symbols begin to break apart. Before that break is complete, the ecclesiastical defenders of dogma fight vigorously and even viciously for the authority of their lifeless version of truth. So long as this group has the social and political power to do so, they will excommunicate, force recantations, put on trial for heresy, depose, even burn at the stake, those who seek new truth or even new versions of the old truth. There will in fact be victims in this struggle. One has only to remember Galileo or Copernicus, or the Right Reverend William M. Brown, the Episcopal bishop of Arkansas, who was deposed for believing in evolution in the early years of this century.

However, when the ecclesiastical institution begins to lose its social and political power, as is the case today, its counterattacks against new revelations will be limited only to such tactics as harassment, ridicule, marginalization, or misrepresentation. This was the tactic used by Samuel Wilberforce (Soapy Sam), the bishop of Oxford, in his campaign against Charles Darwin in the latter years of the nineteenth century. It has been the privilege and fate of such heroes of mine as John A. T. Robinson, bishop of Woolwich, and David Jenkins, bishop of Durham, both from the United Kingdom, and James A. Pike, bishop of California. It has also been, thankfully enough, my fate in that wonderful but not always courageous American Episcopal Church. Beyond my tradition it has been the fate of my questioning Roman Catholic sisters and brothers in faith—Hans Küng, Charles Curran, Rosemary Ruether, and Matthew Fox.

Watching ecclesiastical leaders today dance gingerly around the question of how to understand the traditional ecclesiastical claim that the Bible is the Word of God is both amusing and sad, for in their heart of hearts, they know that this claim is not sustainable in any literal form. The legitimacy of slavery, the chattel status of women, the flatness of the earth, the understanding of epilepsy as demon-possession, all asserted in the Bible, simply will not be saluted in the twentieth century. Most religious leaders just do not have the honesty to say so publicly. Hence, what comes forth is rhetoric that uses the traditional words but suggests that they mean something quite different from what they were understood to mean in the past. It is an understandable strategy, but it will never win the day. Such tactics are reminiscent of rearguard battles where skirmishes are fought in an inevitable retreat into oblivion.

Only those whom the traditionalists mistakenly call liberals carry within themselves the seeds of renewal and future life for the religious traditions of yesterday. A title more proper than "liberal" might well be "open" or "realist." They are the ones who know that the heart cannot finally worship what the mind has already rejected. They know what fundamentalists do not seem to know, namely that literalization guarantees death. They also seem to know what secularists do not, namely that to abandon the historic symbols is to abandon the doorway through which our ancestors in faith found the meaning by which they lived. Those symbols must be taken seriously, but they cannot be taken literally.

Some years ago I engaged in a sidewalk-café debate over coffee with an American priest and religious journalist, Carroll E. Simcox. In time Dr. Simcox would exit the Episcopal Church for a conservative splinter group, with the claim that the church had actually left him, not the other way around. But at the time, which was in the early 1970s, his position did not appear to himself, or to many others, to preclude his being able to remain inside the broad Anglican household of faith. He argued, on that memorable day, that every phrase in the church's historic creeds had to be taken as a matter of literal, factual history or one had no right to claim to be a Christian.

At first I thought he must be kidding, so strange was this conclusion to the twentieth century view of reality. I discovered as the conversation went on, however, that he was quite serious. "Come on, Carroll," I joshed, "what about the line 'he sitteth on the right hand of God?' How literal is that?" My image of that phrase has been forever colored by the story of the Sunday school lad who told his mother that God was wonderful. Accepting his conclusion and praising her son for his theological wisdom, she nonetheless pressed for the details that lay behind the lad's affirmation. "Well, Mother," the boy responded, "God created the whole world with just one hand." "Who told you that?" his mother inquired. "I learned in Sunday school today that God could use only his left hand because Jesus was sitting on his right hand!" Under the pressure of that question, Dr. Simcox did admit that this phrase was a figure of speech and not quite literal, but that was his only concession and the only compromise he was willing to make in his literalized creed.

My counterassertion was that there is only one literal fact of history in the historic creeds of the church, and that is found in the phrase "he suffered under Pontius Pilate, was crucified, died, and was buried." That is the phrase that ties Christianity to history. Everything else in the creeds constitutes an attempt to put into words an experience of God that was beyond history and to explain theologically just who it was who suffered and died, why he was of importance, and why his life had meaning far beyond its historic and finite limits. The creeds are also a faith affirmation spelled out inside a premodern worldview of a three-tiered universe that hardly makes sense to a space-age generation. That creed has so many coming downs, descendings, risings, and ascendings that one can imagine a giant escalator uniting the three floors of the universe. Literal truth the words of the creed are not! Yet profound truth is that to which these words point us. I did not impress Carroll Simcox, but history reveals that he, with his point of view, found life inside the bounds of the Episcopal Church no longer possible, and so he departed.

It would not occur to me to seek to define the church so stridently that efforts would have been taken to purge its ranks of people like Carroll Simcox. Time takes care of that point of view, as a simple reading of a theological textbook, twenty-five to one hundred years old, will readily reveal. The church has always tolerated its traditionalists, no matter how dated their words become, but the church always attacks, and sometimes kills, those who seek to lead it into new truth.

The Vatican's debate in the twentieth century over whether to remove its condemnation of Galileo is illustrative of this strange folly. The problem is not with Galileo, it is with the church. The only question before the church in regard to this issue should be how abject the apology to Galileo will be, and to all those whose pursuit of truth was hindered by their fear of ecclesiastical reprisal, and how honest the confession of the church will be regarding its own incompetence and ignorance on this and similar issues. Such actions are not to be expected, however, from a body in which truth is regularly prohibited in order to preserve such strange claims as biblical inerrancy and papal infallibility.

To bring this discussion back to the focus of this book, I am asked from time to time how I can as a bishop continue to say the creeds of the church with integrity if I do not accept as literal truth the various phrases of those creeds. The implicit suggestion is that I must be dishonest. Certainly I do not believe that the birth of Jesus of Nazareth involved a biological process different from the natural means of procreation that has one sperm from a male impregnate one egg from a female to produce a new life. I have tried to demonstrate that the virgin birth narrative, if literalized and treated as biology, becomes nonsensical. It would violate everything we know about biology, genetics, and reproduction. It is clearly shaped by the other virgin birth traditions that circu-

178

lated widely in the Mediterranean world at the dawn of the Christian era.

In many ways I regret that this was the symbolic means by which the second generation of Christians came to frame their story of Jesus' origin. The price required of both men and women, but especially of women, paid as sacrifices on the altars of this literalized legend, has been extremely high, as I shall attempt to demonstrate in the final chapter of this book.

I would be the first person, however, to oppose removing the phrase, "He was conceived by the Holy Spirit and born of the virgin Mary" from the creeds. I do not think any of us can rewrite history. It is through the virgin birth narratives that Christians have historically interpreted our experience of Jesus. My vote would be to keep the historic creeds intact but to allow, indeed to encourage, the cracking open of the literalized symbols so that the truths to which the symbols point can be entertained, entered, and lived.

Beyond the limits of biology there is the realm of theological speculation and truth. Theology cannot invalidate biology, but its truth cannot be bound by biology's limits. The theological truths to which the language of the virgin birth narratives point are, in my opinion, profound. The birth tradition proclaims, first, that in the divine-human encounter the initiative is always on the divine side. For this to remain true, the story does not have to be literalized into a tale of divine sexual aggression, acted out upon a compliant Jewish peasant girl, who responded, "Be it unto me according to your words"(Luke 1:38). Second, the language of the virgin birth narrative speaks volumes to the human question born in the adult experience of the historic Jesus of Nazareth. So intense was the integrity of his humanity, so complete was the self-giving quality of his life, so total was the life-giving power of his love that men and women found themselves when in his presence to be in the presence of nothing less than the Holy God. Out of that experience came the affirmation of faith that pointed to the truth that human life alone could never have produced what they experienced in Jesus. Jesus was of God. I assert that this is true for me, and that this is the truth which the virgin birth story seeks to establish. Since I believe that I meet God when I meet Jesus of Nazareth, I say the creedal statement about his origins as a powerful symbol of that reality.

This realization, hinted at earlier, dawned in its permanent form in the experience of Easter. Then it began its inevitable pilgrimage, which I have traced in this volume, from Easter to Jesus' baptism, to Jesus' conception, and ultimately into the tradition of Jesus' preexistence with God. All of these accounts are true to the experience of Christian people, but none can be literalized without losing the essential elements of that truth.

So it is that I say the Christian creeds in worship every week. At Christmas I sing the hymns and carols inspired by the birth tradition. (I do confess to being put off by the docetic and therefore heretical language of "veiled in flesh the Godhead see.") I decorate my home at Christmas with several versions of the creche scene. (I do try to keep wise men away from the manger.) I attend at least one children's Christmas pageant each year, complete with bathrobes and bath-towel turbans on the heads of the shepherds. I have seen the baby Jesus represented by everything from a light bulb to a baby doll to a live baby girl. I have watched blond-headed Marys and listened to wise men whose one chance in life to sing a solo was on their stanza of "We Three Kings of Orient Are."

All of these are symbols, beautifully romantic and nostalgic symbols, of the profound truth that the birth of Jesus of Nazareth means many things for human life. It means that

God could be experienced fully in human history. It means that the whole created order proclaims constantly the reality of God. It means that people the world over are always drawn to that place where heaven and earth seem to meet and to that life where the divine and the human flow together as one. It means that by faith we perceive in the life, love, and being of Jesus the life, love, and being of God. It means that we believe that human life alone could not have created the power that Jesus possessed. It means that the ancient ecstatic cries that grew out of the Christ experience can still be exclaimed by us today. Jesus is Lord! "God was in Christ reconciling the world to himself [*sic*]!"

I accept the meaning behind the symbol, but it was meaning that became available to me only when the literalism of the symbol had been destroyed. By making available in this book to the nonprofessional reader the research and scholarship of such people as Raymond Brown, Herman Hendrickx, Michael Goulder, Rosemary Ruether, and Jane Schaberg, among many others, I hope to call my readers into a similar experience, in which the broken symbols can lead us to new meaning and even to a new and joyous experience of God, while making them equally aware that literalized symbols offer but a one-way ticket to the death of Christianity itself.

But what really happened in history at the time of Jesus' conception and birth? No one can ever know for certain. My best guess at this time would be that Jesus was actually born in Nazareth and not Bethlehem. Bethlehem is too obviously part of the interpretive apologetic. The weight of biblical evidence also seems to suggest that in the birth of Jesus there was a significant sense of scandal. Otherwise I do not understand why the virgin birth tradition developed as it did with the story of Joseph wanting to put Mary away quietly. I suspect that Mary's husband, Joseph, [if that was his name] was a far more significant figure in Jesus' early life than either Scripture or tradition has affirmed. He threw his arm of protection over his vulnerable and pregnant wife-to-be. He named the child and thus claimed him as his son, and, at least in part because this man did these things, God was revealed through this Jesus as in no other life that history has ever known.

To gain some insight into exactly what Joseph might have meant to Jesus, I once took every reference in the four Gospels attributed to Jesus in which he refers to God as Father and analyzed them to see if I could discover in these texts a glimmer or a glimpse of a pattern that might reveal how Jesus perceived fatherhood. If Joachim Jeremias is correct, and the use of the Aramaic word *Abba* as a reference to God is the one aspect of Jesus' teaching not found, or at least not emphasized, in some other parts of the Jewish heritage, then this by itself presents a powerful witness.

Abba is a deeply familial word, a word of great affection. If translated to catch its emotional tone, it would be rendered not as "father" but as "daddy" or even as "dear daddy." Surely if that was the word Jesus applied to God, its meaning must have grown out of his relationship with an earthly father figure who was loving, kind, affirming, and life giving. If Jesus was not Joseph's blood son, then the power of their relationship, if deeply caring, would be even more an act of grace and self-giving.

When checking Mark's references to "father" on the lips of Jesus, we learn that a father was for Jesus a source of identity (Mark 1:20; 15:21). A father was someone to be left for a vocation (Mark 1:20; 10:19) or for a wife (Mark 10:7). A father was a source of strength, love, and protection to a child (Mark 5:40; 13:12; 14:36). A father was one to be honored and cared for (Mark 7:10–12). A father was not to be spoken of maliciously by a son (Mark 7:10; 8:38), and even, it was said, the son was to be the glory of the father (Mark 8:35). One forgives others, Jesus said, with the same generosity that the father forgives (Mark 11:26, 27).

Moving to Matthew we find many of these Marcan ideas affirmed but with an intensity added to the note that the father was glorified by the works of the son (Matt. 5:16, 45). It was the son's duty to bury the father (Matt. 8:21), and the spirit of the father spoke through the son (Matt. 10:20). No one, Jesus said, knows a father the way a son does (Matt. 11:27). The father who saw in secret but rewarded openly (Matt. 6:4) gave good gifts (Matt. 7:11) and was to be honored (Matt. 19:19). The will of the father was that none should perish (Matt. 18:14), and honor was the father's gift to give (Matt. 20:23).

For Luke there was the added note that paternity was not complete until the son lived the father's values (Luke 3:8). A father was anxious, concerned, merciful, and caring (Luke 6:36; 8:51; 11:11, 13). In Luke's parable of the prodigal son, the father was drawn with tender love and yearning for his son's return, while still responding to the demands of the elder brother that the laws of inheritance not be broken. The elder son would receive all that was his due, but the father still called that brother to rejoice that "your brother was dead, and is alive; he was lost, and is found" (Luke 15:32).

I wondered, on reading that parable anew, if the elder brother bore any of the identity of James, the Lord's brother who presumably would have been the eldest natural son if Jesus had not been part of that family. I also wondered whether the prodigal son bore any of the identity of Jesus. Jesus was thought by his brothers to have been associating with thieves and harlots. If he were not a full brother, his economic claims on his father's possessions, which came from being the firstborn, would be compromised. The envy that this prodigal got anything might have appeared in Jesus' brothers. Perhaps there were some autobiographical notes in that parable.

Once you enter the midrash tradition, the imagination is freed to roam and to speculate. Trying to search the "father" references in the Gospels to discern what an earthly father might have meant to Jesus is one fascinating way to enable that speculative imagination to play.

John adds a few additional notes to this pilgrimage into the word *father*. A son could do only what he saw the father doing (John 5:19). A father who loved the son showed the son all that he was doing (John 5:20). Is this a reference that was born in a carpenter's shed? The father transferred his power to his son so that son and father were honored together (John 8:44; 14:13). Is this the way Joseph incorporated the illegitimate child? When Jesus said, in John, I live because of the father (John 5:26), or I speak as the father has taught me (John 8:28), was he speaking on both an earthly and an eternal level? Could Jesus have spoken of the oneness he possessed with his heavenly father (John 17:11) if he had never known any sense of oneness with his earthly father, Joseph?

I do not want to press this line of thought too deeply, but from the vantage point of a psychologically sensitive generation, I think we must entertain the possibility that Joseph, whatever his physical ties were with his son Jesus, did in fact give Jesus a relationship of such substance and beauty that it shaped his very understanding of God.

Perhaps the church has done Joseph a disservice by relegating him to near obscurity, by minimizing his contribution, and by suggesting that he must have died while Jesus was quite young. If Jesus had Joseph only until his early teenage years, the relationship could still have been both sustaining and enriching.

Perhaps Joseph's knowledge and presence made the persons making excessive claims about Jesus' origin uncomfortable, so Joseph was expunged from the memory of the Christian church. Surely that fate befell Mary Magdalene, as we shall shortly see. It could certainly also have befallen Joseph. Yet this monument to Joseph's influence remains massive and powerful in the very use of the word *Abba* as Jesus' way of thinking about God. It is even more powerful if in fact Jesus was the child of Joseph's violated betrothed, a woman who became known as Mary the "virgin" from Nazareth. But this possibility can never be more than speculation.

Are these scandalous thoughts? They might once have been so for me, but they are so no longer. A God who can be seen in the limp form of a convicted criminal dying alone on a cross at Calvary can surely also be seen in an illegitimate baby boy born through the aggressive and selfish act of a man sexually violating a teenage girl. A God who can call Amos from the tending of his sycamore trees in Tekoa, a God who can teach Hosea the meaning of the infinite quality of divine love in the human experience of an unfaithful wife, a God who can turn an insecure fisherman, Peter, into a courageous disciple—this God can also turn the possibility of illegitimacy and the actuality of public execution of a convicted criminal into the means through which God's infinite love is experienced and by which salvation becomes the divine gift of the world. Such a realization and possibility is quite enough to make me sing "O Come All Ye Faithful, come and adore him."

13

Suppose Jesus Were Married

He was born of a woman. He was a man. Both the woman who was his mother and the man, Jesus, were dehumanized in Christian history. Part of that dehumanization was their portrayal as sexless persons. Making Mary a sexless woman also served to preserve the image of Jesus as somehow beyond human sexual connotations. We have examined the biblical portrait of Mary from this perspective. Before moving on to examine the implications of that portrait for all human beings, but especially for women, I want to look at the life of Jesus and focus on his humanity, including his sexual nature and the experience of his life. Far more than most of us realize we define sex negatively, as evil and dirty. Yet I hope that subject can be approached with an open mind. I can best do that by posing what is for some people a startling, and even irreverent, question.

Was Jesus married? Was there a primary female figure in the earthly life of the Jesus of history? Let me state the obvious first. There is certainly no overt claim in the New Testament of a marital status for Jesus. Furthermore, the tradition of two thousand years of church history is that

Jesus was a single man. Of course the primary interpreters of this Jesus of history have been the priests of the church, and the church required of that vocation for most of those two thousand years the status of being single. This would certainly provide a major impetus toward maintaining the definition of Jesus as the high priestly model of unmarried celibacy.

Yet throughout that history there has always been an undercurrent that linked Jesus with Mary Magdalene in a romantic way. Medieval literature was filled with this speculation, and it has reemerged in the last half of this century. In the 1960s two Broadway hit shows, "Jesus Christ, Superstar" and "Godspell," carried this theme. In "Superstar" Mary Magdalene sang a touching romantic ballad to Jesus that began "I don't know how to love him!" In the late 1980s this theme reappeared in a highly debated film, "The Last Temptation of Christ." The scenes of Jesus with Magdalene constituted the most controversial aspects of this film.

Without seeking to be titillating or salacious, I would like to raise this question in a serious and scholarly way, recognizing at the very outset its high level of speculation. I think this can be done at the dawn of the twenty-first century in a way that could not have been done before because we live in a time of revolution in our sexual consciousness. We have broken images and stereotypes and have been forced to entertain new definitions of what it means to be male and female. Women biblical scholars, shaped by this new consciousness, now read the sacred texts and see things that men, blinded by the definitions of yesterday, have never before been able to see. The biblical record was written by men and interpreted by men almost exclusively until this generation. So this new vision brings new insights, new questions, and perhaps even new revelations.

To suggest some relationship between Jesus and Mary Magdalene inevitably evokes a strong response. There is in many of us an immediate visceral negativity that does not want even to entertain this possibility. If the suggestion is that Jesus and Magdalene were lovers the negativity toward the idea is easy to understand. That idea would fly in the face of the moral values espoused by the church through the ages, and it would deeply violate our understanding of Jesus as incarnate Lord and the Holy Sinless One. But the negativity that surrounds the idea that Jesus might have been married is increasingly strange in our age. It reflects the residue of that deep Christian negativity toward women that still infects the church. It suggests that marriage is not appropriate for one who is defined as Holy, as the God-man. Given this sense that even marriage is a compromise with sin, one might suppose that any suggestion that Jesus was other than single would have a hard time surviving in the church's anti-female worldview that I seek to challenge. As part of that challenge, I believe we must examine anew any data that might lead to the conclusion that Jesus was married. Are there hints in the Gospel record itself that might now be seen because the negativity of the church toward women is receding?

With newly opened eyes we turn again to examine the sacred text. In I Corinthians (9:1ff), Paul is defending his claim to be an apostle of Jesus. In the midst of that defense he asserts, "Do we not have the right to be accompanied by a wife, as the other apostles and the brothers of the Lord and Cephas [Peter]?" At least in the early church, Paul was saying, wives accompanied the apostolic leaders. Was that a new pattern? A careful reading of the synoptic gospels suggests that this pattern of wives, or at least of women, accompanying the disciples actually began during the earthly life of Jesus. These texts however have been generally ignored by the church. Yet here in the gospel record itself is clear evidence that the disciple band was accompanied both in Galilee and in Judea by a group of women. Indeed, the texts even state that these women provided for the disciples and for Jesus out of their means, a point one of our female bishops loves to make publicly.[1] When we read the record of the presence of these women we cannot help but note in these texts the prominence given to the one called Magdalene.

"There were also women looking on from afar, among whom were Mary Magdalene, and Mary the mother of James the younger and of Joses, and Salome, who, when he [note the singular: Jesus] was in Galilee, followed him, and ministered to him; and also many other women who came up with him to Jerusalem" (Mark 15:40).

"Mary Magdalene and Mary the mother of Joses saw where he was laid" (Mark 15:47).

"There were also many women there, looking on from afar, who had followed Jesus from Galilee, ministering to him; among whom were Mary Magdalene, and Mary the mother of James and Joseph, and the mother of the sons of Zebedee" (Matt. 27:55–56).

"Mary Magdalene and the other Mary were there, sitting opposite the sepulchre" (Matt. 27:61).

Describing the early Galilean phase of Jesus' ministry Luke writes: "Soon afterward he went on through cities and villages, preaching and bringing the good news of the kingdom of God. And the twelve were with him, and also some women who had been healed of evil spirits and infirmities: Mary, called Magdalene, from whom seven demons had gone out, and Joanna, the wife of Chuza, Herod's steward, and Susanna, and many others, who provided for them out of their means" (Luke 8:1–3).

"And all his acquaintances and the women who had followed him from Galilee stood at a distance and saw these things" (Luke 23:49).

190

"The women who had come with him from Galilee followed, and saw the tomb, and how his body was laid; then they returned, and prepared spices and ointments" (Luke 23:55–56).

Somehow our mental image of the early life of Jesus and the disciples needs to be expanded. The Gospel record seems to indicate that Jesus and the disciples were accompanied on their journeys by a group of women. I mean nothing suggestive in these comments, but I must note that given the rules governing women in first century Jewish society a group of women who followed a male band of disciples had to be wives, mothers, or prostitutes. Paul's reference seems to suggest that the disciples, the brothers of the Lord, and especially Peter, were accompanied by wives. What then, we must ask, was the role of Mary Magdalene? In this context that becomes an interesting question for she is certainly given the priority position in every passage. In the first century a women's status was directly related to the status of the man in her life. In the Gospels Mary Magdalene is always listed first, and that would seem to argue that she was related in some way to the one who clearly was the focus of each Gospel, Jesus of Nazareth.

When we embrace this picture of the women in Jesus' movement then the Gospel portrayal of the role of women in the resurrection story becomes less of a surprise. Somehow we have come to think that the women in the resurrection accounts arise out of no previous history. Clearly that is a misperception. In the resurrection tradition once again Mary Magdalene is the central figure. The Gospels vary as to which women went to the tomb at dawn on the first day of the week, but every one of them includes the name of Mary Magdalene first (Mark 16:1; Matt. 28:1; Luke 24:10; John 20:1).

There are other hints in the fourth Gospel that might be explored. Only in John is the story told of the wedding feast

191

in Cana of Galilee (John 2:1–11). This is a strange story in many ways. Jesus appears to be still living at home. Jesus and his mother are at the wedding together along with his disciples, says the text. But at this point in John's story the disciples include only two of John the Baptist's disciples, one of whom was Andrew who went and got his brother, Peter, and Philip who went and called Nathaniel. So Jesus, his four associates, and his mother are all at this wedding in Galilee near the village of Nazareth. When two generations are present at a wedding it is almost always a family affair. I have never attended a wedding with my mother except when it was the wedding of a relative. The only time my mother and my closest friends were at a wedding together with me was my own wedding!

So John tells us that at this wedding Jesus, Jesus' disciples, and Jesus' mother were all in attendance. Whose wedding was it? The narrative does not say, but the narrative does say that the mother of Jesus was quite concerned that the wine supply was exhausted. Why would that have been a concern to the mother of Jesus? Do guests at a wedding become upset about such details? No, but the mother of the bridegroom, who would be the hostess at the wedding reception, certainly would be upset. Indeed, Mary's behavior in this vignette would be totally inappropriate had she not been in that role. Is this an echo not fully suppressed of the tradition of Jesus' marriage?

The fourth Gospel leaned on the authority of John Zebedee though it was not written by him. It was written, most scholars believe, by a disciple of John Zebedee. As such, it had access to an eyewitness. On the basis of this source of authority this Gospel countered the other Gospels on some specific details in Jesus' life such as the length of Jesus' public ministry (three years said John, one year said Matthew, Mark, and Luke), and whether or not the Last Supper was a

Passover meal (no, said John, yes, said the others). These specific, somewhat intimate details in which the fourth Gospel seems to correct the others gives to that Gospel a sense of authenticity. Is there recorded in this work the memory of this apostle whom the church seemed to acknowledge lived to a ripe old age? (John 21:20–23). Is not this sense of an authentic memory missing in the other gospels, none of which are thought to be written by eyewitnesses?

Other hints can also be lifted out of the Johanine text. Nathaniel calls Jesus, Rabbi (John 1:49). That may not be an accurate historical name for Jesus, but it must be noted that in first-century Jewish life a requirement for a rabbi was that he had to be married.

The most dramatic passage of all in this Gospel, however, is John's portrayal of Mary Magdalene at the grave of Jesus. In this Gospel she comes to the tomb alone (John 20:1ff), she finds it empty, she reports this to Peter and the beloved disciple, with whom she appears to have a place of honor and importance. Peter and the beloved disciple, acting on her message, come to investigate. Peter enters the tomb first, the beloved disciple follows. They see the grave clothes lying neatly. They depart. Mary Magdalene then returns to the grave. She is weeping. Stooping down she looks into the tomb through her tears. She sees angels who inquire as to the cause of her tears. "Because they have taken away my Lord, and I do not know where they have laid him."

The phrase "my lord" is a striking one. This episode in John is before the resurrection. The empty grave does not mean resurrection to Mary, it means someone has stolen the body. Yet, of this deceased Jesus, Mary uses the phrase, "my lord." Does this mean that Mary Magdalene came to the realization that "Jesus is Lord" before his resurrection? Was she making at this early moment what later came to be the church's creedal affirmation? If so, she is the only one to whom such a confession of faith in the not-yet-risen Lord is attributed. Or does this phrase on Mary's lips in this context mean "my lord" in the way a first-century Jewish woman would refer to her husband? Once again this is an interesting speculation based on data present in the text but hidden from blinded eyes for centuries.

John's narrative does not stop there. Mary Magdalene turns, and through her tears, sees another figure in the early morning darkness that she takes to be a gardener. This figure repeats the angelic question, "Woman, why are you weeping? Whom do you seek?" (John 20:15). Mary responds, "Sir, if you have carried him away, tell me where you have laid him, and I will take him away" (John 20:15). Note these words! Mary is claiming the right to the body. In first-century Jewish society to claim the body of the deceased, especially for a woman to claim the body of a deceased man, would be totally inappropriate unless the woman was the nearest of kin! Mary Magdalene is the primary female figure in the gospel narrative. She is the chief mourner, she refers to Jesus as "my lord," and she is the one who lays claim to the body of Jesus. These data certainly raise questions about her relationship to Jesus.

John's story moves on. Jesus, in this text says, "Mary." She turns in recognition and says, "Rabboni!" It is a familiar form of the Hebrew word for teacher. Those who use the familiar forms are expressing a relationship of intimacy. Then try to imagine what happens next. The text simply has Jesus say "Mary, do not hold me" or "do not cling to me." Clearly Mary embraced this figure. Women did not embrace or touch men in Jewish society unless they were married and even then it was done in the privacy of one's home. Reading these texts with a new consciousness brings new possibilities into the imagination.

194

Moving over to Luke's Gospel for a moment, there is the story of Mary and Martha who live in a village and receive Jesus into their home (Luke 10:38ff). John also writes about these two sisters and identifies the village as Bethany, and he says that these two sisters have a brother named Lazarus (John 11:1ff). John also identifies the sister named Mary as the one "who anointed the Lord with ointment and wiped his feet with her hair" (John 11:2). It is interesting to note that John does not give us this story until chapter 12, verse 3, though he refers to it in chapter 11.

Mark also told a story of a woman in Bethany who anointed Jesus with "pure nard," pouring the oil over his head. In Mark, the woman is not named but Jesus called this action "a beautiful thing" (Mark 14:6). There is no hint in either Mark or John that this was anything except a gesture of intimate love. Luke however tells a very similar story (Luke 7:37ff), and Luke makes the woman out to be "a woman of the city, who was a sinner." In the first century that was a common description of a prostitute. Jesus' detractors in Luke's narrative say, "If this man were a prophet, he would have known who and what sort of woman this is who is touching him, for she is a sinner" (Luke 7:39).

Luke does not identify this woman with Mary the sister of Martha, as John does. But when Luke tells his story of Jesus visiting in the home of Mary and Martha, other interesting data emerge. Not only is Jesus a guest in their home but Martha is busy in the kitchen preparing for her guest while Mary is busy listening to Jesus. Martha comes and demands that Jesus order her sister Mary to assist her in the kitchen. What was the relationship between Jesus, a guest, and Mary, Martha's sister, that would cause Martha to assume that Jesus had the authority to command and that Mary would obey? That authority did exist in Jewish society in the first century in the marriage relationship. If this Mary can in fact be identified with Mary Magdalene, as many scholars suggest, then the intimate role of anointing Jesus' head with oil, kissing Jesus' feet, and wiping Jesus' feet with her hair would have been things done to Jesus by Mary Magdalene. These actions would be appropriate only in one of two roles; Mary was either his wife or she was a prostitute.

John and Mark treat this episode as an intimate moment inside a very close circle with no hint of impropriety. Luke treats this episode as if the woman is a woman of the street. At the same time, Luke treats Mary the sister of Martha very positively and does not identify Mary with the woman "who is a sinner." Indeed, the woman of the city in Luke is nameless. Do we have in Luke the first hint of the need to push Mary Magdalene out of Jesus' life by tarnishing her reputation while slowly but surely elevating the virgin mother to the role of the primary woman in the Christian story? Luke does treat Mary the mother of Jesus kindly, indeed more kindly than does Mark. In Luke the mother of Jesus "kept all these things, pondering them in her heart" (Luke 2:19). She is also present at Pentecost (Acts 1:14). Furthermore, Luke has quite purposefully softened Mark's criticism of Jesus' mother (compare Mark 3:31–35 with Luke 8:19–21). Does this begin to fit a pattern? There is still more to consider.

What does Magdalene mean? The common wisdom is that the word Magdalene comes from the village of Magdala. However, no one has ever been able to identify such a town. It is mentioned nowhere in the Hebrew scriptures or in the writings of Josephus. One scholar has suggested that Magdalene was derived by Mark from the Hebrew word *magdal*, which means great or large.[2] If that is accurate then Mary Magdalene originally meant Mary the great, or the great Mary. If this Mary is the great Mary and the mother of Jesus is a secondary Mary, what must Magdalene's relationship to

Jesus have been? Is not the role of wife the only female role that would rank above the role of mother?

Obviously these data are not conclusive but they do constitute a cumulative argument that suggests that Jesus might well have been married, that Mary Magdalene, as the primary woman in the Gospel story itself, was Jesus' wife, and that this record was suppressed but not annihilated by the Christian church before the Gospels came to be written. Yet so real was this relationship that hints of it were scattered all over the Gospels and these hints now beg for explanations.

The final piece of supporting evidence seems to me to be the way Mary Magdalene has come to be treated in Christian history. There is not one shred of biblical evidence that Mary Magdalene was a prostitute. Luke, who seems most prone to damage her reputation, says that Mary Magdalene was a woman out of whom Jesus cast seven demons (Luke 8:2), but no other Gospel corroborates that tradition. Luke also portrays a woman who is a sinner coming to anoint Jesus in the home of a pharisee in Bethany, but he does not identify her with a woman named Mary. John, however, says that this woman was in fact Mary but that this episode took place in her own home with her sister Martha and her brother Lazarus. When John tells the story there is no hint of sinfulness in that act. Even Luke has no negativity whatsoever when he relates the account of the two sisters, Mary and Martha, portraying them rather as close friends of Jesus.

By the turn of the first century there was in the life of the Christian church a clear need to remove Mary Magdalene, the flesh and blood woman who was at Jesus' side in life and in death, and to replace her with a sexless woman, the virgin mother. The record of history is that this was accomplished by portraying Magdalene as a prostitute and thus assassinating her character. I am led to wonder why it was that Mary Magdalene became such a threat to the church. Why is there still a continuing sense, ranging from dis-ease to revulsion, that arises in us when we hear the suggestion that Jesus might have been married? I suggest that far more than any of us realize we are subconsciously victimized by the historic negativity toward women that has been a major gift of the Christian church to the world. So pervasive is this negativity that unconsciously we still regard holy matrimony to be less than the ideal, and we still operate out of an understanding of women that defines them as the source of sin, the polluter of otherwise moral men. For only in the service of this attitude would we greet with fear and negativity the suggestion that Jesus was married. Somehow both his perfect humanity and his complete divinity feel compromised by this suggestion.

In my opinion these negative attitudes toward women did come into the Christian story in the early years of the second century. I also believe that the primary vehicle through which these definitions of women entered Christianity was the figure of the virgin Mary. Furthermore I suggest that women have been the victims of this tradition and that in the church today we are beginning the process of breaking out of this age-old stereotype. Surely this stereotype will be broken, and as a direct consequence the male-created and male-imposed figure of the virgin Mary will not survive our revolution of consciousness. This new consciousness will have to engage the possibility that Jesus himself might have been married.

As I shall now seek to demonstrate, the figure of the virgin has in fact been employed as a male weapon to repress women by defining them in the name of a God called Father, to be less human than males, to be the source of a sexual desire that was thought to be evil, and therefore to be guilty just for being women. My conviction is that if Christianity is to live as a force in the twenty-first century the negative female image centering on the figure of the virgin must be destroyed. If that is true then the portrait of the Virgin Mother of Jesus, which was the gift of the birth narratives to the history of Christian thought, must be challenged openly and its destructive elements exposed.

14

The Cost of the Virgin Myth

Sexual harassment rises out of two realities. The first is an unequal distribution of power that has historically placed women into dependent, subservient roles. The second is the primary definition of women as sexual objects who exist for the purpose of providing men with sexual pleasure, a definition that pervades the life of our society. A major contributor to this pejorative view has been the Judeo-Christian faith story.

This faith story began by proclaiming in its account of creation that only the male bore the image of God. The female, according to this myth, was a second level of creation. She was actually taken out of the male's body, specifically from his rib. The creation story said it was only after the man failed to find a proper friend from among the animals that the female was created. The purpose of the woman in the mind of her Creator was clearly to be a fit companion and helpmate to the lordly male, but she could not and did not share his status.

With that definition of a woman firmly fixed, this faith tradition continued its sexist development, culminating ultimately in a narrative that featured a virgin pure and mild who produced a baby without violating her virginity. In time this virgin mother was enthroned in this tradition as the "ideal" woman, thus rendering every other woman immediately inadequate. Because the book that contained these definitions of women came to be regarded as the "Word of God," and the faith tradition out of which this book grew became the world's dominant religion, the results of these definitions as they were lived out in history have not been morally neutral. The Bible in general and the birth narratives in particular became a subtle, unconscious source for the continued oppression of women. The cultural assumption was made that the only proper way for a moral woman to conduct herself was to remain safely inside the sexually protective barriers provided first by her father and second by her husband.

So deeply were these concepts accepted on both conscious and unconscious levels that when women in the twentieth century finally did begin to step out of those barriers to enter the workplace, males assumed that they did so only because they no longer wished to retain their chaste, sexless status. Such women were, in the minds of males, asking for sexual attention and even sexual harassment. This definition of women became the parent of political behavior that marked the male-female working relationship. Since a woman's employment depended first on a man's willingness to hire her and then on the woman's ability to please her male boss, the environment for sexual exploitation was quickly established. Working women were powerless people.

Far more than most of us have been willing to admit, this stereotype in large measure grew out of the myth of the virgin Mary, who began her pilgrimage through written history when she was installed in a prominent position in the birth narratives of Matthew and Luke.

202

Some years ago a book appeared in religious circles with the simple title *Ideas Have Consequences*.[1] Throughout my study of the birth narratives that title has been in the back of my mind. I hasten to admit that not all of the consequences of these narratives have been negative, but the destructiveness that only now is becoming obvious has always been present.

On the positive side, for example, is the fact that these birth narratives stood in contrast to the normal policy of the ancient world that by and large kept wives and mothers of famous people nameless.[2] Mary was identified by name, and this in itself is an indication of a liberalizing tendency present at the dawn of the Christian faith story.

The biblical portrait of Mary has also been, for some people, a symbol to identify with in suffering. Given the violence and insecurity that marked the history of the world, it has been the common fate of many a mother to mourn her dead son who had been either killed in battle or murdered trying to protect his own. Since even Mary was not spared this fate, Mary's life became, in the human history of pain, a source of comfort for many.[3]

Douglas Edwards, a conservative Christian writing early in this century seeking to justify his literalism, went so far as to argue that the birth narratives alone made it possible for the Greek world to hear and to respond to the story of the Incarnation.[4] In this manner Edwards justified his call to an uncritical view of all the symbols included in those narratives. God set it up that way, he rather weakly suggested, to serve God's apologetic and missionary agenda. He concluded that critics of literalism should therefore abandon their criticism and accept God's plan as necessary to serve the needs of a bygone age. It was a simple and intriguing argument possessing a grain, but only a grain, of truth. The fact that the imposition of this naive literalism rendered belief difficult to impossible for many then, and even more today, was, however, for Edwards a price worthy of payment.

Others, when confronted by this literalism, twisted valiantly in an attempt to preserve their intellectual integrity. Some did this by trying to narrow the focus. They argued that Jesus' nativity was not a virgin birth at all but a virginal conception and a normal birth. It was hardly a helpful distinction though one with which both Matthew and Luke would have agreed. Given the rolling tide of history, however, even this distinction was lost in the sea of the rapidly developing myth. The believer's need to literalize the myths was greater than the church's commitment to truth and scholarship. The negative and destructive results of the birth tradition that we observe today have risen out of this literalism.

As the negativity toward women present in these narratives rose slowly to consciousness in this century, the feminist theologians increased their attack upon the literalizing tendencies.[5] Defining women primarily in biological categories as the Bible does, they argued, has served to legitimize as God-given the second-class status of women in Western history. Such insights have caused many, like me, to wonder aloud what would have been the shape of Christian theology and history if birth narratives had never been included in the writings of Matthew and Luke. Would sex and guilt have been so intimately associated? Would infant baptism have become the rule? Would women have been allowed access sooner to ecclesiastical power and position? Would the monastic movement have been born or become as powerful? Would birth control have been looked upon as evil? Would celibacy have become the norm for priesthood? Would the feminine side of the nature of God have been promoted and ennobled? It would be too much to argue that all of these realities stem directly from the birth narratives. It would be too little, however, to ignore the major contributions the virgin of the birth narratives has made to these identifiably Christian traditions.

Ideas do have consequences. The fact is that Christian writers did place the idea of a virgin mother, who could give birth to a divine child by the operation of the Holy Spirit, into two early pieces of Christian writing. These narratives of Jesus' origin, with all their sexual assumptions, did in time exert a powerful influence on Western history. The consequences flowing from these realities were, and are, enormous. I write to raise some of these to our consciousness, to challenge them, and finally to counter them.

Given the patriarchal structure of the times, it was inevitable that the Christian faith would assume the flavor, the values, the shape, and the form of that patriarchal world. Hence no female deity was allowed into the Christian pantheon. God was a male called Father. Jesus the Christ was a male Son. These two male deities made up two prongs of the Christian Trinity. With that heavy a masculine image, one might think that the third aspect of the Trinity would be allowed to embrace the feminine side of life. But it was not to be. The patriarchal value system acted to prevent a female image from emerging anywhere in this theological formulation.

In Eastern religious legends, a father, a mother, and a son were thought to constitute the complete picture of the divine image. In the masculine Christian religion of the West, however, supplementing the Father and Son in the divine image was not the feminine figure of a mother; rather, this third position was taken by the Holy Spirit, who was difficult to define sexually but, in most instances, was interpreted as one more masculine figure. In Christianity's early years there were protests against this total identification of God with masculinity, but, despite those efforts, the exclusive masculine image of God prevailed and became the dominant divine definition.

A group of Christians known as the Gnostics were the primary minority voice in the early years of Christianity. The Gnostics argued that the word *spirit* had ancient feminine connotations. In the Greek language the word *spirit,* as noted in chapter six, is not a masculine but a neuter word. In the Hebrew tradition, to the degree that spirit was identified with wisdom, it was in fact a feminine word. However, the virgin birth story in both Gospels placed the Holy Spirit into the narrative in the place normally occupied by the father or the male agent, thereby making the masculine definition of spirit primary. The Gnostic insights were viewed as an attack on the divine nature of Christ and were opposed vigorously in orthodox circles. A feminine understanding of God was thus condemned as heresy.

So with a God defined overwhelmingly as male, Christianity began its journey through history. The female half of the human experience was ignored at best, denied at worst. However, that part of reality cannot finally be suppressed. As the Chinese have observed, the masculine yang can overwhelm the feminine yin for a period of history, but it can never annihilate it. In time, covertly if not overtly, the yin will reappear. There was in fact at the dawn of the Christian era a feminine vacuum in the heart of the Christian story that cried out to be filled. In time it would be, but given the nature of the power of patriarchy, that vacuum would be filled with a version of femininity that was primarily a male construct.

As I mentioned in the previous chapter, the female figure who seemed destined at the beginning of Christian history to be the primary woman in the Christian story was not Mary the mother of Jesus but Mary Magdalene. Mary Magdalene was a far more powerful figure in the biblical drama of the New Testament than was Jesus' mother.

Indeed, as I have noted, when placed beside Mary Magdalene, Mary the mother of Jesus is a pale, shadowy figure in the early Gospel accounts. But in time this early record was countered and the woman who appeared to have been at Jesus' side during his earthly life was removed. History was rewritten to exalt the sexless virgin as the primary woman in the Christian story and to assassinate the character of the threatening Magdalene by portraying her in Christian tradition as a prostitute. This was exactly the kind of shift that Rosemary Ruether argues did in fact occur in the life of the early church.[6] Women have paid the price for that shift from that day to this.

By the time the first years of the second century began to pass, Mary the mother of Jesus dominated the field. She was portrayed as understanding, faithful, cooperative, and docile, and this image of what a woman is became the replacement for the dangerous love model reflected in Magdalene. Mary the virgin was not only loyal but was so pure that she could not experience either lust or carnal desire. Real feminine power was suppressed, and a woman who was manageable took that place in the tradition. Undergirding this shift was a constant appeal to the birth tradition recorded in both Matthew and Luke.

This suppression of the natural and normal aspects of femininity was not originally a dominating Jewish idea. There was little Jewish denigration of the flesh, no Jewish Queen Victoria, and little Jewish puritanism. No tradition that had God look out on all physical creation and pronounce it good (Genesis 1), or that made the lusty Song of Songs part of its sacred literature, could ever finally call the appetites of the body evil. But the anchor provided by this Jewish understanding of sexual reality was torn loose from Christianity when Jerusalem was destroyed in 70 c.e. Christianity was set adrift in a gentile sea with no Jewish moorings to guide it.

The gentile world of the Mediterranean basin spoke the language of Greece and thought in categories shaped by the Greek mind. There Christianity confronted and was absorbed by the dualism of the predominant Neoplatonic school of thought. In this Greek world, idea was separated from substance, and mind was separated from body. The lower human nature identified with the animal appetites of the flesh and its carnal desires came to be thought of as evil. The higher human nature associated with the aspirations of the soul came to be thought of as the ultimate good. As these values emerged, it became clear why Mary Magdalene represented the lower nature that had to be repressed and why the virgin mother represented the value of the higher nature that had to be enhanced.

So powerful were these Greek influences that in time Jesus' very humanity had to be defended. The mother of Jesus, strangely enough, became an ally in this struggle. A group of thinkers known as the Docetists began to put forth spokespersons who argued that Jesus only seemed to be human but was in fact a visiting deity. The Greeks, supported by their popular mythology, found it easy to conceive of a God who would take upon himself the appearance of humanity and walk the earth. The Christian idea of Incarnation, first advanced by the fourth Gospel, seemed to many to be amenable to such an interpretation.

Valentinus, an early Gnostic writer, even suggested that the divine Jesus had only passed through Mary, like water passing through a pipe.[7] To counter this threat to Jesus' humanity, the Christians built an apologetic defense line around the phrase "born of the Virgin Mary." Jesus was real, he was historical, he was born, the Christians asserted. When attacks came from the other side of the divine-human debate with the suggestion that Jesus was but a good human being—so good in fact that God had adopted him into divinity[8]—the Christians countered with the other emphasis of the birth narrative. He was not just a good human being, they asserted, "he was conceived by the Holy Spirit."

In the constant attempt on the part of the early Christians to define the nature of Jesus, the birth story became a significant weapon, and therefore these narratives grew in use and power. As they grew, the portrait of Mary also began to grow. She became, certainly by the early years of the second century, the dominant female figure in an otherwise heavily masculine religious system. Because Mary was present now in the tradition, she had to be defined. We need to remember that only men were allowed to participate in the defining process. The way Mary was understood and the virtues attributed to her were shaped by the male value system and reflected the things that men appreciated in a woman. She was a mother who was pure. She was a virgin who was obedient. Those words became the foundation stones on which the ecclesiastical legend of Mary came to be built.

Paul had once referred to the Christ as the new Adam. "As in Adam all die, also in Christ shall all be made alive" (1 Cor. 15:22). "The first man was from the earth, a man of dust; the second man is from heaven" (1 Cor. 15:47). This fascinating reference was to echo throughout the early church, and it was destined to be developed in very interesting ways that had nothing to do with either Adam or Christ but was suggested by both.

Iranaeus, a second-century Christian theologian, fastened on this Pauline connection. For both Adam and Christ, Iranaeus suggested, God had used a virgin substance. God had molded Adam from the virgin mother earth, which had never yet been plowed, and God had formed Jesus from the virgin womb of Mary.[9] This comparison of Adam with Christ soon gave way to a comparison of Eve with Mary, and it proved to be an infinitely more popular contrast. Once more the stature of Mary grew and expanded. This comparison lent itself to homiletical zeal and thereby was repeated and developed in seemingly endless ways by the itinerant preachers of the day. Again it served that constant male agenda that perpetually desired to dominate and control the female.

At the time of the fall, when, according to the literal text, sin entered God's good creation, Eve too was a virgin. Adam did not "know" her until they were both banished from the Garden of Eden (Gen. 4:1). Childbirth, the result of Adam's "knowing," was part of Eve's punishment (Gen. 3:16). Sex, guilt, sin, and punishment were coming together in a way that was to defy any power to separate them for almost two thousand years. Eve, the first woman, was disobedient, so this account went. She ate the forbidden fruit (which in fact became a euphemism for sex). She thus brought sin and death to Adam as well as to herself, and through their progeny she became the ultimate source of sin and death for all humankind. Sin, according to this explanation, had entered life through the woman, the weaker sex.

In contrast to Eve, Mary, the holy virgin woman, had been obedient to the Father God. Her response to the angelic message was a docile "Be it unto me according to your will." Mary thus reversed the Eve effect and became the means through which salvation became available to the entire human race. Eve turned away from God into rebellion. Mary listened, responded, and received God into herself. Eve was sexual and evil. Mary was sexless and good. The disobedience of one virgin was set right by the obedience of another virgin. Iranaeus never lost sight of Mary's humanity. She remained for him the earthly mother of Jesus, not the super-historical goddess,[10] but he did pave the road (or greased the skids) that later Christians traveled into an ascetical understanding of life and a not-so-thinly veiled masculine condemnation of feminine sexuality.

The Gnostics, and especially that school of Gnostics known as the Manichaeans, became the first to identify the "most chaste virgin" with the spotless church or with the new Jerusalem.[11] That spotless church was, of course, called Mother, but it was under the total control and lived in obvious obedience to an all-male priesthood and hierarchy. To obey the dominant male, exemplified in both Mary and the church, was portrayed as the highest virtue that could mark the life of any woman. Mary the virgin mother was the prototype of docile obedience, and she had, so the mythology proclaimed, lived this pattern perfectly.

Increasingly the ascetic Greek tradition began to connect with and to be incorporated into the story of the virgin. Purity and chastity became the primary female attributes that elicited male admiration. Mary's virgin purity was contrasted to the carnal lust that issued in childbirth. Virtue was identified with virginity. The only way a woman could overcome the effect of Eve's sin, the church asserted, was to live the life of a virgin. The underlying assumption of that message was that the flesh of a woman was evil, the passion a woman seemed to elicit from a man was evil and was, interestingly enough, the woman's fault. Sexual desire, both that of a man for a woman and that of a woman for a man, was pronounced evil. Sexual desire thus began to be attacked vigorously by the moralizers and was variously referred to as "carnal," "lustful," and "beastly." The early Fathers can be quoted again and again to make this point clear.[12] Virginity had become the higher calling. Marriage was a compromise with sin. Jerome, a fourth-century theologian known best for

211

his translation of the Bible into Latin, attacked vigorously a man named Jovinian for simply suggesting that virginity and marriage were equal callings.[13] With that mentality winning the day, it was just a matter of time before perpetual virginity for Mary became established.

One complication obviously had to be dealt with before the perpetual virgin status of Mary could be affirmed. In the Gospels (John 7:2; Mark 3:31) and in the writings of Paul (Gal. 1:19), brothers and sisters of Jesus were mentioned. Slowly but surely these siblings were removed.

Near the end of the second century a book known as the *Protevangelium of James (the Gospel of James)*[14] made its appearance and placed into the developing Christian tradition a narrative about Mary's birth, early years, and betrothal to Joseph.[15] Mary in this narrative was a child born miraculously to her parents, Joachim and Anna, in their old age. They dedicated her to God, and she was raised in the temple by holy men. Prior to the onset of puberty, and therefore to keep her from polluting the temple with a menstrual flow, she was entrusted finally to an aged widower named Joseph, who already had grown children. Her permanent virginity was therefore preserved, and Jesus' brothers and sisters were, in fact, merely her stepchildren. Sexual intercourse, even in marriage between Mary and Joseph, was also ruled out, making even married love appear to be tainted and profligate. Sex was declared not necessary to human life, a compromise with our carnal nature. The biblical concept of the goodness of God's creation had been rendered null and void. That attitude now combined with the movements of history to create a mighty force and a definitive sexual stereotype.

Christianity came out of the catacombs on the wings of its official recognition by Constantine in 313, and thus the church had to rejoin the world now as a dominant force. Prior to 313, the church had been a persecuted minority fighting a battle for survival. All its energies were galvanized to defeat the common enemy represented by the empire but called the world. When that enemy surrendered, the energy for battle, born of years of persecution, had no focus.

Under the relentless pressure of those earlier centuries that had identified the desires of the flesh with evil and the aspirations of the soul with goodness, a new enemy on which to focus Christian energy was quickly identified. The soul was in a mortal struggle with the flesh, the church asserted. Worldliness, rather than "the world," became the name of the new enemy.[16] Christianity became a call into the higher spiritual self. The Christian life thus required a renunciation of the world, the flesh, and the devil. The carnal, fleshly desires were the point of humanity's weakest vulnerability, so the ascetic life was assumed to be the best chance for defeating the devil and gaining eternal reward. That ascetic life called for renunciation of the world, and, more important, it identified the celibate life with the virtuous life. The converse was also established. The sexual life, even the married sexual life, was at best a moral option only for the weak.

Monasteries and nunneries proliferated. Celibacy in the priesthood was on the way to becoming both mandatory and the norm. Even Joseph, at this point, began to be thought of as a virgin, and his children were transformed from half-siblings into Jesus' cousins.[17]

In the preaching and literature of the church, the model for the chaste life for both men and women was overwhelmingly the virgin mother of the birth narratives. Many males, but especially celibate priests, could safely adore the virgin with passionate prayers and romantic meditations that posed no threat to their celibate virtue. She was the desired but unreachable ideal whose perfection kept their lust from being sinful. To Mary they poured out their hearts. For

213

women Mary became the male-imposed model of holiness to which all women were told they should aspire. Gradually the star of Mary rose to new heights, and she began to rival even her son Jesus as the popular subject for the devotion of the pious.

Few people stopped to realize that the woman who was being hailed as the ideal model was a woman who had been totally defined by men. That a permanent virgin can be an ideal woman only to a celibate male did not appear to be obvious as the values of the church were presented as objective revealed truths. Theological discussions continued to rage around Mary in the male citadels of theological learning. Without exception all of these discussions led to the further erosion of Mary's humanity.

The more evil the flesh was thought to be, the more Mary's virtue needed to be protected. She became not just the virgin but the perpetual virgin and then the postpartum virgin. It became an issue of great import to prove that Mary retained her unbroken hymen through childbirth. The male theologians were equal even to that task. They searched the Scriptures in a paroxysm of wild exegesis to find texts to undergird postpartum virginity. The prophet Ezekiel had once written (ca. 580 B.C.E.), "This gate shall remain shut; . . . and no one shall enter by it; for the Lord, the God of Israel, has entered by it; therefore it shall remain shut" (Ezek. 44:2). Without so much as an apology, this text was fastened on to prove the now-popular claim for postpartum virginity. It had been, the fathers shouted, preshadowed even in the prophets! Midrash separated from the Jewish tradition that created it had become absurd.

Then those same male exegetes looked again at John's resurrection narrative and saw new meaning in the revelation that the risen Lord had been able to pass through the locked and barred doors and windows of the upper room

(John 20:19–23). If the Lord could do that, they argued, he could also pass through the unbroken hymen of his mother, Mary, on the day of his birth. Stories about the ease with which Jesus was born now began to circulate in varying levels of fantasy. It was childbirth as only a male who had never experienced it could describe it.

The next major step in the relentless march of Mary out of humanity came under the influence of the fifth-century philosopher and theologian Augustine, bishop of Hippo. More than any other figure in Christian history, this man shaped the theological categories that have defined Christianity even up to this very moment. Augustinian categories were still dominant in my own theological training. Augustine gave us the primary Christian myth. In that myth, God created a good world that centered in the Garden of Eden. For Augustine, Adam and Eve were both historical persons and the primeval parents of all humankind. Through these two people the goodness of God's creation was violated and ruined by sin. The fall of humanity occurred, Augustine argued, when the great ontological original sin of disobedience was committed in the Garden of Eden. The sin came through the woman, but it corrupted the man. Because they were the literal first parents, the seed of all future human beings was thus corrupted. All human life, therefore, was born stained with sin. Without the intervening action of God, all people were destined to die in sin. Men and women were defined as self-centered creatures with broken wills, at the mercy of forces over which they had no control, standing in need of a savior. Prior to his baptism, Augustine had identified himself with the school of Manichaean philosophy, which accepted a radical dualism about human life. The Manichaeans tended to divide human life somewhere about the diaphragm, pronouncing the lower body parts evil and the higher body parts good. Augustine, in his pre-Christian days, had lived out of wedlock with his lover, by whom he had produced a son. His conversion led him to renounce his flesh, abandon his lover and their child, and take up the "higher calling" of a Christian ascetic, ultimately becoming a priest and bishop. The fate of his paramour and son seemed to be of little concern to him.[18] After all, she was only a woman, and the child was the product of lust. They were expendable for the righteous Augustine. His primary spiritual task was to remove the stain of his sexual desire. He thus became the great theologian of guilt and sin, but, as is so often the case, he remained blind to the price that others had to pay for his righteousness.

Evil, the sin in life, was for Augustine located in the flesh. It was transmitted through sex. The sins of the fathers and mothers were quite literally passed to the new life through sexual intercourse that resulted in conception. The only hope was for the divine rescuer to be sent by God to break the power of sin by paying the price of sin. This rescuer had to be outside the sinful human stream. He had to be of God. Yet he had to make real contact with those he came to save. The virgin birth story gave Augustine and, through Augustine, the entire church the mechanism needed to develop the primary Christian theology of guilt and grace. From that day to this, the church has trafficked in guilt and enhanced its power by raising ever higher the levels of sexual guilt in both men and women.

The virgin was pure. She had been prepared to be the womb of the new creation. God, who also was pure, could thus enter history without benefit of the corrupting pattern of sexuality. In those terms, Augustine saw the birth of Jesus, the divine rescuer. On the cross this Jesus took upon himself the sin of the world, defeated it in his resurrection, and offered to men and women the gift of salvation through the ongoing male-dominated church, called the body of Christ.

216

The church could thus wash away the power and stain of sin by baptizing the corrupted humanity of a newborn baby. If the baptism of that infant was postponed or denied, and the child happened to die, there was no hope of salvation.

This was a powerful threat in a believing age. The baptized and confirmed adult could deal with his or her continuing sin by going to confession, receiving the sacrament of Christ's body and blood, and living in the hope of heaven. A bit of purgation might be required before entry into the eternal city, but the expectation of salvation was nonetheless present. To dedicate one's life to chastity, to cling to one's virginity or one's celibacy, to spend one's life doing acts of mercy—these things were to build merit that guaranteed a heavenly reward.

The sinlessness of Jesus that made salvation possible depended, for Augustine, on the virgin status of Mary, so the birth narratives of Matthew and Luke became all-important. Augustine's scheme also involved a literalistic understanding of the fall, which linked every life to Adam and Eve in sin. It was this literal linking of Adam and Eve to sin in every person that caused the church first to resist and then to ignore the work of Charles Darwin. For when Adam and Eve were finally relegated to the realm of mythology, the Augustinian system, based on sexual guilt, was mortally wounded. Mary's virginity, which neither Paul nor Mark had mentioned and which the fourth Gospel actually seemed to deny, had become, for Augustine and for those who would be shaped by Augustine for the next fifteen hundred years, a theological necessity that could not be ignored. It was a short step from this attitude in Augustine to the doctrine of the Immaculate Conception, which guaranteed that Mary's human flesh was not corrupted by Eve's sin.

When the dogma of the Immaculate Conception was promulgated in 1854 by Pius IX, Mary was said to have been "preserved immaculate from all stain of original sin by the singular grace and privilege granted her by Almighty God."[19] In 1950, almost a century later, when the dogma of Mary's bodily assumption was proclaimed by Pius XII, the humanity of the central feminine figure in the Christian mythology was completely removed. The argument in that document was unique: Since the relics from the bodies of lesser saints created miracles and since no miracles have ever been reported from the body of Mary, therefore her body must have been assumed.[20] Carl Jung rejoiced that the feminine had finally been placed into God in Western religion. He called it one of the most important decisions in human history. But Jung was talking about symbols, not historical truth. That became obvious when he further stated that all that was now needed was for evil, or the shadow side of life, to be incorporated into God.[21] A view of history, however, reveals that the price of Mary's bodily assumption was the sacrifice of her sexual identity. She entered the realm of the gods as one deprived of her humanity. She was a virgin bride, a virgin mother, a perpetual virgin, and a postpartum virgin. She was immaculately conceived at birth and bodily assumed at the moment of death. Clearly she was not a real woman.

Yet this Mary was proclaimed by the all-male hierarchy as the ideal woman. Who can be such an ideal? Who can be a virgin mother? A virgin mother is a contradiction in terms. If that was to be the feminine ideal, accepted and saluted by church and world alike, then in one stroke every other woman was and is rendered inadequate, incomplete, incompetent. Celibate males who constituted the decision-making body of the church had succeeded in defining the ideal woman in such a way as to universalize guilt among women. Women are guilty if they feel desire; guilty if they marry; guilty if they are not obedient to father, husband, or priest, for in this world a male always held the authority. Even a

218

convent that was under a mother superior had to answer to a male bishop and a male warden, who guaranteed male control. Furthermore, the sisters were dependent on a male priest if they were to have the sacraments that they were taught were necessary to salvation.

Since no one save Mary could achieve the ideal state of virgin mother, all other women were taught that they might approach virtue by being either virgins or mothers. They could join the nunnery and live out the role of virgin purity, or they must be perpetual mothers producing as many off-spring as God would grant, regardless of the impact of a large family on the health and well-being of the mother. Sex had no saving purpose except reproduction. Jerome once proclaimed that the only saving grace of marriage was found in the possibility that such a union would produce more virgins.[22] Strange logic indeed.

Out of this same mentality has come the present prohibition against the use of any means of birth control other than total or cyclical abstinence. It has also given rise to such unusual statements as the one uttered by Pope John Paul II condemning a man who might "lust after his wife."[23] Sex clearly, said the church, was not designed for joy, for love, or for recreation. Sex was evil save as a means for keeping alive the human race. The sexuality of the woman was the most evil of all, for she was the source of male desire. All of these attitudes were part of the legacy that arose at least to some degree from the birth narratives, in which a virgin was placed at the center of the Christian story.

Marina Warner, in her analysis of the role the virgin has played in history, suggested that in those lands where the virgin was particularly popular the status of women was particularly low.[24] James Freeman drives home this same point when he suggests that "mother-goddess worship stands in inverse relationship to high secular status for women." The mother-goddess is unconscious compensation, he argues, for women's actual role. It is an ineffective form of rebellion against the denigration of women.[25]

The emancipation of women has come primarily in those parts of the world in which the Protestant Reformation kicked over the sexual stereotypes of both virgin Mary and Mother Church. Corazon Aquino was one of the rare women in the twentieth century to achieve political power in a predominantly Roman Catholic country, and she had three things going for her that made her situation unique. She was the widow of the primary political rival to Philippine dictator Ferdinand Marcos. Her husband was in fact murdered by Marcos, and therefore she became his political and spiritual heir. She was backed by James Cardinal Sin, the head of the Roman Catholic Church in the Philippines. Finally, she had the backing of key military generals. Without all three of those sources of male power she could not have achieved her position. Indeed, her public demeanor of simple piety, obedience to the church and military, and the absence of personal political ambitions made her a "safe" female candidate, a symbol easily controlled behind the scenes by powerful males. Her hold on political power was always tenuous and rested upon the willingness of the background male figures to continue to offer support. Compare that to the figure of Margaret Thatcher, the "Iron Lady" of Protestant England's politics in the 1980s, who ruled, won elections, and scuttled her enemies in her own name and with her own power. She even appointed the archbishop of Canterbury and the bishop of London and bent the Church of England to her own political purposes.

Corazon Aquino and Margaret Thatcher reveal vastly different definitions of what it means to be a woman. Those definitions, I argue, rise out of the still-alive denigration of women that marked traditional Christianity in the case of Mrs. Aquino and a rebellion against that traditional Christian definition of women that was part of the Reformation, which produced Mrs. Thatcher. My point is that beginning with the birth narratives of Matthew and Luke and carrying on through the rise of Mary as a figure in Christian theology, we are not dealing with the image of a real woman in Christian history. Mary is a male-created female figure who embodies the kind of woman dominant males think is ideal—docile, obedient, powerless.

The power given to Mary in Christian thought is twofold. Her power of intercession includes her ability to identify and sympathize with petitioners. Her power of compassion includes approachability. To put it crudely, Mary's power historically is the power of "pillow talk." Because of her intimate, female, manipulative relationship with the Father God and with the Son, who had become the Judge, Mary could intercede on behalf of those who appealed to her sympathy. She could plead for mercy for those who were frail and weak and, though sinful, were now penitent. They could approach Mary when they could not approach the Father or the Son. The male, either Father or Son, who had the real power could be moved to leniency by the intercession of the pure, docile, obedient virgin mother, who had their ear. Mary's constant advice was based on John 2:5: "Do whatever he tells you." Even in various apparitions throughout history, Mary's message remains, do what my son tells you. She is not a power center. Clearly the male was king.

In the patriarchal family structure of Europe, especially southern Europe, where the virgin myth remained the strongest, intercession (pillow talk) was also the power of the human mother. Again and again the role of Mary was to legitimize the patriarchal value system and to keep women

221

in a controlled behavior pattern in which the primary purpose of a woman, and therefore the primary value of Mary, was to serve the needs—physical and emotional—of the dominant male. The power of the male was based upon his ability to define women in terms of biology, a capacity to associate sex with evil and guilt, and a refusal to allow women into positions of influence.

The real ally of males in this battle to subjugate women was the assumption that these male definitions of women were divine, unchanging, and imposed by God. The church, run by an all-male hierarchy, had spoken. Any attempts to challenge these assumptions or to suggest some other possibilities were immediately condemned as a sin against God, the Bible, or the divine nature of creation. Any attempt to open the ecclesiastical hierarchy to women was met by screams that God's will, expressed through an unbroken, all-male sacred tradition, was being violated. The emotional response betrayed the irrationality of the fear as well as the weakness of the argument.

Ideas do have consequences. In some significant measure these ideas that defined God, established sexual stereotypes for both men and women, and came to be thought of as expressions of the divine will have at least a part of their origin in the lovely and romantic narratives that we popularize in church and secular society alike every Christmas season. Because Matthew and Luke, for a variety of reasons, placed a virgin into their drama concerning Jesus' origins, women down through the centuries have paid, in my opinion, a very high price. How different it might have been if Matthew and Luke had followed the lead of Paul and Mark and told the Christ story without reference to a virgin.

The church certainly cannot argue today that the virgin concept was or is necessary to the divinity of Jesus, for surely

222

the Christology of Paul, who knew not the virgin tradition, and of John, who seems to deny the virgin tradition, is far more profound and even more divine than the Christology found in Matthew and in Luke. But it does raise the question of what effect the women's revolution will have on the fate of the organized, institutionalized Christian church, where sexist attitudes are still used to define God, Jesus, human life, and human virtue. Those sexist attitudes can be challenged only by challenging the doctrine of God, the meaning of Christ, the definition of sin, the role of the Savior, and the structure of the church on which they are based.

Catholic Christianity in its Anglican form has now begun to ordain women to the priesthood and to consecrate women to the episcopacy. Catholic Christianity in its Roman form, which is still a predominantly Western church, cannot escape being drawn into a rigorous debate on these issues. That debate has been enjoined on subterranean levels across Europe and America even if the hierarchy publicly rules out such a possibility forever. Forever will prove to be a very brief period of time, I suspect. Catholic Christianity, in its Orthodox form, because of its eastern and southern European origins, will be a bit slower in coming to new and more inclusive sexual definitions. The world today is too small and too interdependent, however, for even this tradition to escape the whirlwind of change.

A literalized Bible produced a literalized theology, which produced a Christianity that believed itself, in its various forms, to be inerrant and/or infallible. But that institutionalized Christianity with its infallible theological pronouncements and its claims of an inerrant Bible is now confronting a new consciousness, an unwillingness to leave unchallenged the faith and practice of our fathers from which our mothers were systematically excluded. The feminine aspect of God so

223

long oppressed by the masculine patriarchy is roaring back into our awareness, sweeping away our male prejudices and even our male definitions of the ideal woman.

The only hope for the survival of the virgin Mary as a viable symbol is her redefinition by the new consciousness. A male-dominated church will resist this with its dying breath. If that resistance succeeds, however, the church will die. The church will have won the battle only to discover it has lost the war. Only the church that manages to free itself from its sexist definition of women, anchored significantly in the virgin Mary tradition, will survive. The virgin of a literal Bible, the virgin of the annunciation, Bethlehem, and the manger, corrupted by the years of an overlaid male theology, will have to go. But the feminine side of God in some new incarnation will inevitably arise to take her place. When that occurs, the church of Jesus Christ will be more whole, more inclusive, and more reflective of the reality for which the word God is a symbol.

I welcome the dawn of this deeper and higher human consciousness. The rewards that it will bring promise to be worth the journey we must make to a new Bethlehem, where we can once again worship and adore the God who is met in the heart of our humanity incarnate as male and female. Perhaps there we will discover even a God who could be experienced in the life of one who entered this world through either a natural birth or through what we have called the route of illegitimacy. If we do, a new star will appear, and wise men and wise women, led by that star, will come and worship anew.

Notes

Chapter 1. *Escaping Biblical Literalism*

1. Jerry Falwell on ABC-TV and John Ankerberg on a national cable network.
2. See the text of my book *Rescuing the Bible from Fundamentalism* (San Francisco: Harper San Francisco, 1991) for further documentation.
3. The Right Reverend William Wantland, Episcopal Diocese of Eau Claire.
4. Joseph Campbell with Bill Moyers, *The Power of Myth* (Garden City, NY: Doubleday, 1988), chap. 1.
5. Marina Warner, *Alone of All Her Sex* (New York: Alfred A. Knopf, 1976). On page 38, Warner quotes Tertullian, who died ca. 230, as saying, "The whole fruit is present in the semen." Tertullian, *Apologia* 9:8.
6. Wolfhart Pannenberg, *Jesus, God and Man* (Philadelphia: Westminster, 1978), pp. 141–150. Emil Brunner, *The Christian Doctrine of Creation and Redemption*, Dogmatics, vol. 2, trans. Olive Wyon (Philadelphia: Westminster, 1952), p. 352ff.
7. The Right Reverend Maurice Benitez, Episcopal bishop of Texas.
8. The Right Reverend William Frey, retired Episcopal bishop of Colorado.
9. For the purposes of this chapter I accept the traditional naming of Mary's husband as Joseph. However I am aware that there is a significant debate about whether this name has any literal accuracy at all.

Chapter 4. *From the Scandal of the Cross to the Scandal of the Crib*

1. Even this title "zealot" might be a reading back into history of a later group of Jewish guerrilla fighters who resisted Roman domination in the revolution that resulted in the destruction of Jerusalem in 70 C.E.
2. Michael D. Goulder, *Luke, A New Paradigm*, vol. 1, Journal for the Study of the New Testament Supplement Series 20 (Sheffield; JSOT Press, 1989), chap. 5, p. 147.
3. This phrase was popularized by the German Lutheran theologian Dietrich Bonhoeffer.

Chapter 5. *The Development of the Birth Tradition*

1. Raymond E. Brown, *The Birth of the Messiah* (Garden City, NY: Double-day, 1977), App. IV, p. 517ff.
2. Joseph Fitzmyer, *The Gospel According to Luke, I–X*, Anchor Bible Series (Garden City, NY: Doubleday, 1981), p. 305.
3. John Drury, *Tradition and Design in Luke's Gospel* (London: Darnton, Long-man & Todd, 1976). In this book Drury argues that Luke has simply changed Matthew to suit his purposes. To transform wise men into shepherds is a striking feat. Even if that were granted, the other differ-ences make Drury's arguments, in my opinion, difficult.
4. Goulder, *Luke, A New Paradigm*. In this book Goulder argues vigorously against the existence of Q and for Luke's dependence on Matthew. Schil-lebeeckx, who opposes this thesis, goes so far as to develop an analysis of the theology of the Q document.
5. Brown, *Birth*, pp. 34, 35; and Herman Hendrickx, *Infancy Narratives* (London: Geoffrey Chapman, 1984), p. 4. Although this list can be put together with ease by comparing the two narratives, I have benefited here from Raymond Brown's analysis and by a similar listing by Hen-drickx.
6. Eusebius, *The History of the Church* (New York: Dorset Press, 1965), p. 54 (Tr. by G.A. Williamson)
7. Edward Schillebeeckx, *Jesus* (New York: Crossroad, 1981), pp. 409, 411ff.
8. Thomas Sheehan, *The First Coming* (New York: Random House, 1986). A particularly intriguing analysis of this development is given by Professor Sheehan, who sees this development to be contingent upon Christian-ity's historic pilgrimage from Aramaic-speaking Jews to Greek-speaking Jews to Greek-speaking Gentiles.
9. Philo, vol. 2, ed. T. E. Page. On the Cherubim, XII, 41, p. 33; XIII, 47, p. 37 (London: William Hememann; New York: Putnam & Son, 1929). A similar though not exact reference is found in vol. 1, allegorical inter-pretation III, 88–90, p. 361.
10. Brown, *Birth*, p. 156.

Chapter 6. *Matthew's Story, Part I*

1. Brown, *Birth*, p. 46.
2. Brown, *Birth*, p. 66ff. Raymond Brown spells this threefold sonship out in much more detail.
3. This idea has come first from B. W. Bacon, in his book *Studies in Matthew* (New York: Holt, 1930), and is criticized by Raymond Brown, among others. I, however, find the Bacon argument to be far more substantial than Brown does.
4. Hendrickx, *Infancy Narratives*.

5. Brown, *Birth*, p. 67.
6. Raymond Brown's table of the monarchical period of the genealogies, on p. 78, makes these points visually.
7. The historical analysis of these varying arguments leans upon Brown's work, pp. 71–74.
8. Hendrickx, *Infancy Narratives*, p. 25.
9. Ibid., p. 26.
10. Elaine Pagels, *The Gnostic Gospels* (New York: Random House, 1979), p. 53. Her quotation is from the *Gospel of Philip* 55:25–26.
11. For a fuller explanation of this point, see my earlier book, *This Hebrew Lord* (San Francisco: Harper & Row, 1974, 1987), Chap. 2.
12. Jane Schaberg, *The Illegitimacy of Jesus* (San Francisco: Harper & Row, 1987). Ms. Schaberg argues this case persuasively.
13. The Reverend Jerry Falwell, *Finding Inner Peace and Strength* (Garden City, Doubleday, NY: 1982), p. 126, 127.
14. Justin Martyr, *Dialogue with Trypho*, ed. A. Roberts and J. Donaldson, The Ante-Nicene Fathers, vol. 1 (reprint, Grand Rapids, MI: Eerdmans, 1979), pp. 194–270.
15. Goulder, *Luke, A New Paradigm*, pp. 208.
16. Brown, *Birth*, p. 145ff.
17. Hendrickx, *Infancy Narratives*, p. 28.

Chapter 7. *Matthew's Story, Part II*

1. Most scholars do not include all of 40–66 in Second Isaiah. A more familiar division would be to place chapters 40–55 in Second Isaiah and chapters 56–66 in Third Isaiah. When Matthew wrote, however, the whole of Isaiah was regarded as a single work by one author.
2. Hendrickx, *Infancy Narratives*, p. 37.
3. Brown, *Birth*, p. 190ff.
4. Brown, *Birth*, p. 193.
5. Hendrickx, *Infancy Narratives*, p. 39. Hendrickx is here quoting from Jewish written midrash tradition.
6. Brown, *Birth*, p. 543.
7. Brown, *Birth*, p. 171, 172.
8. Josephus, *Antiquities* xvi v. 1, 136–41, quoted from Brown, *Birth*, p. 174.
9. Hendrickx, *Infancy Narratives*, p. 39.
10. W. F. Albright and C. F. Mann, *Matthew*, Anchor Bible Series (Garden City, NY: Doubleday, 1971), p. 13.
11. Pliny, *Natural History* xxx v. 16–17, quoted from Brown, *Birth*, p. 174.
12. Hendrickx, *Infancy Narratives*, p. 49.
13. Brown, *Birth*, p. 217.
14. Brown, *Birth*, p. 219ff.

Chapter 8. *Behind Luke—An Original Pageant?*

1. Haenchen, *The Acts of the Apostles, A Commentary* (Philadelphia: Westminster, 1971), p. 112ff.
2. Brown, *Birth*, p. 280.
3. Michael Goulder in his fascinating commentary on Luke does argue powerfully for Luke's dependence on Matthew and, therefore, has no need for the Q hypothesis. I am increasingly impressed by his argument. However Goulder has not yet changed the mind of the major New Testament scholars outside England, though I do not mean to suggest that he will not do so. Time will tell.
4. Brown, *Birth*, p. 451.
5. Schaberg, *Illegitimacy*, p. 144.

Chapter 9. *Luke's Story, Part I*

1. John A. T. Robinson, *The Human Face of God* (Philadelphia: Westminster, 1973), p. 88. This point is clearly drawn here.
2. Spong, *Rescuing the Bible from Fundamentalism*. I spelled out this theme in detail in my chapter on Luke in this book.
3. Brown, *Birth*, p. 283ff.
4. Brown, *Birth*, p. 284.
5. Brown, *Birth*, p. 266.
6. Goulder, *Luke, A New Paradigm*, pp. 214–15.
7. Hendrickx, *Infancy Narratives*, pp. 54, 55.
8. Goulder, *Luke, A New Paradigm*, p. 21.
9. Brown, *Birth*, p. 288.
10. Hans Conzelmann is so sure of this that he does not even treat Luke 1 and Luke 2 in his book *The Theology of St. Luke* (London: Faber & Faber 1960).
11. Brown, *Birth*, p. 300.
12. Schaberg, *Illegitimacy*, p. 201. Goulder, *Luke, A New Paradigm*, p. 252.
13. Schaberg, *Illegitimacy*, p. 201.
14. Schaberg, *Illegitimacy*, p. 135ff.
15. Brown, *Birth*, p. 321. I lean heavily in this section on the research of Raymond Brown, whose fuller exposition may be found in the section of his book noted here.
16. Brown, *Birth*, p. 350–55. Raymond Brown's detailed discussion of the Anawim community, its history, ideas, and influence on the early Christian church is found in this section of his book. Michael Goulder argues the contrary point of view.
17. Goulder, *Luke, A New Paradigm*, p. 230ff.

Chapter 10. *Luke's Story, Part II*

1. Goulder, *Luke, A New Paradigm*, p. 260.
2. Goulder, *Luke, A New Paradigm*, p. 250.
3. Hendrickx, *Infancy Narratives*, p. 94.
4. Brown, *Birth*, p. 547. See his App. VII.
5. Goulder, *Luke, A New Paradigm*, p. 246ff.
6. I attribute this to Rosemary Ruether but I am not certain. It was passed on to me verbally and not taken from a written source.
7. Brown, *Birth*, p. 416.
8. Hendrickx, *Infancy Narratives*, p. 102.
9. Brown, *Birth*, p. 419.
10. Goulder, *Luke, A New Paradigm*, p. 251.
11. Brown, *Birth*, pp. 420–31.
12. Brown, *Birth*, p. 447.
13. Goulder, *Luke, A New Paradigm*, p. 255.
14. Brown, *Birth*, p. 457ff.
15. Brown, *Birth*, p. 460ff.
16. Brown, *Birth*, p. 468. Married as a young girl at 14, married for seven years until 21, widow for 84 years brings the total to 105. See Brown's notes on Luke 2:36, p. 412.
17. Brown, *Birth*, p. 469. Brown suggests that Luke was unwilling to "posit a growth in the Spirit for one who was conceived in the Spirit."
18. Goulder, *Luke, A New Paradigm*, p. 264ff. Goulder argues powerfully that this story is necessary to the story line that binds Luke's narrative together.
19. Unless the story in John of the wedding feast at Cana of Galilee can be considered part of such a tradition. I will suggest this in Chapter 13.
20. Josephus, *Antiquities* 11:6, no. 230.
21. Brown, *Birth*, p. 495.

Chapter 11. *Birth Hints from Mark and John*

1. Schaberg, *Illegitimacy*, p. 161.
2. Schaberg, *Illegitimacy*, p. 162.
3. Schaberg, *Illegitimacy*, p. 157.
4. I have expanded these ideas significantly in my chapter on the fourth Gospel in *Rescuing the Bible from Fundamentalism*.

Chapter 13. *Suppose Jesus Were Married*

1. The Right Reverend Barbara Harris of Massachusetts.
2. Dale Miller and Patricia Miller, *The Gospel of Mark as Midrash on Earlier Jewish and New Testament Literature* (Lewiston, NY: Edwin Mellen Press, 1990) p. 370.

Chapter 14. *The Cost of the Virgin Myth*

1. Richard Weaver, *Ideas Have Consequences* (Chicago: Univ. of Chicago Press, 1948).
2. Douglas Edwards, *The Virgin Birth in History and Faith* (London, Faber & Faber, 1943).
3. David Flusser, *Images of the Mother of Jesus in Jewish and Christian Perspectives* (Philadelphia: Fortress Press, 1986).
4. Edwards, *Virgin Birth.*
5. People such as Rosemary Ruether, Elisabeth Schüssler Fiorenza, Margaret Miles, and Jane Schaberg.
6. Rosemary Radford Ruether, *Mary, the Feminine Face of the Church* (Philadelphia: Westminster Press, 1977).
7. Hans von Campenhausen, *The Virgin Birth in the Theology of the Early Church*, Valentinus is quoted from Irenaeus, *Haer.* iii, p. 23.
8. Marcion was one example of the group known as the Adoptionists. Actually, Paul, in Romans 1:4, and Mark, in his story of the baptism, were sometimes quoted on the side of adoptionism.
9. Irenaeus, *Haer.* iii 21:10; quoted from von Campenhausen, p. 41.
10. von Campenhausen, *The Virgin Birth*, p. 43.
11. von Campenhausen, *The Virgin Birth*, p. 44.
12. John S. Spong, *Into the Whirlwind* (New York: Winston Press, 1983), p. 92, 105ff.
13. Jerome, *Against Jovinian*, quoted from von Campenhausen, p. 72.
14. Edgar Hennecke, *A New Testament Apocrypha* (Philadelphia: Westminster 1959), p. 374–88.
15. Hennecke, *A New Testament Apocrypha*, p. 381; James 8:2.
16. Spong, *This Hebrew Lord*, chap. 3, p. 51ff.
17. Jerome argues in this manner in the piece entitled *Against Heloidius.*
18. This point is made powerfully dramatic in a one-woman play *All That I Am*, written by Irene Mahoney, and presented by Roberta Nobleman when I saw it in Newark, New Jersey.
19. *Ineffabilis Deus Munificentissimus*, 1854, p. 204.
20. *The Christian Faith in the Doctrinal Documents of the Catholic Church*, ed. J. Neuner and J. Dupuis (New York: Alba House, 1950).
21. Carl Jung, *Psychology in Western Religion* (Princeton, NJ: Princeton Univ. Press, 1984).

230

22. Jerome, Letter 22 to Eusto Chium in *A Select Library of Nicene and Post-Nicene Fathers of the Christian Church*, second volume. Translated with prolegomena and explanatory notes, under editorial supervision of Philip Schaff and Henry Wace (New York: The Christian Liturgy Co., 1890–1900), 6:29.
23. Quoted in news releases from the Vatican in 1980. Subsequently Vatican sources attempted to clarify the pope's intentions. The clarifications, however, only served to reveal anew the sexist attitudes that prevail in the Vatican.
24. Warner, *Alone of All Her Sex*, p. 183.
25. James W. Freeman, "The Cross-Cultural Study of Mother Worship," in *Mother Worship*, ed. James J. Preston (Chapel Hill: Univ. of North Carolina Press, 1982).

Bibliography

Albright, W. F., and C. S. Mann. *Matthew*. Anchor Bible Series. New York: Doubleday, 1971.

Aron, Robert. *Jesus of Nazareth, The Hidden Years*. Trans. Frances Frenaxe. New York: William Morrow & Co., 1962.

Bacon, B.W. *Studies in Matthew*, New York: Holt, 1930.

Benson, Richard Moeux. *The Virgin Birth of Our Lord Jesus Christ*. Boston: Damrell & Upham, 1910.

Bonhoeffer, Dietrich. *Letters and Papers from Prison*. 2d English ed. Trans. by Reginald Fuller. London: SCM Press, 1956. Also published under the title *Prisoner for God*. New York: Macmillan, 1959.

Boslooper, Thomas, D. *The Virgin Birth*. Philadelphia: Westminster Press, 1962.

Brown, Raymond E. *The Birth of the Messiah*. Garden City, NY: Doubleday, 1977.

———. *The Gospel According to John*. Garden City, NY: Doubleday, 1966–1970, 2 vols.

Brown, Raymond E., ed. *Mary in the New Testament: A Collaborative Assessment by Protestant and Roman Catholic Scholars*. Philadelphia: Fortress Press, 1978.

Brunner, Emil. *The Christian Doctrine of Creation and Redemption*. Dogmatics, vol. 2. Trans. Olive Wyon. Philadelphia: Westminster Press, 1952.

———. *Eternal Hope*. Trans. Harold Knight. Philadelphia: Westminster Press, 1954.

———. *God and Man*. Trans. David Cairns. London: SCM Press, 1936.

———. *I Believe in the Living God*. Trans. and ed. John Holden. Philadelphia: Westminster Press, 1961.

Campbell, Joseph, with Bill Moyers. *The Power of Myth*. Ed. Betty Sue Flowers. New York, London: Doubleday, 1988.

Carrol, Michael P. *The Cult of the Virgin Mary, Psychological Origins*. Princeton, NJ: Princeton Univ. Press, 1986.

Christ, Carol P. *Diving Deep and Surfacing: Women Writers on Spiritual Quest*. Boston: Beacon Press, 1980.

Christ, Carol P., and Plaskow, Judith P. *Womanspirit Rising*. San Francisco: Harper & Row, 1979.

The Christian Faith in the Doctrinal Documents of the Catholic Church. Ed. J. Neuner and J. Dupuis. New York: Alba House, 1950.

Coggins, R.J., and J.L. Houlten, eds. *A Dictionary of Biblical Interpretation*. New York: SCM, Trinity Press, 1990.

Conzelmann, Hans. *The Theology of St. Luke*. Tr. by Geoffry Buswell. London: Faber & Faber 1960.

Crain, Orville E. *The Credibility of the Virgin Birth*. New York: Abingdon Press, 1925.

Daly, Mary. *Gyn/ecology: The Metaethics of Radical Feminism*. Boston: Beacon Press, 1978.

Danielou, Jean. *The Infancy Narratives*. Trans. Rosemary Sheed. London: Burns & Oates, 1968.

Dictionary of Classical Mythology. Ed. Pierre Grimal. New York: Blackwell, 1985.

Dinkler, Erich. *The Anthropology of Augustine*. Stuttgart: W. Kohlhamer, 1934.

Drury, John. *Tradition and Design in Luke's Gospel*. London: Darnton, Longman & Todd, 1976.

Edwards, Douglas. *The Virgin Birth in History and Faith*. London: Faber & Faber, 1943.

Eliade, Mircea, ed. *The Encyclopedia of Religion*. Vol. 6. New York: Macmillan, 1987.

Eusebius. *The History of the Church from Christ to Constantine*. Trans. by G. A. Williamson. New York: Dorset Press, 1965.

The Fathers of the Church. Trans. Mary Melchior. New York: Fathers of the Church Press, 1951.

Fiorenza, Elisabeth Schüssler. *Bread Not Stone: The Challenge of Feminist Biblical Interpretation*. Boston: Beacon Press, 1984.

———. *In Memory of Her: A Feminist Theological Reconstruction of Christian Origins*. New York: Crossroad, 1983.

Fitzmyer, Joseph. *The Gospel According to Luke—I–X*, Anchor Bible Series. New York: Doubleday, 1981.

Flusser, David. *Jesus*. Trans. Ronald Walls. New York: Herder & Herder, 1969.

———. *Mary, Images of the Mother of Jesus in Jewish and Christian Perspective*. Philadelphia: Fortress Press, 1986.

Fox, Matthew. *The Coming of the Cosmic Christ*. San Francisco: Harper & Row, 1988.

———. *Original Blessing*. Santa Fe: Bear & Co., 1983.

Goulder, Michael D. *Luke, A New Paradigm*. Vol. 1 and 2. Journal for the Study of the New Testament Supplement Series 20. Sheffield: JSOT Press, 1989.

Graeb, Hilda. *Mary: A History of Doctrine and Devotion*. Christian Classics. London: Westminster, 1963.

Grotzmacher, Richard H. *The Virgin Birth*. New York: Eaton & Mains (Foreign Religious Service), 1907.

Haenchen, Ernst. *The Acts of the Apostles, A Commentary*. Trans. by Bernard Noble and Gerald Shinn. Philadelphia: Westminster Press, 1971.

Hageman, Alice, ed. *Sexist Religion and Women in the Church, No More Silence!* New York: Association Press, 1974. See especially the chapter "Theology After the Demise of God the Father" by Mary Daly.

Hendrickx, Herman. *Infancy Narratives*. London: Geoffrey Chapman, 1984.

Hennecke, Edgar. *New Testament Apocrypha*. Ed. Wilhelm Schneemelcher. Philadelphia: Westminster Press, 1963.

Hodgson, Leonard. *And Was Made Man: An Introduction to the Study of the Gospels*. London: Longmans, Green & Co., 1928.

Jerome. *Select Works and Letters*. Vol. 6 of the Nicene and Post-Nicene Fathers. Trans. by W. H. Fremantle. Grand Rapids, MI: Wm. B. Eerdman's, 1979.

Jung, Carl J. *Memories, Dreams and Reflections*. New York: Vintage Books, 1965.

———. *Psychology and Religion*. New Haven, CT: Yale Univ. Press, 1938.

KisKaddon, J. Fulton. *Scientific Support for Christian Doctrines*. Privately published by the author, 1933.

Konner, Melvin. "The Aggressors." *New York Times Magazine*, August 4, 1988, p. 33, 34.

Küng, Hans. *On Being a Christian*. Garden City, NY: Doubleday, 1976.

235

Lobstein, Paul. *The Virgin Birth of Christ*. Oxford: Williams & Norgate, 1903.

Machen, V. Gresham. *The Virgin Birth of Christ*. New York and London: Harper & Brothers, 1932.

Miller, Dale and Patricia Miller. *The Gospel of Mark as Midrash on Earlier Jewish and New Testament Literature*. Lewiston, NY: Edwin Mellon Press, 1990.

Minear, Paul. S. Monograph. *The Interpreter and the Birth Narratives*. Uppsala: Wretmans Boktryckeri, 1950.

Orr, James. *The Virgin Birth of Christ*. New York: Charles Scribner & Sons, 1907.

Pagels, Elaine. *Adam, Eve, and the Serpent*. New York: Random House, 1988.

————. *The Gnostic Gospels*. New York: Random House, 1979.

Palmer, Frederick. *The Virgin Birth*. New York: Macmillan & Co., 1924.

Pannenberg, Wolfhart. *Basic Questions in Theology*. Trans. George H. Kehn. Philadelphia: Westminster, 1970.

————. *The Idea of God and Human Freedom*. Trans. R. A. Wilson. Philadelphia: Westminster Press, 1973.

————. *Jesus, God and Man*. Philadelphia: Westminster Press, 1968.

————. *Theology and the Kingdom of God*. Philadelphia: Westminster Press, 1968.

Parrinder, Geoffrey. *Avatar and Incarnation*. London: Faber & Faber, 1970.

Preston, James J., ed. *Mother Worship: Theme and Variation*. Chapel Hill: Univ. of North Carolina Press, 1982.

Robinson, John A. T. *The Human Face of God*. Philadelphia: Westminster Press, 1973.

Ruether, Rosemary Radford. "The Collision of History and Doctrine: The Brothers of Jesus and the Virginity of Mary." *Continuum* 7 (1969–70): 93–105.

————. *Mary, the Feminine Face of the Church*. Philadelphia: Westminster Press, 1977.

Schaberg, Jane. *The Illegitimacy of Jesus*. San Francisco: Harper & Row, 1987.

Schillebeeckx, Edward. *Jesus*. New York: Crossroad, 1981.

A Select Library of Nicene and Post-Nicene Fathers of the Christian Church. Vols. 1 to 7 trans. and ed. by Philip Schaff and Henry Wace. New York: The Christian Liturgy Co., 1890–1900.

Sheehan, Thomas. *The First Coming: How The Kingdom of God Became Christianity.* New York: Random House, 1986.

Soltau, Wilhelm. *The Birth of Jesus Christ.* Trans. Maurice A. Carney. London: Adam and Charles Black, 1903.

Spong, John S. *The Easter Moment.* San Francisco: Harper & Row, 1980, 1987.

———. *Living in Sin? A Bishop Rethinks Human Sexuality.* San Francisco: Harper & Row, 1988.

———. *Rescuing the Bible from Fundamentalism: A Bishop Rethinks the Meaning of Scripture.* San Francisco: Harper San Francisco, 1991.

———. *This Hebrew Lord.* San Francisco: Harper & Row, 1974, 1987.

Taylor, Vincent. *The Historical Evidence for the Virgin Birth.* Oxford: Clarendon Press, 1920.

Terrien, Samuel. *The Elusive Presence: Toward a New Biblical Theology.* San Francisco: Harper & Row, 1978.

Thiering, Barbara. *Deliver Us from Eve.* Sydney: Australian Council of Churches, 1977.

Thurian, Max. *Mary, Mother of the Lord, Figure of the Church.* London: Faith Press, 1963.

Trench, B. C., and Richard Chenevix. *The Star of the Wise Men.* Philadelphia: H. Hooker, 1850.

Ulanov, Ann B. *Picturing God.* New York: Cowley Press, 1986.

von Campenhausen, Hans. *The Virgin Birth in the Theology of the Ancient Church.* Studies in Historical Theology. London: SCM Press, and Naperville, IL: Alec R. Allenson 1964.

Warner, Marina. *Alone of All Her Sex.* New York: Alfred A. Knopf, 1976.

Weaver, Richard. *Ideas Have Consequences.* Chicago: Univ. of Chicago Press, 1948.

Worcester, Elwood. *Studies in the Birth of the Lord.* New York: Charles Scribner's Sons, 1932.

Index

Abraham, 68; descendants of, 57, 68, 80, 81, 95, 97–98, 171
Acts, 32, 99, 100, 123, 155; **1**, 10, 54; **1:1–11**, 17; **1:14**, 131, 196; **1:26**, 100, 120; **2**, 54, 150; **2:1ff**, 17; **2:36**, 150; **2:43–47**, 134; **4:32–37**, 134; **5:1–11**, 134; **5:30–31**, 52, 150; **5:36–37**, 142; **8:9ff**, 139; **9:1ff**, 121; **9:19–29**, 100; **10:9–16**, 100; **12:1,2**, 24; **13**, 52; **13:6–8**, 139; **13:33**, 52; **15**, 24; **15:14ff**, 154; **19:3–4**, 115, 122; **28:28**, 154
Adam, 209–10, 215, 217
Adultery, 8–9, 169–70
Ahaz, 77–79
Amos **5:2**, 130
Anawim community, 133–34, 153, 155
Anna, 151, 153, 155
Annunciation, 80–82, 96, 103–4, 105–6, 120–34, 149–50
Anti-Semitism, 7–8
Aquino, Corazon, 220–21
Ascension: of Elijah, 17; of Jesus, 10, 16–18, 20, 52, 53–54, 100, 101
Assyrians, 77–79
Augustine, 215–17

Balaam, 87–89
Baptism, 114
Baptism of Jesus, 124–25; Isaiah and, 135; Luke and, 157; Mark and, 55, 58–59, 72, 80, 116, 166

Bathsheba, 69, 70, 127
Benedictus, 133, 134, 135, 139
Bethlehem, 41, 71–72, 138, 142–50, 181
Biblical literalism, 1–20, 44–45, 137–41, 175–77, 203–4, 223; and biblical contradictions, 5; John and, 166–67; and Luke's story, 112, 118, 132, 135–36, 137–41, 142–44, 157–58; and Matthew's story, 62, 68–69, 72, 75–76, 83–85, 139. *See also* Midrash
"Biblical morality," 7–8
Birth control, 219
Birth narratives, 1–2, 10–11, 21–30, 35, 36–37, 41–42, 59, 178–79; contradictions in Matthew's and Luke's, 48–50; development of, 43–60; John and, 167–69; as midrash, 21, 61, 66, 71, 74, 134–35, 137; in other religious traditions, 26–27, 56–58. *See also* Luke; Matthew; Scandal of the manger; Virgin birth
Brown, Raymond, 45; and Luke's story, 116, 123–24, 126, 133–34, 153, 155; and Matthew's story, 64, 87, 89
Brown, William M., 175
Brunner, Emil, 10

Caesar Augustus, 141, 143–44
Campbell, Joseph, 9
Canticles, 128, 132–35, 138–39, 153–54
Cassius Dio, 92

145, 158, 162–63; Mark and, 162–65; Matthew and, 73, 74, 80, 164
Immaculate Conception, 217–18
Immanuel, 61, 68, 80
Incarnation, 10, 25, 116, 203, 208
Innkeeper, Bethlehem, 144
Iranaeus, 209–11
Isaac, 57, 58, 80, 90–91, 120
Isaiah: **1:3**, 145, 150; **4:3**, 96; **7:2**, 78; **7:4**, 78; **7:12**, 78; **7:13–14**, 74, 76–79; **7:15**, 78; **7:16**, 78; **7:18ff**, 78–79; **8**, 134; **9:5–6**, 149; **11:1,2**, 81; **37:32**, 130; **40–66**, 86, 138; **40:4**, 5; **40:5**, 154; **41:2**, 87; **42:6**, 154; **46:13**, 154; **49:1**, 87; **49:6**, 154; **49:7**, 87; **52:7**, 150; **59:10**, 154; **60:1, 3,6**, 87, 93
Ishmael, 57, 58

Jacob, 48, 154
James, "the Lord's brother," 24, 165, 183
Jeremiah: **14:8**, 144; **14:17**, 130; **18:15**, 130
Jeremias, Joachim, 182
Jerome, 69–70, 211–12, 219
Jesus, 21–22, 29–31, 37–38, 179–80; ascension, 10, 16–18, 20, 52, 53–54, 100, 101; baptism of, *see* Baptism of Jesus; brothers of, 24, 131, 163, 165, 168, 183; chronology of birth, 48; circumcision/presentation/purification, 151–53; conception, 47–48, 57, 71–72, 79, 80, 110, 123–30, 139, 156, 166–72, 209 (*see also* Birth narratives); crucifixion, 37, 38–41, 177; as divine rescuer, 35–37; exaltation, 40, 50–55, 58; family in adulthood, 161–65; father of, 13, 30, 41–42, 47–48, 71–74, 80–81, 125–26, 156, 158, 165, 181–85; as firstborn, 145–46; genealogies, 41, 48, 67–69, 101–2, 126 (*see also* David); as Immanuel, 61, 68, 80; and John the Baptist, 113–36,

143, 156; as king, 35–36, 59, 145 (*see also* David); length of public ministry, 192; as Logos, 110, 166; married, 187–99; mother of, *see* Mary; naming of, 41–42, 48, 74, 96, 182; as Son of God, 25, 51–59, 66, 68, 81, 95, 128, 166; youth, 48. *See also* Resurrection
Jesus (Schillebeeckx), 50
Jews: anti-Semitism, 7–8; Christians among, 62–67, 98, 137–38; Luke's Semitisms, 103, 134, 156; Matthew among, 61–67; Passover, 31, 152; revolution against Rome, 62, 143; Torah, 37, 64–65, 67, 73. *See also* Midrash
John, 53, 156, 165–72, 192–93, 196, 197, 222–23; **1:6–9,14**, 115, 116; **1:14**, 166; **1:20**, 115; **1:31**, 118; **1:35ff**, 114; **1:45**, 29; **1:46**, 94; **1:49**, 193; **2:1–11**, 191–92, 221; **3:4**, 166, 168; **3:5**, 168; **3:6**, 168; **3:30**, 115; **4:12**, 166; **4:32**, 166; **5:19**, 184; **5:20**, 184; **5:26**, 184; **6:1–14**, 6; **6:60**, 167; **7**, 167–68; **7:2**, 212; **7:3**, 168; **7:5**, 168; **7:27**, 169; **7:29**, 169; **7:37**, 169; **7:39**, 169; **7:42**, 148; **7:51**, 169; **7:52**, 169, 172; **8**, 168–69; **8:12**, 170; **8:14**, 170; **8:15**, 170; **8:18**, 170; **8:19**, 170; **8:23**, 170; **8:28**, 184; **8:31**, 170; **8:32**, 170; **8:33**, 171; **8:37–38**, 171; **8:41**, 171, 172; **8:44**, 7, 184; **8:45**, 171; **10:30**, 172; **11**, 20; **11:1ff**, 195; **13:1–11**, 38; **14:13**, 184; **17:11**, 184; **19:26–27**, 168; **20:1ff**, 191, 193; **20:7**, 6; **20:15**, 194; **20:17**, 54; **20:19–23**, 19, 54, 214–15; **21:20–23**, 193
John, Jeffrey, 103
John Paul II, Pope, 6–7, 219
John the Baptist, 80, 103, 106, 153, 155–56, 192; and Jesus, 113–36, 143, 156
John Zebedee, 192–93
Jonah **1:17**, 6

241

244

Wisdom of Solomon **7:4,5,** 145
Women, 201–24; biblical scholars,
188, 204; creation of, 8, 201; definitions of, 1–2, 198, 201–2, 220–23;
disciples, 6–7; emancipation of,
220; ideal, 1–2, 13, 202, 218–19;
with Jesus and disciples, 188–98;
in Matthew's genealogy, 69–72,
127; oppression of, 1–2, 13; priests,
6–7, 223; as property, 8–9; sexual
harassment, 201, 202; sexuality of,
2, 69, 70–73, 208, 210–14, 218–19;
widows, 155; working, 202. *See also*
Elizabeth; Illegitimate birth; Mary;
Mary Magdalene; Virgin birth
Worldliness, 213
Wycliffe, John, 118

Zechariah (in Chronicles), 117
Zechariah (in Luke), 101, 103, 105,
106, 117–21, 131–35, 138, 139, 153
Zechariah (prophet), 117; **11:4–14,** 20

245